D1452785

RELIGIOUS CONFLICT
IN SOCIAL CONTEXT

A Publication of the Leo Baeck Institute

Religious Conflict in Social Context

THE RESURGENCE OF ORTHODOX JUDAISM IN FRANKFURT AM MAIN, 1838–1877

Robert Liberles

CONTRIBUTIONS TO THE STUDY OF RELIGION,
NUMBER 13

Greenwood Press
WESTPORT, CONNECTICUT • LONDON, ENGLAND

Library of Congress Cataloging in Publication Data

Liberles, Robert.
  Religious conflict in social context.

  (Contributions to the study of religion, ISSN 0196–7053 ; no. 13)
  "A Publication of the Leo Baeck Institute"—P.
  Bibliography: p.
  Includes index.
  1. Orthodox Judaism—Germany (West)—Frankfurt am Main—History—19th century. 2. Hirsch, Samson Raphael, 1808–1888. 3. Frankfurt am Main (Germany)—Religion—19th century. I. Title. II. Series.
  BM318.F7L52   1985   296.8′32′094341   84–27981
  ISBN 0-313-24806-0 (lib. bdg.)

Library of Congress Catalog Card Number: 84-27981
ISBN: 0-313-24806-0
ISSN: 0196-7053

First published in 1985

Greenwood Press
A division of Congressional Information Service, Inc.
88 Post Road West
Westport, Connecticut 06881

Printed in the United States of America

The paper used in this book complies with the Permanent Paper Standard issued by the National Information Standards Organization (Z39.48-1984).

10 9 8 7 6 5 4 3 2 1

To Adina
and our children
May they learn of the old while living the new

Contents

Illustrations _____

Series Foreword _____

Most studies of religion in modern times emphasize adjustment and compromise with an eye toward survival. Commonplace interpretations usually stress the ascendancy of secular guidelines and a consequent need for religious accommodation to achieve continued, if somewhat diminished, relevance. This book is not about religion desperate to keep abreast of cultural developments. Instead, it concerns a perspective that dealt with modernity by maintaining a strong position of theological self-awareness in the face of homogenizing trends. Its focus on Judaism further sharpens the picture because this religion has faced modernity in its starkest terms. Since the Enlightenment modern life had tended to make religion largely a cerebral affair, with faith propositions adjusted to social events and scientific advances. It has also nurtured the idea of religion as a matter of private conscience, without many cultic or community roots. Judaism as a way of life clashed with religion as a set of intellectualized abstractions, and as communal existence it resisted the atomization of private judgment. The story of Orthodox Judaism is a particularly significant gauge of how traditional values have endured in the face of modern pressures.

Professor Liberles's contribution to the ongoing shelf of *Wissenschaft des Judentums* brings to light several new and valuable correctives. He helps put to rest the idea that through the 1830s Reform Judaism moved with rapid strides to achieve virtually complete success in German synagogues. Traditionalist leaders had for some time grappled with Enlightenment ferment and with its later expressions in Reform. Such prolonged experience among traditional conservatives produced diverse responses in schools, social experimentation, and new worship arrangements, not the collapse of orthodoxy. This book also revises popular ideas about the nature and extent of what Samson Raphael Hirsch accomplished within Neo-Orthodoxy. Too much has been made of Hirsch as the intellectual defendant whose theological manifestos rescued Jewish traditionalism from bewilderment. Liberles shows that Hirsch made his real mark in communal circles, not philosophical ones, and that Hirsch was but the most visible part of a large movement with many spokesmen. Finally, the author brings a refreshing sense of historical realism to all divisions of his subject matter. Instead of taking a narrow or doctrinaire interpretive line, he remains inclusive and broad-minded throughout. Rather than confine description to theological channels or clashes between isolated personalities, he includes a wide range of factors in broad context. Significantly, he also points to future research by showing that attitudes and policies of civil governments were crucial to the ebb and flow of religious endeavor. This candor is refreshing in religion studies; it has the tang of historical reality to it, while it raises more questions about why such relationships were there.

Probably the most satisfying quality of this study is its combination of different analytic perspectives. Liberles examines religious conflict within its social context, and he views social differences from the angle of religious debate. Neither viewpoint provides a comprehensive explanation by itself, but together their complementarity reaches truly beneficial dimensions. So this important history covers not just a survey of embattled ideas seen through rabbinic sermons and pamphlets. It is not a simple chronicle of shifting politics where opportunists grasped for local advantage. The combined perspectives allowed Liberles to enlarge his horizons to include Jews from all walks of life and to bracket interests ranging from liturgy and theology to vocations and voting rights. His finished work presents a realistic and concrete picture of Jewish life in nineteenth-century Germany. It depicts the flesh-and-blood struggles over central issues in a religion that had to face hard choices inherent in modernized existence. Thanks to this seminal study, we are now in a better position to understand how religious change and political developments were interwoven in the fabric of European historical experience a century ago.

Henry W. Bowden

Preface _____

This study of Orthodox Judaism in Frankfurt had its beginning in 1970 when I started my studies in Jewish history under Professors Gerson Cohen and Ismar Schorsch at the Jewish Theological Seminary of America. During a most stimulating course on the modern tools available to the historian, we had occasion to tour the archives of the Leo Baeck Institute in New York City with its director, Dr. Fred Grubel. Among its treasures, we examined two cornerstone documents of the Orthodox *Israelitische Religionsgesellschaft* of Frankfurt. The methodology I had been studying and the opportunity provided by those documents combined to give rise to this study. In the years that followed my teachers continued to stimulate my pursuits, but even more significant was the model they both provided in combining intellectual courage with scholarly caution. Their legacy is now enriching Judaic studies both in America and in Israel.

Professor Sigmund Diamond of Columbia University contributed his critical insight to the growth of this work. Valuable comments were provided by Professors Gershon Bacon, Mordechai Breuer, Rivkah Horowitz, Paula Hyman, Michael Meyer, and the late Daniel Duman, my dear friend and colleague at Ben Gurion University. Dr. Max Grunewald and Dr. Fred Grubel of the Leo Baeck Institute (LBI) continually demonstrated much interest in the development of the study. I am particularly gratified that the completed work is being published under the auspices of that fine institution. Dr. Marion Kaplan of the LBI has provided sage advice and much assistance in preparing the final draft.

The research was completed with the assistance of the librarians and archivists at the Jewish Theological Seminary, the Leo Baeck Institute, the Judaica and Frankfurt divisions of the Stadts- und Universitaetsbibliotheck of Frankfurt, the Stadtarchiv of Frankfurt, the Central Archive for the History of the Jewish People, and the Jewish National Library in Jerusalem. Dr. Dietrich Andernacht, director of the Frankfurt archive, was most gracious and helpful during my various trips to Frankfurt.

I am grateful to a number of funds for their support: the Jewish Theological Seminary, the Memorial Foundation for Jewish Culture, the Deutscher Akademischer Austauschdienst, the School of Humanities and Social Sciences of Ben Gurion University of the Negev, and the Spiegel Fellowship in Modern Jewish History at Tel Aviv University.

Publication of the book has been supported by the David Baumgardt Memorial Fund of the Leo Baeck Institute. Sections of chapter four appeared previously in the *Association for Jewish Studies Review*.

My wife Adina has provided untiring support in seeing this project through its various stages.

Scholarship is enriched through collaboration, and I feel that I have been most fortunate to benefit in this way at all stages of this work from my teachers, my colleagues, and most especially from my students at the Jewish Theological Seminary, at Ben Gurion University, and now as a visiting professor at Yale.

RELIGIOUS CONFLICT
IN SOCIAL CONTEXT

Introduction ⎯⎯⎯⎯⎯⎯⎯⎯⎯⎯⎯⎯

THE CONTEXT OF RELIGIOUS CHANGE

Until its demise, German Jewry spoke for Judaism in modern times. From Moses Mendelssohn to Leo Baeck, German soil produced the spokesmen that would explain, defend, rationalize, and even alter the content and form of the Jewish expression for the Western world.

Why Germany? There were countries in which Jews were better accepted and less accepted, but there was no other country more ambiguous in its relations with its Jews in the nineteenth century than Germany. Were Jews acceptable as citizens? Did Judaism represent an appropriate set of beliefs for citizens of the state? These questions were asked elsewhere. They were never resolved in Germany.

The English Deists posed the issue as early as the seventeenth century, but by the middle of the nineteenth century, English society had, on the whole, lost interest in Judaism. It advanced the emancipation of the Jews and seemed satisfied with their religion—or their lack of it.[1]

The French were less easy to please than the English, but more precise than the Germans in their dissatisfaction. Napoleon spelled out the issues that had been emerging for over twenty years and used the forceful means to which he was accustomed to convey his message. In 1806 he brought the Jewish leadership together to Paris and transmitted a list of twelve questions on the attitudes of the Jews toward French society. He then convoked, in 1807, a conference of the rabbis of France and occupied territories known as the Sanhedrin and once again demanded answers to these questions. The beginnings of emancipation in France were shaky, but Napoleon chose to press harder on the Jews through special decrees, but affirming the basic principle of Jewish citizenship.[2]

In Germany, Judaism itself remained a matter of controversy. The proponents of emancipation deemed it unfit to be the religion of a citizen; the opponents extended that judgment to Jews themselves. Judaism was put on the defensive, and it remained there. Hence one reason for the emergence of spokesmen in Germany to defend it.[3]

One could suggest that the diverse responses to the pressures of emancipation implied an unclear message of expectations from those Germans who supported emancipation. But the message really was quite clear—it was simply not acceptable. If the Jews had followed Wilhelm von Humboldt's program, Judaism would not have been defended, and emancipation in Germany would have been less controversial. Converts could become full citizens; Jews could not.[4] Hence the controversy, and hence one reason for the diversity. Having rejected the price, Jews argued the terms among themselves. Some were more anxious than others to attain legal equality, and, hence more willing to provide religious accommodation, but others determined that caution and reserve would eventually prove the more effective means. These were the opposing approaches of the Reform and Orthodox parties within German Jewry.

What historians of German Jewry have rarely appreciated is that Orthodoxy had a point: On the whole, German society demonstrated little patience for the assimilationist's path. This attitude dated back to the very beginnings of the emancipation debate. When Christian Dohm, a ranking Prussian civil servant and friend of Moses Mendelssohn's, issued his call for increased rights for the Jews in 1781, the Protestant theologian and orientalist Johann Michaelis responded with a sharp critique of Dohm's position. After explaining why the observant Jew was unfit for citizenship, Michaelis proceeded to cast distrust on the nonobservant Jew as well: One who has been unfaithful to his religion cannot be relied upon as trustworthy in other matters. "If I see a Jew eating pork as an affront to his religion, then, since I cannot see into his heart, I find it impossible to rely upon his oath." Of course, according to Michaelis, a Jewish oath had been unreliable for 1,800 years, but if the Jew did not even believe in the Jewish religion, then how could one rely even on the special oath?[5] That theme continued throughout the emancipation debate. Jacob Katz wrote of the conservative opponents of emancipation that

> It was typical of the exponents of the concept of the Christian state that whatever position they allotted the Jew in their scheme of things, the Jew they wished to have dealings with was of the old type, the old Orthodox Jew.[6]

Katz brought the examples of Constantin Frantz (1844) and Philipp Wolfart (also 1844). Both protested against the use of religious reforms in order to attain civil rights. A convert from Judaism, Wolfgang Fraenkel, also attacked Reform Judaism with complaints of the loss of religious authority and the resultant religious anarchy.[7]

By the next decade, opposition to the reformers and to assimilation in general had been transmitted to the leaders of the emerging antisemitic movement like Herman Wagener, editor of the arch-conservative *Kreuzzeitung*. For Wagener, Reform Jews presented both a political threat to the state, as well as a religious threat to Christianity, but primarily he criticized their attitudes and behavior. "Once the tenacious energy of their nature has been directed away from religion the bulk of the nation is bent only on acquisition and pleasure."[8] But this distrust of the Reformers and relative appreciation of the traditionalists was not an extreme position in German society. The same theme reappeared in a simple, but revealing expression that has direct bearing on our study. In 1851 the Prussian representative to the Diet of the German Confederation in Frankfurt wrote to his wife:

> I picked the enclosed leaves for you in old Amschel Rothschild's garden. I like him because he's a real old Jew peddler, and does not pretend to be anything else; he is strictly Orthodox and refuses to touch anything

but kosher food at his dinners. . . . He is a short, thin little man, and quite gray. The eldest of his line, but a poor man in his palace; he is a childless widower, who is cheated by his servants and despised by conceited Frenchified and Anglicized nephews and nieces who will inherit his wealth without any love or gratitude.[9]

The writer was Otto von Bismarck, and Orthodoxy's staunchest supporter in Frankfurt was Amschel Rothschild. The bond between them contained a message too often overlooked: Not assimilation, but steadfast loyalty was the value appreciated most by conservative Germans, and, as we shall see, by a number of German governments as well. But such loyalty did not always reap the rewards of improvement, and not all Jews were prepared to or could afford to bear a process that seemed endless. If German Jewry spoke for Judaism, it did so with diverse tongues. The religious legacy of German Jewry bequeathed ideologies and institutions ranging from radical reform to modern orthodoxy. Only the orthodoxy of seclusion did not remain vibrant in the German religious spectrum. Those Jews most anxious for an improved status turned to religious reform in pursuit of social change.

EXPLAINING RELIGIOUS DIVERSITY

Diversity in Jewish religious life in the form of movements and sectarian groups was one of the main spheres of interest of the nineteenth-century scholars of the *Wissenschaft des Judenthums*, the science of Judaism. The interest held by the *Wissenschaft* scholars derived from the very diversity of religious life in their own century. To paraphrase Louis Finkelstein in his book on the Pharisees, after a long period of disrepute, it suddenly seemed that all sides in the nineteenth-century controversies between reformers and traditionalists claimed to represent the contemporary Pharisaic spirit.[10]

Reform leader and scholar Abraham Geiger dealt extensively with the Pharisees and Sadducees in his writings,[11] but perhaps the most striking example of such interest was Isaak M. Jost's *Geschichte des Judenthums und seine Sekten*, published in 1857–1859, a full history of Judaism and its sectarian digressions. Interest in the Karaites was also strong long before the end of the nineteenth century as demonstrated by the work of Simchah Pinsker and later by A. Harkavy. Beginning with Pinsker's work published in 1860, Karaism gained esteem as a major intellectual force in medieval Jewish history.[12] The interest in the Pharisees and Sadducees of the Second Commonwealth and in medieval Karaites and Rabbanites expanded still further in the wake of the major archival and archeological finds of the Cairo Geniza and the Dead Sea Scrolls during the past century.[13]

By our own times, the strong interest in religious movements has expressed itself with regard to the movements of the nineteenth century as well. Yet, despite the growing literature on the subject, there persists a sense of bafflement at the appearance of these movements, and that bafflement is revealed in at least one of the most popular interpretive models that have been employed. Altogether, I would delineate four approaches that have been used by scholars to explain the historical origins of religious movements in the nineteenth century. Those approaches are:

1. What can be called "subterranean anti-nomianism," or the reawakening of an earlier manifestation of religious deviance.

2. Christian religious influence.

3. Migrations that carried with them the ideological kernel on which movements arose.

4. The social context in which movements arose.

It is the first of these factors—the subterranean anti-nomianism—that reveals a sense of total wonder at the appearance of religious movements. It is as if these movements are the products of creatio-ex-nihilo; they simply seem to come from nowhere and can be explained only by asserting or assuming spontaneous combustion. But, of course, religious movements need not be quite so mystifying, and an increasing amount of historiography has managed to shed light on the gaps that surround the origins of these movements.

Subterranean Anti-nomianism

In explaining the rise of Karaism in the ninth century, several scholars, beginning with Abraham Geiger, have suggested that Karaism represented a reawakening of the earlier Sadducean sect of the period of the Second Temple.[14] Such an extreme suggestion that a sect had remained alive for centuries without historical signs of existence highlights some of the questions that must be asked in discussing the relationship even between two closer-ranged movements such as the relations between the messianic Sabbatian movement and the growth of Reform Judaism in central Europe or between Sabbatianism and Hasidism in eastern Europe.

In asserting a causal role played by Sabbatianism in the rise of these two later movements, Gershom Scholem underscored his conception of the centrality of Sabbatianism in the breakdown of the traditional Jewish world in modern Europe.[15] Sabbatianism, according to Scholem, thrived not only during the lifetime of Sabbatai Sevi in the seventeenth century, but long after, giving rise to subsequent movements that continued to eat away at the traditional Jewish framework. Scholem's suggestion with regard to Hasidism has received some critical attention, but only recently has a historian of Reform Judaism confronted Scholem's interpretation that Sabbatian influence on religious life had sustained itself even into the nineteenth century.

In that discussion, Jacob Katz argued against Scholem's views based on a number of difficulties posed by the empirical evidence.[16] Thus, Katz argued that there was little geographic overlap between the centers of Sabbatian activity and the centers of Enlightenment and later Reform, since Jewish Enlightenment centered in Berlin, where there had been little trace of Sabbatian activity. While Scholem emphasized the importance of Hamburg in building a connection with Reform, Katz correctly countered that other centers of simultaneous Reform activity again showed no connection. Why explain the phenomenon one way for one location and another for all the others? Moreover, Katz argued that only one personality active in the early growth of Reform, Aaron Chorin of Hungary, was suspected of Sabbatian tendencies. Katz went on for several pages to dispute even this claim, but it would seem that we have already struck the earth of irrelevancy. One individual does not prove a theory, nor can he give rise to a religious movement.[17]

Of the four approaches to the study of Jewish religious movements that I have listed, the suggestion that earlier movements were sustained and then resurrected in a later period is the only one that has failed to supply any empirical basis for its conclusions. It has failed to explain how these ideas were transmitted from one period to another and most especially why the ideas were suddenly activated into renewed existence.

Christian Religious Influence

According to some historians, developments taking place within the realm of Christianity have frequently influenced subsequent developments within Judaism. The reference here is specifically to parallel religious developments and not to other streams of influence originating within the larger society such as official government policies. As an example, Michael Meyer, who is now preparing the first new comprehensive history of Reform Judaism in eighty years, has suggested Christian influence in several places in his writings. For example, in discussing the radical reform circle, the *Verein der Reformfreunde*, founded in Frankfurt in the early 1840s, Meyer suggested the influence of Young Hegelians like Ludwig Feuerbach and Bruno Bauer upon the radical reformers, but, in the end, Meyer himself concluded on a rather minimal note: "The direct influence of the Christian movements on the Reformfreunde seems to have been limited, though the similarity of name with the Protestantische Freunde is striking."[18]

A second example of this approach can be found in Lou Silberman's analysis of the events in Charleston, South Carolina, in the 1820s. The Reformed Society of Israelites marked the first attempt to introduce religious reforms of any substance in America. Silberman's primary thesis was to suggest that the Charleston reformers were influenced by an earlier schism within the local Protestant community that led to the establishment of a Unitarian congregation: "What happened in Charleston was derivative and its proximate source is to be found within the context of Protestantism in Charleston in the years immediately preceding the founding of the Reformed Society."[19]

The approach of interpreting Jewish religious movements in the light of developments within the Christian world provides an intrinsic explanation for the time and possibly for the place of the Jewish development. Indeed, this model has certainly precipitated examples of scholarship, like those I have discussed, that must be incorporated into our understanding of the historical processes.What I suggest is missing from these interpretations, as well as from the category of subterranean antinomianism, is the notion that Jews were actively responding to their own circumstances. Most writers combine the question of Christian influence with other factors, but to the extent they rely on this interpretation the reader is given no sense of what prompts the Jews in question to act, of what promotes their receptivity to the related developments in the Christian world. In sum, each of these first two lines of interpretation appears frequently in the study of Jewish religious movements, but each ignores the relevance of the contemporary situation of the Jew as an active force in the shaping of his own history.[20]

Migration and Social Context

Movements of populations, whether that movement represent a transatlantic journey or a change of domicile from a rural area to an urban center, have presented a favorite avenue of interpretation to social historians to explain the phenomenon we are discussing—the origins of religious movements.

In the classic case, it has been argued repeatedly that American Reform Judaism prospered from a wave of German-Jewish migration in the mid-nineteenth century. The fact that many of the first Reform rabbis came from Germany was to explain the initial strength of Reform in organizing in America, thus ignoring the importance of the immediate context in explaining how the movement attracted its constituency and support. Only recently, Leon Jick has developed an alternative formulation that explains the growth of Reform in America in terms of increasing affluence and acculturation.[21]

A further example of the tendency among social historians toward the migration factor can be found in Steven Lowenstein's comprehensive and valuable essay on the spread of Reform Judaism in Germany in the 1840s and the weakening of that momentum in the later forties and fifties.[22] The strength of Lowenstein's presentation lies in its broad synthesis of the dynamics of religious change and conflict and in tracing the locations of Reform activity. However, Lowenstein paid only minimal attention to the historical context in which these developments were taking place.

In Lowenstein's concluding argument, he asserts that the political events of the 1840s had little effect on religious developments. "The upheaval of the Revolution of 1848 . . . did not usually favour either the Reform or the Orthodox party. . . . The only real effect, then, which the Revolution had on Reform was to undermine most of the efforts for co-ordination, and to return the initiative to the individual community." The subsequent decline of Reform in rural communities was caused "by the fact that the 'progressive-minded' were more likely to move to the cities, while the more conservative usually remained in villages and small towns." Thus, migration explained the depletion of Reform strength in the rural areas.

Religious direction within the Jewish community was not always voted on in the most democratic manner. State governments in Germany intervened most actively in the internal matters of the Jewish community, and this intervention was stronger, not weaker, during the politically turbulent years of the 1840s and early 1850s. Based on the idea of a gradual change due to the urbanization process, Lowenstein observed that "a number of communities which sent rabbis to the Reform rabbinical conferences of the 1840s had Orthodox rabbis in the twentieth century" (p. 273). But the change was at times far more abrupt, and as we shall see, a number of these communities already had more conservative rabbis by the early 1850s. In Prussia, Mecklenburg, and in Frankfurt too, it was in the aftermath of the revolutionary years that the authorities came to the support of the Orthodox Jews. Government involvement in internal religious affairs was a matter of recognized practice in Germany, and the regimes bore much greater, direct responsibility for

Catholic and Protestant affairs in the different states than they exercised in Jewish matters.[23] Within this atmosphere of active intervention, I would suggest that government policies had considerably more relevance for the decline of Reform in certain areas than the migration of a few leaders, who, themselves, may well have been imposed upon the community a decade earlier.

The tendency toward the migration factor by social historians may be partly understood by a desire to explain a Jewish religious development within the context of the inner Jewish world: hence, a hesitation by some scholars to invoke non-Jewish influence or to place the events in question in a broader historical context. In fact, this study shares the view that the emergence of a Jewish religious movement ought to be studied as an act meant to meet the needs of its constituents, but it was not only migrants who had such needs. Some religious movements were constituted by Jews on the rise; some by Jews on the decline; but all were spearheaded by Jews in conflict with their surroundings.

Migration may represent one attempt to return Jewish history to the Jew, but we can go further if we can demonstrate—as I believe we can—that Jews responded actively to their historical circumstances. Even in modern times, religious movements were a frequent expression of that response.

A SOCIAL PERSPECTIVE

The conflict between Reform and Orthodoxy in nineteenth-century Germany has usually been portrayed as a battle of literary pamphlets, sermons, and declarations. However, rabbinic enunciations from both sides represented but the exposed peak of a bitter struggle between individuals. Each side had its adherents who for one reason or another cared about the course and outcome of events. Some cared for religious reasons, some for social or political, some out of economic concerns.

These religious movements were historical phenomena. They were movements like any other. They had origins, patterns of growth and decline, interactions with other movements or groups, and constituencies. They evolved through stages of formation and establishment. They went through combatant periods and reached plateaus of quiet and consolidation. Each had periods of internal unity and of internal dissent.

The Reform movement has been by far the better studied of the two movements, with several factors contributing to this situation. Reform attracted historical attention because it was the movement of change, a subject more perceptible to the historical eye than a movement identified with the status quo. Further, the Reform movement itself was immersed in a historical outlook concerned with describing religious developments in the past. From the 1850s on, Reformers also encouraged the writing of their own history as a measure of accomplishment and an agent of legitimacy. Descriptions of German-Jewish society of their own century with an emphasis on rampant assimilation were now invoked in support of their program of innovations.[24] Orthodoxy, on the other hand, tended to be far more ahistorical in its outlook, opposing the concept of religious evolution and presenting arguments steeped in rabbinic tradition. Finally, Reform has been the better studied because it has been generally assumed that it eventually won the conflict and that it spoke almost exclusively for German Jewry. As we shall see, this assumption was far from accurate.

This study will focus on Orthodoxy as it emerged during the century, and by so doing will contribute toward a more complete picture of Jewish religious life in nineteenth-century Germany. Orthodoxy was a viable religious movement almost everywhere in Germany for most of the century. Its influence was not restricted to certain regions where modernity's inroads were late or blunted. Indeed, every major urban community hosted a flourishing Orthodox congregation. However, it is not just the *religious* profile of German Jewry that can profit from a study of Orthodoxy. Religious conflicts, when examined from a social perspective, can provide an opening into a far broader context of *social* conflict and unrest. This is especially true in a traditional society where religion serves as a central focal point for the concerns of the members. As we shall see, it was still true of Frankfurt in the mid-nineteenth century that there existed a bitter hostility within the Jewish community during those revolutionary years that was expressed primarily in religious terms. Significantly, no previous social history has discussed that hostility, and it took a religious history of the period to bring the story to light.

Although German Orthodoxy was besieged in the 1830s and 1840s, it did not collapse. Some smaller cities and, of course, rural areas remained unscathed by the onslaught of Reform. In the major cities, struggles took place, but in none of them did Orthodoxy disappear. By mid-century, Orthodoxy was restrengthening its position, recouping some of its losses, and reorganizing in a number of communities. The resurgence of Orthodoxy in Frankfurt symbolized the turning point for all of German Orthodoxy.

How could this turnabout be explained? The mystery of countermovements in history runs deep. Friedrich Engels put it well, writing shortly after the period with which much of this study is concerned, when he warned that the forces of counterrevolution tend to be greatly simplified.

That the sudden movements of February and March 1848 were not the work of single individuals, but spontaneous, irresistible manifestations of national wants and necessities, more or less clearly understood, but very distinctly felt by numerous classes in every country, is a fact recognized everywhere; but when you inquire into the causes of the counter-revolutionary successes, there you are met on every hand with the ready reply that it was Mr. This or Citizen That who "betrayed" the people.[25]

Engels was, of course, arguing that counterrevolutions must be the result of wide-ranging social forces no less than revolutionary movements. This formulation presents a new set of problems, for we must ask not only what historical processes enabled Orthodox Judaism to reassert itself after mid-century, but also where had its supporters been during the preceding troubled years? In other words, what had changed in the social constellation of forces that now allowed Orthodoxy to respond to the Reform challenge although it apparently could not do so earlier? The answers to these questions derive from the fundamental thesis of this study: The religious changes of the 1840s and 1850s were more than parallel developments to the political trends of those same years. The two were intrinsically interwoven. Indeed, the governments of a number of German states played a major role in the struggle between Reformers and Orthodox. It was characteristic of those turbulent years that these same governments frequently changed their position, at times totally reversing their previous stance. The reassessment by the authorities in Frankfurt and elsewhere of their position in the late 1840s and early 1850s enabled Orthodoxy to reassert itself in the conflict.

However, Orthodoxy was able to do this because even during its weakest years its adherents had spent their time well, maintaining their strengths as best they could and laying the seeds of organization that would prove useful later on. Such reorganization can give the appearance of being a set of isolated, random events, scattered across the dispersed communities of divided Germany. Indeed, it was one of the tasks of this study to synthesize specific events into the more comprehensive processes that gave rise to the Orthodox reemergence. However, it must be added that the groundwork for an Orthodox response to the challenges of the nineteenth century had been laid even earlier in the century. Orthodoxy was prepared for the Reformers because it had begun long before to confront the problems of modernity posed by the Enlightenment and only later by the Reformers. To be precise: Although Neo-Orthodoxy as a party emerged only later in the century as a result of the confrontation with Reform, its program originated much earlier and derived from the influences of the Enlightenment at the very beginning of the century.

THE BEGINNINGS OF NEO-ORTHODOXY

The men of the Jewish Enlightenment centered in Berlin in the latter half of the eighteenth century were, on the whole, observant Jews, who nevertheless had their criticisms of traditional Jewish life and society. They opposed the system of education steeped in rabbinic literature, the consequently narrow occupational base of the Jewish community, and the continuing power of the rabbis to control the very thoughts of their constituents.[26] Nevertheless, Orthodox criticism of the Enlightenment, known as the Haskalah, was at first muted. Moses Mendelssohn, considered to have been the father of the Haskalah, was not subjected to bitter opposition, "partly because he was an observant man, partly because of his standing in German society, and partly because of his defense of the Jews against various hostile elements."[27]

It was no accident that Orthodox opposition was sharper against the educational reformer and Hebraist Naphtali Herz Wessely than it had been against Mendelssohn. Wessely, by proposing new directions and values to Jewish education, had, in the words of Raphael Mahler, transformed the Haskalah into a social movement. However, the rabbis also realized the need for educational reform, and when Wessely later softened his revisionist program, the opposition was again quieted.[28]

Nevertheless, the new schools which were opened by the leaders of the Enlightenment over the next decades provided an institutional framework for influencing a generation of children inculcated with secularized values. The broadening of the economic base as encouraged within these schools necessitated increased contact with the non-Jewish world and thereby weakened attachments to the traditional Jewish life-style. The religious atmosphere within the schools also made it difficult for the graduates to participate later in a traditional service. Worship hours inculcated a sense of aesthetics that could not be found in regular synagogal worship, and the increased importance of manual labor necessitated more flexibility in the time of services than the traditional community could provide.[29] The establishment of these progressive schools in Berlin (1778), Breslau (1791), Seesan and Dessau (1801), and Frankfurt (1804) marked the first stage in the spreading of the ideas of the Enlightenment to broader circles of the Jewish community in Germany.

Napoleon's armies provided the second stage. The policies toward the Jews that emerged during the Napoleonic period in Germany represented a combination of those policies imported from France with the values and concerns already developed by the Jewish Enlightenment in Germany. The legal position attained during the Napoleonic hegemony derived from the emancipated status of French Jewry. True, the status of the Jew differed in the various German states during this period, but on the whole, it represented a quantum leap forward from the disabilities of the previous laws.[30]

On the other hand, educational reform had become a prominent concern earlier in Germany than in France, and this was subsequently reflected in consistory policies during Napoleonic rule. Whereas in France the empire denied the consistories the right to open Jewish schools, in Germany such moves were encouraged and supported, for example, in Westphalia and Frankfurt. Here the Westphalian example is instructive, for while Israel Jacobson had already opened an elementary school in Seesan in 1801, the later consistory under his leadership opened additional schools and established a teachers' seminar in Cassel.[31]

It was also during the Napoleonic period that religious reforms were first introduced into German synagogues, when Israel Jacobson established a consistorial synagogue in 1810. Traditional Jews could privately object to the innovations, but given Jacobson's official status as head of the consistory and the authoritative nature of the regime, there seems to have been little they could do in protest.[32] It was, therefore, in this setting, under the wings of Napoleon, that the religious reforms envisioned by the figures of the Enlightenment were first translated into practice in Germany.

A broader movement for reform originated in 1818 with the establishment of the Hamburg Temple.[33] Reform in Hamburg differed from the short-lived experiment in Westphalia in that the movement in Hamburg was both free and enduring, representing an expression of popular will. It also differed from Westphalia in that Orthodox opposition was freer to respond—and did.

There were two dimensions to the Orthodox response to the Reform endeavors in Hamburg. Orthodox opposition to the Enlightenment had been brewing for more than three decades, and the forming of the Temple brought the reaction into the open. Yet the Orthodoxy of the polemics represented primarily a defense of the status quo and derived extensively from beyond German borders through the participation of Hungarian rabbis.[34] A second development in Hamburg of that time was far more indicative of the paths to be adopted by German Orthodoxy. With the appointment of Isaac Bernays as rabbi in Hamburg in 1821, traditional Judaism in Germany initiated a process of adaptation that became known as Neo-Orthodoxy.

The birth of modern Orthodox Judaism, often referred to as Neo-Orthodoxy, is frequently dated to the year 1851 when Samson Raphael Hirsch, its ideologue and spokesman in the nineteenth century, assumed the position of rabbi of the newly formed *Israelitische Religionsgesellschaft* of Frankfurt am Main.[35] Hirsch was born in Hamburg in 1808 and studied under Hamburg's rabbi Isaac Bernays and later under Jacob Ettlinger, then of Mannheim. In the 1830s, Hirsch issued two works in defense of Orthodox Jewish tradition, *The Nineteen Letters of Ben Uziel* and *Horeb, Essays on Israel's Duties in the Dispersion*. With these works, Hirsch demonstrated that the message of Orthodoxy could be translated into the nineteenth century, symbolically represented by the *Nineteen Letters*. Yet, there was little to the Neo-Orthodox program that had not been introduced previously by Bernays, as he undertook a program of innovation under the influence of the Enlightenment, affecting both school instruction and the synagogue service.[36]

However, Bernays was not a free agent in his dealing either with reforms or Reformers. The board of the Hamburg Jewish community was strongly sympathetic to the Reform program and at times curtailed Bernays' attempts to oppose them. More important, they strongly pressed Bernays to undertake a program of change within the traditional synagogue. Bernays' very appointment depended on his accommodations, even on his agreement to the title of *Hacham* and the somewhat debilitating German title *"geistlicher Beamter."* Before accepting the position, Bernays complained concerning the stipulated conditions that "never has a rabbi been so dependent in his office on a Board, as I shall be."[37] Hence, Hamburg provided an early and prime example of modern observant Judaism, but Bernays lacked the independence to represent modern Orthodoxy as a distinct and aggressive party in Judaism. In fact, Hirsch himself was a product of that Hamburg environment. Bernays and Hirsch's grandfather Mendel Frankfurter were two of the cornerstones in Hirsch's development.

That Hirsch and not Bernays was seen as the founder of Neo-Orthodoxy derived primarily from factors beyond the content of their similar religious programs.[38] As we shall see, the essence of Hirsch's contribution to the growth of Neo-Orthodoxy lies not in the intellectual sphere, but in the communal. The emergence of Frankfurt as a center for European Orthodoxy must be traced not only to Hirsch's intellectual abilities and to his charismatic leadership, but also to a combination of broad historical factors.

Orthodoxy's survival in Germany was supported by the change in the political milieu of the late 1840s. But the Orthodox resurgence was also based on latent strengths and loyalties that had survived the Reform growth of the thirties and forties. Orthodoxy had not collapsed in that period; it had simply lain dormant. The Orthodox of Germany had maintained the struggle, but the times had not been appropriate to their success. Numerous historians have commented on the significance of 1848 for German-Jewish history. However, there were also those Jews for whom 1849 marked a year of relief and even of religious, if not political, liberation. Such Jews shall play a major role in this study.

The strength of Orthodox Judaism in Germany described in this study still runs counter to a widely accepted idea of the extent of assimilation of German Jewry into their surroundings. That description of German Jewry has proven remarkably convenient for diverse segments of contemporary Jewry and the historians who represent them. Spokesmen of Reform Judaism often emphasized the degree of assimilation in Germany, thus legitimizing their orientation toward religious change by demonstrating the heavy losses that German Jewry would otherwise have suffered. Zionists, beginning with Moses Hess, constructed their ideology on the axiom of the impossibility of a secure Jewish life in the diaspora. They continue to do so, reenforcing their claim by describing as totally assimilated a community that suffered so much as Jews. In that scenario, no community could have done more to pay the price of emancipation, only to be rudely awakened by the tragic turn of events.

Strangest of all, however, was the reenforcement of this picture of German Jewry put forth by the German Orthodox themselves, for they too described German Jewry in the first half of the nineteenth century as having all-but-totally abandoned the fundamentals of traditional Jewish life. As I have argued elsewhere, much of that view derived from a hagiography greatly influenced by the writings and teachings of Samson Raphael Hirsch, who had emphasized the small number of Orthodox Jews remaining in Frankfurt by mid-century.[39] His followers, supported by the strong communal ties examined in this study, continued to transmit this view. Ironically, it contributed greatly to the picture of German Jewry that I believe must be challenged.

The ghetto of Frankfurt, best known for the financial power that was seated within its walls, has come to symbolize the closed doors and locked gates that German Jews strove to open from the period of the Enlightenment to the attaining of emancipation.

In 1800 Frankfurt Jewry numbered approximately 3,000 Jews. By 1850 it had climbed to 5,000 Jews, and in 1875 it had reached about 12,000 Jews. Despite this growth, the Jewish percentage of the total population remained in the vicinity of 10 percent throughout the period of this study.

Legally, Frankfurt Jewry in the early nineteenth century was still governed by a set of ordinances dating back to 1616 that severely restricted rights of occupation, domicile, and freedom of movement within the city. In later discussions of the Jewish situation in Germany Frankfurt was frequently cited as a blatant example of restrictions still imposed on Jews.

French armies brought these questions to the forefront. The ghetto walls were battered during various battles in the 1790s, and the question of their renovation led naturally to more basic discussions of the position of the Jews. Frankfurt am Main was known as the capital of southern Germany, but in fact, it is centrally located between the north and south. Hence, it was caught in the crosswinds between modernization and traditionalism that characterized the two halves of Germany.

Each swing of the political pendulum during the nineteenth century encouraged a new religious endeavor. No Jewish community reflected the changing trends of religious life in Germany better than Frankfurt, and few communities were as active as Frankfurt in bringing about those changes. The long struggle began when the first hopeful rays of freedom shone over the Main River during the Napoleonic occupation, and the leaders of the Jewish community took steps to alter the image held by the general public of both Jews and Judaism.

If the developments we are analyzing were part of the broader context of German-Jewish history, then why continue the emphasis on Frankfurt that has been portrayed in traditional historiography? This study will put the events in Frankfurt in perspective, but there can be no question that Frankfurt made a unique contribution to the growth of Neo-Orthodoxy. Even more important, the historical forces that contributed to the growth of Neo-Orthodoxy were most blatant in Frankfurt. The traditional emphasis was not misplaced, only the interpretation.

The Triumph of Reform

The Reform takeover of the institutions of the Frankfurt Jewish community was neither as rapid nor as one-sidedly complete as is usually portrayed by all sides. Even Orthodox mythology depicts a total collapse of the traditional position in order to enhance the mission of rescue later accomplished by Samson Raphael Hirsch. But the conquest was, in fact, painfully slow for the Reformers and took effect only over a number of stages.

The turning point in Reform tactics took place in the late 1830s, when demands became more adamant for renovation of the synagogue building and for the election of a second rabbi to preach during the services. The new militant position contrasted with a decades-long posture of moderation in which members of the community board had satisfied themselves with a separate service conducted under the auspices of the Reform Philanthropin School, while the communal synagogue itself remained completely traditional.

In Frankfurt and throughout Germany, as the early Reformers gave way to their successors, the cosmetic changes of the former were enhanced by more sharply defined conceptions of both platform and strategies. The call for a systematic theology of reform denoted not only further intellectualization, but an actual rejection of earlier tactics within the communal conflicts. The unfolding of the slow-moving Frankfurt scenario reveals the changing strains and expectations which influenced the course of Reform in the early nineteenth century.

EXCLUSIVE REFORMATION

The Napoleonic occupation of Frankfurt occasioned in 1808 a restructuring of the local Jewish community that benefited the supporters of Reform. The board of the community was now dominated by men who sought to transform both the status and style of Jewish life. The principal achievement of the early Reformers was the establishment and continued expansion of the Philanthropin School, later known as the Realschule. Founded in 1804, the school, like those in Berlin (1778), Breslau (1791), Seesen (1801), and Dessau (1801), combined secular studies with a progressive religious education.[1] The Philanthropin and many of its sister institutions, by educating German youth in the values and perspectives of Reform thinking, helped mold a generation that could later assume leadership in the broader Jewish community.[2] These schools also provided both an opportunity and framework for establishing a Reform service. The *Andachtstunde*, a weekly hour of prayer and discourse conducted by the Philanthropin first on Sundays and later on Saturdays, was one of the best known of these school services.

Yet this religious experience was not the sole objective of the Philanthropin's education, just as religious reform was not the only area of concern for those Jews who sought a more integrated role in Germany society. As the negative economic image of the Jew had caused much harm in the past, a diversification of the occupational distribution among Jews now became a matter of the highest priority. In 1807 new city regulations allowed Jews to learn and ply various trades. The Philanthropin responded to the opportunity by arranging to send its pupils to Christian masters, while the school's teachers were instructed to emphasize the importance of handicrafts. In Frankfurt and elsewhere, leaders of religious reform continued to be active in organizing and supporting *Handwerkervereine* whose task was to support youth, especially orphans, in learning a trade.[3]

The Philanthropin was originally founded to provide for the education of orphans or children of poorer families, although the school had to encourage the entry of students whose families could afford the tuition fees as well.[4] There are several possible explanations for this emphasis on educating the poor. Wealthier children would receive their education from private tutors, but those whose families could not afford the expense would be unable to escape from the traditional Jewish occupations.[5] Worse yet, they might prove unable to earn an income at all and become a burden upon the community and society. Another motive often present, most noticeably in the establishment of Jews' Infant School in London, was to avoid the temptation to poorer families to send their children or charges to Christian schools, thus alleviating their responsibility, but at the price of the possible—even probable—conversion of the child. Reform leaders were no less adamant than traditionalists in their opposition to such conversion attempts by Christians.[6]

In sum, the early Jewish integrationists of Frankfurt, those who sought an expanded role for the Jews within the general society, were as involved in the reform of Jews as of Judaism. Concern over religious innovation in the early nineteenth century was manifested only within a restricted context, the Philanthropin's *Andachtstunde*. In other words, religious reform was significant at this time only as a limited part of a broader package.

The *Andachtstunde*, or hour of prayer, was instituted by Michael Hess, the school's director, in 1811. The services then took place on Sundays until Josef Johlson, teacher of religion, persuaded Hess in 1814 to change the service to Saturday and to allow community members to participate. By 1815 Hess reported that more adults than children participated in the service. In 1824 Michael Creizenach assumed the preaching role and the importance of the service began to increase. In 1828 new facilities were provided, and in the years that followed a number of illustrious preachers addressed the services, among them David Einhorn, Abraham Geiger, Leopold Stein, and Leopold Zunz.

Several sources refer to the large number of adults attending the service and, accordingly, it has become accepted that the service made a significant contribution to religious life within the community.[7] Actually the situation was quite different. The prayer room may have been crowded, but we are informed by several sources that its physical capacity was also limited. Mendel Hess, a leading spokesman for the radical wing of the Reform party, could even write of Frankfurt in 1841 that no beginning had yet been made toward improvement of the synagogue serv-

ices, adding parenthetically, "although very highly respected
men preach there, the *Andachtstunde* cannot satisfy the general
needs because of its limited premises and its separation from
the community synagogue."[8] The fact is that participation was
restricted to parents, teachers, school committee, and board
members. Few remaining places were available.[9] If there were
other community members who sought synagogue innovations,
then the board of the early nineteenth century ignored them
and contented itself within its own closed congregation.

The board of the early decades seems considerably more passive than that of the thirties and forties, which actively contested
the religious authority of the rabbinate. Actually, the objectives
and spheres of combat of the earlier board were quite different.

Jacob Katz has observed in his study on Jews and Freemasons
that between 1817 and 1832 all members of the Frankfurt Board
were also members of the Morgenroethe Freemason Lodge, an
independent lodge with a heavy majority of Jewish members,
organized because of the prohibitions Jews faced in their attempts to join other lodges in Germany. Founded in 1808, its
leading figure was Sigmund Geisenheimer, who four years earlier had been the primary force behind the founding of the Philanthropin. Geisenheimer described in a letter to Ludwig Boerne
how Masonic lodges might serve as a significant medium for
increasing Jewish-gentile interaction.[10] Since the doors of the
existent lodges were closed to Jews, Geisenheimer and others
took the initiative in forming the Morgenroethe. They thought
that official recognition would entitle the Jewish members of the
new lodge to the right to visit the meetings of the other lodges.[11]

A strong link existed between the lodge and the Philanthropin.
In addition to Geisenheimer, Michael Hess, the school's director
for fifty years, and Michael Creizenach and Isaac Marcus Jost,
both leading teachers at the school, were members, as were in
the years that followed Leopold Beer, Herman Zirndorfer, Jacob
Auerbach, and Theodore Creizenach. Hence, those community
leaders that favored religious reform, both the board and the
teachers of the Philanthropin, were also identified with the Jewish Masonic lodge.[12] Their efforts in one sphere were not to be
separated from their achievements in the other. Katz quoted an

evaluation of their endeavors in 1837 by a group of Christian Masons in Frankfurt:

The men are known to all of us . . . they constitute the kernel of the good, learned, and enlightened among the Jewish community. . . . . The projects begun and completed by it are now clearly shown to have been not only for the benefit of the lodge and those belonging to it, but for the good of the nation as a whole. These Israelite brethren are no longer the Jews of 1789, they are Masons . . . who are devoted in all respects to the true veneration of God, to knowledge, to the virtues which adorn civil and family life . . . we are forced to admit that their participation in Masonry has made all their culture stride forward with giant steps.

Most relevant was the observation of one Masonic leader who praised the Morgenroethe members "for their intentions to bring Judaism closer to Christianity by the founding of schools and houses of worship."[13]

The early integrationists, as we have suggested, fought their battles on a number of fronts. Men like Geisenheimer simultaneously attempted to improve education, to achieve a balanced occupational distribution, to provide the poor with an independent livelihood, to reform religious services, and to provide opportunities for mixed social intercourse. Religious reform was, in those years, but one aspect of an extensive campaign aimed at breaking down the barriers between Jew and gentile.

The members of the Morgenroethe were not militant in their campaign for acceptance within the Freemason organization and followed for several decades a path of quiet diplomacy based, in part, on the distinctive social position of its membership. For this, it was severely criticized by a second Jewish lodge, *Zum Frankfurther Adler*, founded in 1832, which adopted a more aggressive policy than that followed by the older lodge. The differences between the two lodges followed classical patterns— the exclusive and cautious Morgenroethe, contrasted with the more open and more militant Adler. The Morgenroethe had been discriminating in its acceptance of members, both in order to enhance the prestige of membership in the lodge and as part of its strategy to attain recognition for the lodge itself. In contrast, the Adler was more open in its admission policy, especially in accepting nonresidents of Frankfurt. In Katz's words, the Adler was "a reception center for candidates unable to gain entry to the veteran lodge."[14]

The early Reformers of Frankfurt constituted a somewhat defined, exclusive group with several outlets for social gathering. Among these various institutions was one that filled the religious dimension—the *Andachtstunde*, which was intended to provide a religious service appropriate to the circle of Jews who sought most actively to break down the barriers of separation between them and gentile society. It was exclusive and limited, as was the Masonic lodge that served much of the same constituency.

Members of the community board of Frankfurt, who were an integral part of this semi-closed social group, were accused on a number of occasions of ignoring the desire of the larger community for the introduction of reforms.[15] It is indeed rather remarkable that thirty years passed before a Reform-dominated board finally entered into a serious struggle with the rabbinate over innovations in the service. We can now understand that the board members were, in fact, turning elsewhere for their own religious needs.

The pattern of development in Frankfurt was followed elsewhere as well during the early years of Reform. In most places, the first generation of Reformers worshiped in schools or in private synagogues. This was the case in Berlin, where services were conducted in private homes, and the most important institution founded during this period was the Hamburg temple, also a private association.

In the 1830s, the Reformers of Frankfurt and throughout Germany changed their tactics and began a more active campaign to bring innovations to the entire community. The new strategy derived both from the failure of their quest for social emancipation and from the renewed attention in Germany to the prospect of political emancipation.

The inability of the Morgenroethe to attain acceptance of Jewish Freemasons was only one example of the many attempts which had failed to provide entry into German social circles in the early decades of the nineteenth century. The concerted effort to legalize the political and social status of the German Jew in the middle third of the nineteenth century was a consequence of his failure to integrate via free and casual paths of intercourse.[16] An ironic anecdote appearing in the press reveals the lesson to be learned from these failures. It dealt with the father who precipitated a major conflict in Frankfurt between the Jewish parties over the question of circumcision.

The Jewish banker Floisheim who precipitated the debate by not allowing his son to be circumcised, had himself nominated for membership in the Casino, where it is well known that Jews are not allowed. A Christian banker commented: "We want no Jews, *keine beschnittene und keine unbeschnittene*"; and Floisheim was unanimously rejected.[17]

The continued failure of such individual attempts to gain social acceptance decreased the value of isolated, individual strides toward acculturation. "We want no Jews," declared the banker and that echoed the warning that the battle could not be fought on an individual basis, but only for the community as a whole.

The need to effect a change in the general image projected by the Jew was necessitated as well by the increasing emphasis on political emancipation. By the late 1830s, the interest in attaining full political emancipation for the Jews of the various German states had been aroused out of its post-Napoleonic dormancy. The 1815 Congress of Vienna had been unable to ensure the Jews of the "restored world" outside France the liberties they had received during French hegemony, and as reaction set into both "throne and altar," Jewish emancipation efforts decreased. But by the late thirties and early forties, ideas of political change returned, and with them Jewish interests in equal rights. The renewed struggle was manifest in the speeches and writings of the lawyer Gabriel Riesser, and no less in the diversified activities of Ludwig Philippson, rabbi in Magdeburg and founder and editor of the *Allgemeine Zeitung des Judenthums*.[18]

The case of Frankfurt Jewry had served as a notorious example of the continuing inferior legal position in Germany. Their plight had been a major item of contention between Frankfurt and its fellow German states at the Congress of Vienna. As late as the 1840s, a number of primitive restrictions remained. As the rest of German Jewry undertook an intensive effort for political emancipation, the Jews of Frankfurt still faced restrictions on the number of marriages permitted the community per year.[19]

By the late 1830s Frankfurt Jewry had reason for muted optimism. The horizons of the proud and independent free city had been broadened in the earlier years of the decade by its affiliation with the Prussian Customs Union and with the proposal of a number of railroad schemes connecting Frankfurt with neighboring centers.[20] Jewish horizons were broadening as well throughout Germany during this same period. Their very lack of rights helped to bind together the Jews of the various states, and a German-language Jewish press emerged to provide weapons and support for the renewed battle. Even while German Jewry argued that it did not constitute a separate national entity within German borders, its press reported extensively on the progress and setbacks of Jewish communities across Germany in the struggle for legal equality from without and in the drive for religious innovations from within. Through the medium of the press, a brotherhood of like-minded Jewry emerged, ironically unified as Jews by their desire to be treated equally as Germans. Political liberals thirsting for change had created a vocabulary of national unrest and Jews were following their model with moderation. The conservative authoritarianism of the reactionary age had found its opposition among elected officials and in popular demonstrations. The presence of the German Confederation's Assembly in Frankfurt provided a constant stimulus to liberal protests and the city became a center for revolutionary activity.[21]

Within the changing political atmosphere, the liberals were gaining strength; yet it was the conservatives, still dominating local politics, who had brought Frankfurt out of its sustained isolationism. The leadership for this shift had been provided by the young Edouard Souchay, who first entered the Senate in 1831. Souchay maintained that Frankfurt's future economic strength depended on its adaptations to new trends in industrial development and monetary systems. He had an immediate impact on Frankfurt's policies, and Richard Schwemer, chronicler of Frankfurt's history, wrote that by the late 1830s Souchay was already "the most significant personality in the Frankfurt Senate." While liberal activity emboldened Jewish tactics, these early steps of modernization by the still predominantly Conservative regime increased Jewish expectations and by the late 1830s, there were public expressions of Jewish discontent with their legal status.[22]

The renewed effort to attain full political rights required an intrinsic change in tactics. The early integrationists had thought that they could win social acceptance on an individual basis, and theoretically they were correct. Invitations to lodge memberships and tea are not granted en masse. Their error lay in not grasping that such invitations could, however, be withheld en masse. Political emancipation was different. The state's interest in emancipation was to diminish the importance of subgroups within its society and to provide open opportunities for all its citizens. As various groups were being absorbed into the general society, the Jew remained a blatant exception, which, as such, could not be tolerated. Only rarely did legal acts of toleration or emancipation distinguish between Jewish residents, for such discrimination would have hindered the objectives of the enactments themselves.[23] The struggle for political emancipation required, therefore, that the state be prepared to grant rights to all Jews and that the Jewish community—as a whole—project an image of being worthy of those rights.[24]

Once they realized that it was the face of the entire community that must be transformed, the second-generation Reformers focused their efforts on the cause of religious change. The reform of Judaism was emerging more and more as the primary focus of attention in proving Jews suitable for full emancipation. Much had already been accomplished in the economic sphere, but as long as society saw Jews only as part of a collective group, the Reformers realized that the image of the Jew could be altered only by reforming the Judaism which bound them together in the public eye. The change in emphasis could be felt in the birth of the Jewish press, in the increasing number of communal struggles over religious change, and in the institution of rabbinical conferences. By 1837 with the appearance of Philippson's *Allgemeine Zeitung des Judenthums* and the rabbinical conference called by Abraham Geiger in Wiesbaden, the second generation of Reformers were bursting into activity. Bitter community struggles between Reform and Orthodox parties soon followed, as the Reformers now sought to expand their influence and to alter the practice of Judaism in communal institutions.

In Frankfurt, the Reformers could no longer be satisfied with a separate service which filled their own needs but left the community synagogue untouched. In the late 1830s they responded to the new conditions and undertook a campaign to bring about innovations in the community's main synagogue.

COMMUNAL STRIFE

The enhanced ambitions of the Reform party in Frankfurt for new directions within the community's religious life conflicted with the traditionalist outlook of the rabbinate and of a sizable segment of the community itself. In 1838 both camps petitioned the Senate for a reexamination of the communal structure. The board expressed dissatisfaction with the existing limits of its authority, while the Orthodox loyalists in turn accused the board of usurping authority beyond their legitimate confines of interest,[25] objecting primarily to the board's encroachment into matters dealing with "church and religion." What were the claims of the board in moving for a redistribution of authority and what did the Orthodox fear as the board sought to expand its power? We do not possess the board's memo, but we can nevertheless reconstruct the atmosphere of conflict from the materials at hand.

The Orthodox petition responded to the Board action, first, by asserting that religious matters were legally outside the realm of the board and, second, by nominating a committee of five community members to assume responsibility in these very matters. This specific proposal was branded as "arrogant" by supporters of the board.[26] A group of initially only ninety-nine members out of a community membership of some seven hundred families, totally self-constituted and certainly unrepresentative, selected five men not only to represent its interests, but to be empowered to make decisions for the entire Jewish community as well.[27]

The basis of the Orthodox case was clause #8 of the 1812 community regulations:

The official function of the Board extends, *with the exclusion of all actual church and religious matters*, solely over the internal administrative affairs of the religious community, as well as over all educational and charitable institutions of the community.[28]

The Orthodox petitioners acted with transparent motivation, but they appear to have been well justified in referring to the indicated exclusion of the board from authority in religious matters. The Board, however, rejoined that the Jewish community had certainly been intended to be a religious entity, and that it represented the legally constituted body of authority. In short, the board insisted that it was the Board of a religious community.[29]

The Frankfurt rabbinate was headed at this time by Solomon Trier (1758–1846), who became a member of the rabbinical court in 1794. In 1807, while Frankfurt was occupied by Napoleonic troops, Trier served on the delegation to the Parisian Sanhedrin, and in 1817 he became Frankfurt's chief rabbi.[30] The last decade of his long career was devoted to the vigorous strife with the Reformers that was now brewing.

By 1838 the board and rabbinate of Frankfurt had come to a stalemate in a conflict over renovation of the community's main synagogue. In March 1834 the board announced a campaign to gather subscriptions for the necessary improvements. The physical structure of the building was central to the ensuing conflict. Sources refer to the existence of two synagogues within the single building, separated by a wall. One of the synagogues was known as the "*Frauensynagogue.*" The proposal for the building's reconstruction called for demolishing the wall and relocating the women from the *Frauensynagogue* to a gallery in the interior of the new single building.[31] The wall separating the synagogues was, then, nothing more than a partition, separating the sections for men and women, but with each section referred to as an individual synagogue. Trier, as head of the Frankfurt rabbinate, forbade the reconstruction program on the grounds that it called for the destruction of a synagogue, or more exactly, the reduction in the number of synagogues, which he asserted was prohibited by Jewish law.[32] The legal validity of Trier's position is doubtful.[33] He himself thought little of it when in 1843, Baron Rothschild mediated a compromise between the two sides and, in turn, pledged to finance construction of the new edifice, women's gallery and all.[34] In fact, both sides were perfectly aware that they were not fighting over the demolition of a wall, but rather over the aesthetic improvement of the religious services and especially over the authority for making those improvements.

The Orthodox position on renovation was first presented in two memoranda submitted to the board in 1837. The first was a petition signed by the rabbinate and 175 members of the community. The Orthodox petitioners lamented the deplorable state of the two synagogues and the negative impression made on all who entered, but the grandiose reconstruction plan proposed by the board in 1834 had proven unrealistic because of the prohibitive cost. The petitioners further opposed the project because the extent of reconstruction involved would so alter the synagogue building that all the worshiper's recollections of and associations with the past would be eradicated.[35] The latter argument reveals a hint of the underlying basis for their opposition, because the extensiveness of the changes involved would cut the cord connecting present with past and dangerously facilitate the possibility of extensive changes within the ritual itself. There is only the barest hint in this first statement that the reconstruction program was in conflict with Jewish law. Nevertheless, in the second statement issued in November 1837, the rabbinate officially forbade the proposed program. The Orthodox party proposed instead a renovation of both existing synagogues, while the rabbinate pledged to introduce liturgical reforms "whenever possible," thus fully exposing its identification of physical renovation with religious reforms.[36]

The rabbinate was, of course, correct that renovation was a mere stepping-stone for the board and its supporters toward further reforms. Michael Creizenach, teacher of religion at the Reform-oriented Philanthropin and leader of the Reform party, responded to the rabbinical declaration in two letters published in the *Allgemeine Zeitung des Judenthums* in early 1838. Creizenach informed the paper's readers that the Frankfurt Board had on many occasions attempted to beautify the existing synagogue into a worthy house of prayer "and thereby prepare the way for a progressive improvement of the manner of worship."[37]

The board complied with the rabbinate's decision, but it is evident from its announcement delaying the reconstruction program that its members felt their authority circumscribed. The tension over spheres of authority was growing and was soon complicated by a vacancy in the Frankfurt rabbinate. The death of Jacob Silberkron on January 23, 1838, intensified the divisions.

Five candidates applied for the vacant position of deputy rabbi. Of these, one, deficient in his secular studies, was supported by the Orthodox faction. A number of community members, however, petitioned the board to insist upon the gymnasium and university studies required by existing ordinances.[38] We may conclude that the ensuing impasse, combined with the board's inability to proceed with its plan to renovate the synagogue building, resulted in the board's request of March 13, 1838, for a Senate reevaluation of the governing structure of the Jewish community and for greater authority in the religious sphere in order to break the existing deadlocks.

How far apart were the two factions? The rabbinate itself had, after all, openly favored improvements in the synagogue service: "To introduce all liturgical improvements wherever possible." But, in reality, the rabbinate placed serious obstacles in the path of the most elementary innovations, while the introduction of reforms within the Orthodox framework was actually intolerable for the Reformers themselves. The futile attempt to introduce a discourse into the synagogue service exemplifies both points.

Discourses were conducted in Frankfurt under the traditional auspices of the *Tzitzith* Society, a somewhat unusual private association whose *raison d'être* was the distribution of this religious garment to poor religious Jews. As in most cases of an association formed by members of the Jewish community, the *Tzitzith* Society filled a number of diverse purposes.[39] Members assembled in their own facilities beneath the yeshivah after Sabbath and festival services were concluded. There they enjoyed a discourse from their own rabbi, specifically engaged by the society to speak on the "weekly Haphtorah, on contemporary matters, or on the Torah portion of that Sabbath."[40]

Jacob Silberkron, whose death in 1838 precipitated the conflict over the appointment of a deputy rabbi and preacher, had served as rabbi of the society since at least 1821.[41] It was no accident, then, that the dispute broke out with Silberkron's death, since the future of the discourses was now open to question. With the appointment of a preacher unresolved, the rabbinate took steps of its own. After Silberkron's death, discourses in the German vernacular were delivered by three members of the rabbinate, Beer M. Adler, Aaron Moses Fuld, and Abraham Trier (son of the city's chief rabbi). These lectures were still under the patronage of the *Tzitzith* Society, since until this time such lectures had been the exclusive privilege of that association.[42]

Despite the apparent breakthrough made on the question of German discourses delivered in the synagogue, the rabbinate proved unable to come to terms with the innovation. The lectures began one half hour following the conclusion of the service, and the preacher did not occupy the same position in front of the ark used by the rabbi when he himself delivered sermons. Even our source, a traditional correspondent, could not understand why the discourses were not delivered as an integral part of the service and from the proper place of honor.[43] The implication is that once again, as in the renovation of the synagogue, the rabbinate agreed to the reform only on its own terms and in this way attempted to safeguard its own authority.

The Reformers, for their part, were unmoved by whatever progress had been made. Michael Creizenach, in one of his letters to the *Allgemeine Zeitung des Judenthums*, scored the distance in mentality separating the preachers, who continued to center their lives and teachings around the Talmud, from their listeners:

So long as the growing chaos within the religious consciousness of Jews is not improved, so that teaching and life are not brought together in harmony, *every modernisation of the synagogue service remains a bitter irony.*[44]

Creizenach's position here reflects the concern that Orthodoxy would prove capable of thwarting the Reform thrust by offering piecemeal changes, leaving the overall system with its principles intact. "What basic changes in ritual can be expected," he asked, "if the literal letter of the *Shulchan Aruch* must be strictly adhered to?"[45]

The Reformers took active steps to express their opposition. In the middle of 1840, the by-then four rabbis sharing the preaching duties announced that it was not possible for them to continue this responsibility regularly. Our newspaper source tells us that the initiative for this decision came from them and for well-justified reasons.[46] We know nothing more about their decision. One Joseph Isaaksohn of Filehne, in Posen, was appointed provisional rabbi of the *Tzitzith* Society and assumed the role of preacher. The board, however, relocated the lectures once again; now they were delivered in one of the smaller synagogues rather than in the main synagogue. Perhaps the board wanted to indicate that Isaaksohn, despite his preaching role, had not been appointed to the still vacant position of deputy rabbi and was to be considered no more than rabbi of the society.

Even in this more restricted location, Isaaksohn had succeeded in attracting one hundred men, women, and youth to his weekly lectures when *"ploetzlich wie vom Himmel,"* he was called before the police commissioner and ordered to halt them until further notice. The commissioner explained that the orders had originated with the community itself. The press report indicates that upon further inquiry, the orders were traced to the community school board, on which several members of the board served.[47]

The Reformers were blatantly unable to tolerate the possibility of innovation within the Orthodox framework. A Reform spokesman and board member made the point well when, a few years later, he reportedly responded to a request that an Orthodox rabbi with advanced education be called to Frankfurt: "If you would like to have a Polack, that would be fine with us, with a huge beard, who has come out of the Ukraine, but an educated man—at no price."[48] In the Reform view, a fossilized Orthodoxy personified by the long-bearded rabbi clarified the choices available to the Jewish community. But if the Orthodox could succeed in projecting an image of openness to innovation, it would threaten the very self-definition of the Reform platform.

The Reform leaders like Creizenach, in fact, had good reason to fear that cosmetic changes introduced by the Orthodox could seriously weaken their cause and that Reformist energies within the community would be dissipated over mere changes of form. The success of the so-called Vienna Program, with its emphasis on introducing a choir, discourses, and decorum into the services underscored the reality that few Jews, even in Germany, were seriously concerned with liturgical changes that reflected an evolution in theological beliefs.[49]

Both sides from their different perspectives saw the inadequacy of isolated innovations. The Reformers did not reject the

Orthodox attempts—feeble as they were—merely for tactical reasons. Creizenach's letters to the *Allgemeine Zeitung des Judenthums* are indeed very revealing. He saw the specific changes, reconstruction of the synagogue and weekly discourses in the vernacular, within a matrix of innovations and ideological principles that approved of an evolutionary process in Jewish religious practice. He himself could not look upon these same innovations as isolated components; hence, his contention that synagogue reconstruction meant little if the system still depended upon the *Shulchan Aruch*, and that sermons were of limited value if the preachers lacked advanced secular education. The traditionalists of Frankfurt, for their part, were not yet prepared to introduce their own system in which innovations seemed plausible. Hence they too were correct that there was nowhere to go but from one innovation to another, as demanded by the Reformers, since it was still the Reformers' vision that governed the battle. Only at the end of the next decade would the Frankfurt Orthodox emerge with their own system in which innovations would be integrally bound up with a staunch defense of traditionalism.

The Orthodox petition of March 1838 originally received 99 signatures, and a later demonstration of support attracted 212 adherents. Yet, a counterpetition backing the board and its policies received 272 signatures.[50] On March 8, 1839, the Senate, responding to the petitions of both parties, issued a new regulation governing the community's central bodies. The most significant change was the establishment of a bicameral system. A community council was charged with the task of supervising the community's spending, participated in the nomination of new members of the board, and together with the board, had general control over the cultural and religious needs of the community. The board, on the other hand, retained certain independent spheres of authority, especially its relations with the municipal authorities.[51]

The two bodies, each consisting of nine members, were selected by quite different procedures. In each case, the Senate itself chose from a list of three nominees for each vacant position, submitted together with the recommendations of the Senate commissioner for Jewish affairs. But while the nominations for membership to the board were designated by a joint meeting of the board and council, nominations for openings in the council itself were determined by open elections within the community.[52] Taken as a whole, the new structure provided a rather elaborate combination of limited democracy within a framework which remained very much under the direct control of the Senate.

The new regulation dealt as well with the qualifications for rabbinical positions. The incumbent rabbinate was confirmed in its position, but requirements were imposed for the selection of future rabbis. Candidates were expected to be German by birth, to have studied in a German gymnasium and to be familiar with historical and philosophical studies, and to pass an examination given by the chief rabbi or to substitute the approval of the rabbinate of two other major German cities.[53]

The regulation has often been described as favoring the side of the Reformers, but this was not the case. By introducing free elections, the Senate had not judged either party as morally or theologically desirable, but left the decision to the criterion of majority rule. Further, the stipulation requiring of rabbinical candidates a firm background in German life and culture was not a new ordinance, but a reaffirmation of similar rulings which dated back to 1807 and were repeated in 1812 and 1829.[54] If there had been an innovation, it, too, was in support of the traditionalists, for the available sources give no earlier indication of the required examination in Jewish studies, a stipulation that in real terms would require Trier's approval of any selection made by the board for a rabbinical position. On the other hand, the Senate supplied its own way of by-passing the Frankfurt rabbinate with the curious alternative that a candidate could be examined by the rabbinate of two other cities. This ruling may have reflected the board's argument which made reference to the religious advances made in other German states, especially in southern Germany.[55] In the selection of new members of the rabbinate specifically, and in the regulation generally, the Senate wove a delicate path between the factions.

The Orthodox were reportedly happy with the regulation, while, as we shall see, the board was not.[56] Amidst the tension that preceded the actual appearance of the regulation, the Orthodox had developed fears that the Senate would demand changes in the rabbinical leadership. When the Senate did not tamper with the existing ecclesiastical authorities, the Orthodox were relieved and even grateful.[57]

The Protocol Book of the Senate contains a statement issued to both parties upon passage of the regulation, summarizing the Senate's position:

> The necessary provisions have been made through the new regulation ... for the appropriate handling of the religious and liturgical matters of the community, such that both the protection of positive faith and a just toleration of freedom of conscience will emerge out of its stipulations, especially if both parties will only apply themselves harmoniously to such improvements ... that will not harm, but rather will strengthen the ancestral religious order. Both parties are therefore being cautioned in this matter that the Senate will always be prepared to oppose all, which can, in fact offend the conscience of believing Jews and can disturb their traditional service; but on the other hand, will support, for its part, whatever is dictated by the advances of time for the true and essential religious culture.[58]

The statement clarified the Senate's leaning toward positive reforms that would not prove offensive to the community's members. Even more strongly emphasized was the Senate's growing disgust with the tensions dividing the community. On this count, the regulation proved to be a complete failure.

The Senate's neutrality was, according to the contemporary historian Jost, the stuff of which controversy was made. There were German states, especially in the south, where the civil government had strongly supported the introduction of reforms. This was done, as in Wuertemberg and Baden, by the creation of civil authorities responsible for the religious affairs of the Jews. Other states, like Prussia, had also imposed their will on Jewish religious life by prohibiting the introduction of innovations.[59] But in Frankfurt, the Senate did not blatantly support either side. By throwing the question of reform back to the community, it left the way open for continued communal strife.[60]

The Senate's policies toward the Jews for some twenty years, culminating in the new regulations, had been framed by its commissioner for Jewish affairs, Christian Friedrich Ihm. Ihm had earlier been the foremost spokesman for developing close commercial ties between Frankfurt and Prussia. But Ihm in those days had stood alone. His position in the Senate was influential but isolated. When an alliance with Prussia became a matter of necessity, Ihm at last found the majority support he needed, but through a plot of political intrigue, the conservative powers successfully removed him from leadership in 1834. In subsequent years, his role in the Senate diminished, and his influence with the Jewish community waned as well.[61]

A few weeks after the Jewish regulations had been issued, Ihm resigned his position as commissioner for Jewish affairs. The *Allgemeine Zeitung des Judenthums* reported that the board of the Jewish community had expressed its gratitude to Ihm for his long service to the community. Jost, however, observed that the board's commendation was merely an act of formality and that relations between the two had, in fact, not been very cordial. Based on materials from the Municipal Archives, we can go even further: The board had requested Ihm's resignation as commissioner. On January 28, 1839, after Ihm's recommendations to the Senate had apparently become known to the board, it submitted to the Senate a protest against the commissioner. The Senate rebuked the board for its action, but Ihm resigned his post.[62]

The board had reason for dissatisfaction with the new regulations, despite attempted neutrality in their formulations, for the regulations had not solved the board's inability to circumvent the rabbinical intransigence against innovations. Indeed, the board had been entrusted with authority in the religious sphere, but in conjunction with a council whose composition was still unknown and with a rabbinate with which it had been unable to work. Under such circumstances, the board might well have asked how harmony could be returned to the community, as urged by the Senate's warning. Ihm's attempt at neutrality thus failed from the outset.[63]

The Senate passed the Ihm regulations in 1839 with some limited opposition from both liberal and conservative sides.[64] Following his resignation, Ihm was replaced by a commissioner who was prepared to play a more active role in the Jewish community's inner affairs. The appointment of senate leader Edouard

Souchay as commissioner was the first of several events that both facilitated and necessitated the implementation of a more militant policy by the Reformers.

The first Council elections were held in May 1839. Of approximately 720 members entitled to vote, some 640 exercised this right. In accordance with the procedures outlined in the regulation, the names of the twenty-seven men receiving the highest vote were transmitted to the Senate for selection of the nine who would actually comprise the Council. The results for the Orthodox were devastating.

The Reformers received two-thirds of the votes and all of the twenty-seven places.[65] The opposing petitions of 1838 had revealed 272 supporters of the board against 212 Orthodox, or approximately 56 percent versus 44 percent of the number of signatures.

That the Orthodox were incapable of rallying sufficient support behind even one of their candidates indicates how strongly the party lines had now been drawn. The numerical strength of the Reform party demonstrated considerable support beyond the leadership ranks that we have been describing. Approximately 400 community members voted for the Reformers. They comprised the majority of the community membership, and that is almost the only way they can be identified and described, since we do not have lists that would specifically identify them as supporters of the Reform party. On the whole, they were businessmen, although some probably engaged in currency trade as well. The Reformers were primarily a middle-class party, presumably attracted to Reform by a desire for upward mobility. In fact, as we shall see in the example of synagogue construction, despite their numbers, the Reformers did not enjoy considerable financial support.[66] Most did not attend synagogue regularly. A few may have attended the Orthodox community synagogue, and another limited number attended the *Andachtstunde*, but even after the community synagogue introduced a Reform service, it was only sparsely attended.[67] This majority perceived the Reform party as the better representative of their interests and shared a conviction that religious reforms were necessary. It must also be recalled that many community members had over the course of the previous thirty-five years sent their children to the Philanthropin School and by this time a large number had in fact themselves graduated from its ranks, thus increasing the Reformist sentiment in the community.[68] The board had now received a clear mandate to hasten the process of reform, and the Senate now looked more favorably upon the Reform party and entered a period in which it consistently turned its back on the Orthodox.[69] Yet the board remained inactive for several more years. The decisive victory behind, the road was now clear for those men who disapproved of the board's moderation in pursuing reform to press harder for their demands to be fulfilled. The more militant position was publicly espoused by a group small in size, but which succeeded in influencing the content and intensity of the debate over reform in Frankfurt and in all of Germany.

THE FRIENDS OF REFORM

The members of the Frankfurt Society of Friends of Reform, the *Reformverein*, were probably the most notorious of second-generation Reformers. Usually they are discounted as a small, short-lived group, but this underrates the influence that they did obtain.[70] The *Reformverein* did not merely want more reform; it sought a system to the process of reforming. In this sense, it shared Michael Creizenach's criticism against piecemeal innovations introduced by the Orthodox. But the society's program was primarily a critique, not of the Orthodox, but of the early Reformers themselves. The society's leading force was Theodore Creizenach, son of the man who had led Frankfurt Reform in the first generation. Strikingly, the society was formed in late 1842, shortly after the father's death.

The members of the *Reformverein* had their own views on the scope and nature of reform. Their objections to the religious status quo were most eloquently expressed in an essay published anonymously in 1837. The layman author was, according to Jost, a member of the later society.[71]

Jews and non-Jews alike, wrote the author, had been convinced that the political emancipation of the Jew would be an inevitable result of the course of justice. Most Jews unified in the pursuit of emancipation, but only a limited segment under-took religious reform. These few separated from the larger com-munity, while Jews, on the whole, appeared satisfied that their own internal condition would not detract from their chances of political emancipation, labeled by the author, "the most impor-tant objective." The internal matters, they thought, could be left to the processes of time, and they remained indifferent to them. This apathy was the result either of the belief that those elements repulsive to reason had already been fully removed from the religion or from the self-deception that the unsuitability of one's religious attitudes would not hinder recognition by the state.

By 1837 the lesson had been learned that the self-complacency of the community was in error and that the actions of an isolated few would not help attain the desired goal. Progress had been achieved in the cultural and economic spheres, but the religious image of the community lagged far behind. "Jewry has ad-vanced," declared the writer in his most poignant point, "Ju-daism has stood still. So much in the views of a significant number of Jews has changed, so little with regard to the Jewish religion—least of all its external appearance—has undergone any kind of transformation." Despite the activities of individual re-formers, "without a specific declaration of what is meant by pure Judaism and what is unauthorized ornamentation . . . the religion in general remains distorted." It is precisely this false picture which is of significance: The image projected by Judaism as a religious entity was now of primary importance to the emerging Reform school. "As yet, Judaism is understood as every existing and traditional law; the *Shulchan Aruch* with its insatiable commentaries and super commentaries is still recog-nized as its symbol, any deviation from it, is considered equiv-alent to a deviation from the religion itself." The reform efforts of the past had been carried out "in secrecy and evasiveness," and hence, Judaism remained precisely where it had been. There has been no change in the concept of "Jewish-religious."[72]

The greatest disappointment had come from the younger, pro-gressive generation of rabbis, but the author was aware of the pressures heterogeneous communities placed upon the rabbi, hindering him from taking decisive action. The duty therefore fell upon the laymen to issue public declarations of their view to encourage the rabbis to take "decisive steps forward." The author himself proposed a text for such a declaration:

[We] do not feel in conscience bound to invest the prescriptions of the Talmud, to say nothing of those of the later rabbis, in as far as these cannot be proved by scientific exegesis to have been handed down by Moses, with any greater authority than is awarded all other temporary religious institutions whose reasonableness and whose agreement with the spirit of Judaism must first be established.[73]

The formulation of a theological creed might imply a sectarian split, but that was not the author's intention. Expression must be given, however, to the existing differences:

This is no schism, no more than the separation between the supernaturalists and the rationalists in the Evangelical Church. The differences exist: better that they come out openly and together than in the isolated acts of individuals; . . . better that they become the means to progress than the cause of complete disintegration.[74]

The author's logic, combining the open declaration of differences with disavowal of a schism, underscores the new strategy that Reformers must no longer be satisfied with separation, but must undertake the battle for control of the total community.

It is noteworthy that the writer continued to recognize the rabbinate as the legitimate leadership of the Jewish community, while making only passing references to the accomplishments of the teachers of religion at the Philanthropin and elsewhere. These men had been the de facto leaders of Reform in the first generation, editing textbooks and prayerbooks and serving as spokesmen of the emerging movement. Most prominent among them were the teachers of Frankfurt—Josef Johlson and, especially, Michael Creizenach. And yet, while the author applauded their accomplishments, he felt these to be insufficient, isolated acts, albeit in the correct spirit of Judaism. The by-passing of these men in favor of the younger rabbinate indicates the shift of concern away from the separated back to the integral community. The teachers had provided adequate leadership for the early, sectarian phase of Reform development, but the rabbinate was the traditional source of authority and it would be through the rabbis that Judaism's image would be recast.

The *Reformverein* was formed sometime prior to November 1842. Most contemporary reports estimate its size at about twenty members.[75] We possess the names of only a few: the lawyers Goldschmidt and Simon Maas; Joseph Ruetten, a merchant; Schwarzschild, a physician; Theodore Creizenach and M. A. Stern of Goettingen, both academicians.[76] One report was somewhat specific about the occupations of the members—two doctors, two lawyers, two writers—and the society numbered within its membership two members of the community's board.[77] The group's short but eventful history is laden with confusion. The fullest account has been presented by David Philipson, and we follow it here with some revisions.

The first meetings were held privately and the members discussed a statement of the principles that bound them together. An early formulation included five points, three of which were retained by the *Reformverein* in its later declaration. At first, the founders thought to declare their opposition to specific rituals, especially circumcision, but also "ritual, dietary, and other laws concerned with bodily practices." These sections were eliminated, however, so that the declaration would be of a general nature and disagreements on specific questions would not be encouraged.

The society had sought to issue its declaration publicly only after gathering a list of notable supporters. Correspondence relating to the society, however, was leaked to the public, reportedly by a member of the Orthodox party, resulting in considerable attention in both the German and Jewish press. At least in the latter, little of that notice was complimentary, but the negative effect that the premature publication had on the *Reformverein*'s image has been exaggerated. Actually, by the time of the disclosure, the society was already in the process of openly publicizing its position.

On June 21, 1843, *The Frankfurter Journal* printed a brief notice that then spread through the German press and was copied in the *Allgemeine Zeitung des Judenthums*.

A new Jewish sect has been founded here under the direction of Dr. Creizenach. The supporters—and they already amount to a considerable number—do not adhere to any Jewish-Talmudic ceremony of law; do not look upon circumcision—either as a religiously or as a civily obliging act; and believe that the Messiah has come in the form of the German Fatherland. The supporters of this sect are increasing daily and are already circulating lists outside [Frankfurt].[78]

The *Frankfurter Journal* continued to spotlight the *Reformverein*'s activities. A few weeks later, the *Allgemeine Zeitung des Judenthums* described the society more precisely as a "Society for the Reform of Judaism." Theodore Creizenach was identified as organizer, and Gabriel Riesser of Hamburg and M. A. Stern of Goettingen were reported to be participants. Philippson also received information from a private correspondent, which named the same three men and listed the three points that corresponded to those of the later declaration. Opposition to circumcision was no longer listed as a principle, but only as an example of the nonauthority of Talmudic legislation.[79]

In response to these announcements, Riesser composed a public statement on August 1, published in the *Allgemeine Zeitung des Judenthums* on August 14, in which he denied his association with the *Reformverein*. Reisser admitted that he had been contacted by Stern in November 1842, and later by Creizenach and that his views had been solicited. At first, he had informed them of his opinion of the society's program, which was more opposed than in favor; but in February 1843 he had discontinued the correspondence.[80] Within a week after publishing Riesser's letter, Philippson received a copy of the controversial pamphlet containing excerpts from Riesser's correspondence. Although aware that the pamphlet originated from an opponent of the Society, and despite having himself published Riesser's disclaimer of involvement, Philippson welcomed the opportunity to damage the society's reputation.[81]

Stern, especially, was quite open in the correspondence on his objectives in these activities and on his attitudes toward Judaism. He admitted how far removed he was from feeling part of the Jewish community and feared that the bonds of many other Jews, especially intellectuals, were just as tenuous.[82] Intellectuals could not be satisfied with sermons, confirmations, choirs, and "other masquerades." Christianity might easily prove too tempting under these circumstances, since churches had greatly facilitated the process of conversion. Stern was well aware of his final objective—nothing short of the "annihilation of positive revealed religion," but he was less certain of where to begin his attack. A generalized struggle against the Orthodox might have attracted broader support and reduced criticism, but the *Reformverein* had decided to penetrate further with its initial program. On the one hand, Judaism had to be liberated from its Talmudic hegemony; yet, it could not be reduced to a fundamentalist biblical religion. The declaration was formulated to avoid both of these positions, and Stern commented freely on its tenets.

1. Judaism is capable of continuing development, such that it can absorb the latest and highest results of philosophy.

2. The Talmud must be refuted so that Jews can be freed of rabbinic authority, which can be as burdensome as one expects the civil authorities to be.

3. The belief in a Messiah must be negated not only for the sake of progress, but even as a matter of honor for which Jews are obligated to their Christian brothers.[83]

In an important programmatic statement, Stern expanded the argument for laymen taking the initiative by issuing the declaration. The theologians, who would undertake the extended struggle, must first have communities to support them, and such communities can only result from societies paving the way. Here, Stern implied a clear difference between the society, whose function was the winning over of entire communities, and the earlier Reform groups, which had established their own self-contained religious institutions. The point was made even more explicit in a published letter from Stern to Creizenach. There Stern emphasized the importance of the negative orientation of the declaration. A more positive program would amount

to building a house from the top downward and must be left to the future, while we first sow the seeds. Temple and new English synagogue [referring to the Hamburg Temple and the West London synagogue] are not healthy births, but a true abortion of an awakening desire for reform.[84]

Here was the full thrust of the *Reformverein*'s position. The desire for true reform was being strangled—not just by the Orthodox— but through compromise by the Reformers themselves. Rather, the very foundations of the existing system had to be overthrown and only then could a positive new entity be built.[85]

The publication of these documents was seen as severely damaging the society's cause, but this is an exaggeration.[86] The documents revealed very little that the society had not previously stated publicly. Furthermore, the society was clearly not overly concerned with publicizing the contents of these letters. Directly or indirectly, the society itself was responsible for the disclosure. The *Deutsche Allgemeine Zeitung* put it well: "After all, if the correspondence of Stern and Riesser was included in the Society's mailing to its members, it is quite easily explained how [these letters] came into improper hands."[87] The failure of the society to gain any significant, direct support did not result from publication of the correspondence or from premature publication of its program, but rather from a number of broader factors.

The negative approach of the program hurt the society's potential growth because of the deep commitment it implied. The society's leadership was fully aware that a positive program, for example of "sermons, confirmations, and choral singing," could sway larger numbers. The experiences in Hamburg and London had shown that communities could be built by people who sensed a dissatisfaction with the existent religious scene and were attracted to an alternative program. This did not mean, however, that these same people would have a fundamental grasp of the cause of the deficiencies in religious life and would be so committed to their removal as to identify with a nascent movement that went no further than to attack the causes without offering a positive alternative, lest they "build a house from the top downwards." In essence, the *Reformverein* was perceived as nihilistic. German Jewry may have been rapidly becoming religiously indifferent, but not self-destructive.

The *Reformverein* was also hurt by its attacks on the rabbinate, whose role in the religious authoritative system was too significant for Jews to conceive of theological and ritual innovations being introduced without their support. All Reform congregations and societies were founded by laymen, but other than the *Reformverein*, all appointed rabbinical leadership. The 1837 essay had talked of laymen supporting rabbinical systems; the 1843 *Reformverein* merely echoed this strategy but usurped the full initiative for itself.

The failure of the *Reformverein* to attract membership should not imply that it was without influence, for the society had a definite impact on the pace at which reforms were discussed and introduced in Frankfurt and throughout Germany. It accomplished this feat by attracting attention to an extent totally disproportionate to its limited size. The *Allgemeine Zeitung des Judenthums* and the *Orient* frequently attacked; the *Israelit des Neunzehnten Jahrhunderts* no less often defended the society's position. The seriousness with which the society was dealt is explained by a number of factors, the primary one being the coverage the society received in the general press. Philippson explained his position in the pages of his paper:

It would, perhaps, have been better to remain silent on this matter, until it actually proved itself. . . . But the matter has already been reported on too often. The *Frankfurter Journal* has published a number of articles, . . . so this subject must be examined closely.[88]

The *Reformverein* had forced the Jewish community to take notice by releasing its initial information to the general and not to the Jewish press. Whether it did so because it feared the Jewish press would ignore it or because it was precisely the German public that it sought to reach, it is clear that it was not hesitant about the German public knowing of its activities. If it sought to spur Jews into action, it no less wanted Germans to encourage such actions further.

The society's radical program added fuel to the attention and concern it was given. The moderate Reformers grew anxious as they saw the radical paths that might be followed if passivity continued. Most especially, the society's support of the growing opposition to the circumcision ritual raised apprehension. When two cases occurred of fathers foregoing circumcision of their sons, the society came to their defense, and the initial anxiety that had greeted the society grew to condemnation.[89]

Riesser's disclaimer of involvement and the subsequent disclosure of the documents reinforced its position in the public spotlight. Riesser had been forced to take an open stand on their platform, and the turn of events maintained intensive discussion of the program in the press.

Partly by accident or circumstances, partly by intention, the *Reformverein* captured attention. In Berlin and Breslau similar groups followed the Frankfurt society in expressing their dissatisfaction with the pace of rabbinically inspired reform. The rabbis were losing influence in a battle they essentially supported. When the clamor over the *Reformverein* began to subside, the rabbis responded. Ludwig Philippson, who had earlier seen the need for development of the Jewish press, now pressed for convocation of an annual rabbinical conference. The first of three conferences held in successive years was convened at Braunschweig in 1844. In his initial plea for the rabbis to come together and take stands on the issues of the day, Philippson echoed the barrage of criticism aimed at the rabbinate: "Jewish religious life grows weaker from day to day, and the laity asks us: what are you doing?"[90]

In Frankfurt, too, the *Reformverein* had its influence. The "layman" of 1837 had rejected precisely the situation that had developed in Frankfurt. A group of men actively pursuing reform had established their own service, allowing an atmosphere of indifference to permeate the main synagogue. But it was precisely there that the battle had to be fought. If the first generation had been inhibited by a desire to avoid a schism within the community, the laymen replied that the split was there and could no longer be ignored. The *Reformverein* set out to display its strength and to confirm the gap between the communal institutions and the views of the individual members. Various reports indicated that it was not taken very seriously within the Frankfurt community itself. The *Allgemeine Zeitung des Judenthums* reported that, "The entire Society is . . . more visible from a distance; here it is hardly noticed and remains unheeded."[91] A correspondent for the *Orient* drew a similar picture and assured his readers that local response to the society had been totally negative and that membership had not grown beyond forty-five.[92] But the society was not as totally isolated within the community as these views indicate. Two of the nine members of the community's board were, in fact, members of the society and this required the support of a majority of the remaining members of the community's governing bodies.[93]

When, in December 1843, the community took the step it had delayed for so long and appointed a deputy rabbi, there were those who suggested the society's influence in the selection. But whether or not this was the case, the action followed quickly after the society had tested the waters of public opinion in the summer and autumn of that year, and if it did not result from their positive influence, then as Jost suggested, the society's activities at least had hastened the process.[94] The appointment of Leopold Stein as deputy rabbi was a precaution against the anarchistic tendencies of the more extreme Reformers. The specific issue that prompted such concern was the requirement for circumcision for inclusion within the Jewish community. It was once again in Frankfurt that the issue came to the foreground.

CONFLICT OVER CIRCUMCISION

On February 8, 1843, the Health Department of Frankfurt issued a new regulation governing the Jewish practice of circumcising all male infants on the eighth day after birth. The ordinance, whether or not harmlessly intended, resulted in a controversy ranging over the breadth of Germany. The controversy indeed had been long in coming; the new edict provided the framework, and the radicals of Frankfurt provided the case.[95]

The edict of the Health Department required that any future circumcisions be conducted by a properly approved individual who demonstrated the necessary knowledge of anatomy and physiology, as well as the technical skill required for the act. Furthermore, the circumcision was to be conducted in the presence of a fully recognized doctor. The intent of the decree was to safeguard the lives of children from the dangers involved in an improperly conducted medical procedure or from the operation being performed on an unhealthy child. The legitimacy of the state's right to enter the realm of licensing the *mohelim* who conducted the rite was not challenged, as far as I know, anywhere in the ensuing debate. Philippson declared in the *Allgemeine Zeitung des Judenthums* that he favored the law and that he recommended using a Jewish doctor whenever possible. Solomon Trier referred to the law as "a beneficial measure which was soon imitated in those states, where such ordinances did not yet exist."[96]

The provocative section of the law was not legislative, but a mere summarizing statement of what was now required. It began, "Jewish citizens and residents insofar as they wish to have their children circumcised."[97] The civil authority had, with this clause, declared circumcision of a Jewish infant to be an optional act, subject to the discretion of the parents. Although religious observance was not enforced upon Jews by the civil authorities, circumcision had been viewed as a prerequisite for membership in the Jewish community. Since Frankfurt's Jews were classified by the city's law as "Jewish citizens," a category which required membership in the Jewish community, circumcision had been required for all Jewish males.[98] One could not live in no-man's-land. As Philippson put it, the choice had been between circumcision and baptism. In consequence of the new law, however, the father now had the free choice of whether or not to circumcise.[99]

Solomon Trier, still rabbi of the community, explained the gravity of the situation to the Senate in an address dated February 20. Circumcision, Trier explained, symbolized the eternal covenant between God and the descendants of Abraham. The transgressor of this commandment helped destroy that eternal bond and was therefore to be excluded from any Jewish community. In fact, a community was responsible for circumcising a boy if the father did not. Therefore, Trier argued, circumcision was not a commandment that could be made dependent upon the free choice of the individual. He petitioned the Senate to issue a declaration correcting any "misunderstanding" that could arise from the decree.[100] The Senate's answer came on March 10, explaining "that the ordinance in question in no way had the intention of annulling a Jewish religious law."[101] The inadequacy of the Senate's response became apparent when a father, in fact, refused to allow the circumcision of his son. Trier now returned with a more explicit request that the Senate rule that an uncircumcised son would not be recognized as Jewish by the community.[102] The Senate, after long delay, replied on February 13, 1844, that it regretted that individual Jews might cause offense to the community, but that it could not take the action requested.[103] Trier was requested to take his appeal to the community board.

Trier turned to the Senate repeatedly in the latter half of 1843 and early 1844. He did so first over the circumcision and later over the appointment of Leopold Stein as deputy rabbi of the community. The Senate rebuffed him continuously, referring him to the board. At times it lost its patience with him; when Trier persisted in his petition for a ruling that an uncircumcised boy could not be accepted into the Jewish community, the Senate scolded him: "Must Rabbi Trier be reminded of the Senate's previous decision [not to intervene]?"[104] The Senate had discarded its neutrality of the 1830s, employed in designing the community's new regulations. It now not only consistently supported the Reformers as they finally asserted their control over the community, but even supported the program of the more radical *Reformverein* members. Indeed, the origins of the circumcision decree can, I think, be traced to their influence.

During the early 1840s, numerous polemics appeared on the circumcision question.[105] Attacks claiming the ritual to be barbaric, as well as defenses of the ritual, were written and forwarded to the responsible bodies. But the 1843 enactment in Frankfurt did not result merely from literary pamphlets. One of the few members of the *Reformverein* who can be identified by name was a Dr. Schwarzschild, described in the *Orient* as "a general practitioner and obstetrician." In fact, Heinrich Schwarzschild was one of Frankfurt's most popular and influential doctors, a specialist in the area of gynecology, and also a leading spokesman on the political scene for Frankfurt's radical party.[106] In later years Schwarzschild was a member of the Health Department Board itself. The evidence is circumstantial, but one of the *Reformverein* leaders possessed both the position and the connections to influence the Health Department in their policies. Furthermore, such an action would not have been unusual for this period of intensive conflict over reform generally and cir-

cumcision specifically. If the decree did result from Schwarzschild's influence, then however well justified the ruling had been
for reasons of health, its wording was not the error of an un-
involved official.

Jewish doctors played an active role in bringing the circumcision ritual and its dangers to the attention of the public authorities. Dr. J. Bergson, a founding member of the Reform
Congregation of Berlin, composed a comprehensive survey of
interpretations of the origins of the ritual, as well as an elaborate
description of the procedure of operation and his own suggested
reforms for greater safety.[107] Bergson referred to other Jewish
doctors in France and Germany who had publicly opposed the
procedures then in practice. He himself hoped to encourage the
Prussian authorities to increase their role in supervising per-
formance of this procedure. He also sent a copy of his work to
the Frankfurt Senate.[108]

What prompted Jewish Reformers like Bergson and possibly
Schwarzschild in their opposition to circumcision? Some basis
exists for considering their objectives to have been political. An
essay attributed to Josef Johlson, teacher at the Philanthropin,
which appeared during the height of the controversy in Frankfurt, hinted at political objections to circumcision. The commandment in Genesis, the author explained, was the sign of a
specific covenant in which God promised to form a nation out
of Abraham's descendants and to give them the land of Ca-
naan.[109] Bergson too referred to the political interpretation of
Johann David Michaelis, who denied that the ritual had originally possessed any religious significance.[110] According to the
eighteenth-century German Bible scholar, circumcision was a
formal prerequisite for political citizenship in the Israelite nation.
One might easily conclude that the Reformers who sought the
abolition of the practice wished to extinguish another reference
to a Jewish longing for return to Palestine and independent,
political sovereignty. But, as Bergson himself affirmed, whatever
the origins of the practice, it had evolved into a religious institution of sacred meaning.[111] The attempts to annul the practice
did not presume circumcision to have retained any political significance, as the ritual had long outlived the notion of citizenship
in an Israelite state.

Objections to circumcision were raised only by the most radical Reformers, and to understand their reasons it is necessary to distinguish between their position and that of the moderates. Only a small minority of Reform leaders supported abolition of the circumcision commandment. For example, Ludwig Philippson's *Allgemeine Zeitung* vehemently attacked the opponents of circumcision.[112] The mainstream Reformer introduced only moderate innovations into the service, adding a sermon, a choir, and prayers in translation. His objective was to attain political emancipation without sacrificing his Jewish identity. The more extreme Reformers of Germany, however, sought equality through an eventual merging of all religions into a single national religious force. M. A. Stern, spokesman of the *Reformverein*, for example, had written that he sought an end to belief in revealed religion. Sigismund Stern, later principal of the Philanthropin, wrote in 1845:

and when once the pagan world will be destroyed, not only by Christianity, but within it as well, then the separation of both religions will cease, and I can't decide which name the religion of mankind will bear.[113]

The very name *"Reformfreunde"*—"Friends of Reform"— adopted by the Frankfurt radicals echoed the terminology being used simultaneously in Protestant circles, where the supporters of universalism were known as "Friends of Light."[114]

Those few Jews who dreamed of a neutralized, enlightened religion were most insistent upon the elimination of distinctive elements in the traditional service, such as language of prayer and the day of worship. Circumcision, likewise, had to be excluded as a blatant act of distinctive identity. Bergson had written on the opening page of his pamphlet, "[Circumcision] imprints upon [the Jew] an indelible sign, an ineradicable stamp of a specific nature which is the only remaining mark of difference from other nations and religions maintained until this day."[115] The elimination of circumcision in Judaism was supported by those who sought to attain equality through the eradication of religious distinctions.

The Senate's claim that it had no intention of abolishing a

religious practice, but rather that the measure was introduced for reasons of health and safety, was only partly true. There was nothing innocent about the extraneous *"insofern sie wollen"*—"insofar as they desire." The Senate would not at this point even uphold the rabbi's authority within the community in religious matters.[116]

The Senate was now siding with the radical Reformers of Frankfurt. The policy of the previous commissioner for Jewish affairs, Friedrich Ihm, had been abandoned, and with Edouard Souchay in that position, the government intervened in purely religious questions. True, it moved more subtly than certain other German states in its control of religious life. Orthodox services were not prohibited as they were in those states where a civilly binding synagogue ordinance had been introduced. Yet, the radicals in Frankfurt were being encouraged to pursue their program. The Prussian emissary in Frankfurt described the intent of the local authorities in an 1843 report sent to Berlin:

The party of unbelievers is by far the larger and, in particular, has complete control of the community Board and Council, as well as enjoying the favor of the majority of the Senate. Admittedly, it is divided into shades of opinion, but most of its adherents go beyond the mere discarding of the coarse Talmud and they profess not less than the crudest disbelief. The *Reformverein*, representing the majority of those so inclined, lacks any positive basis. The local health police authorities, on the occasion of prescribing the presence of a doctor at every circumcision of a Jewish boy, used a deliberately chosen expression which designated this act as being optional, thereby providing the Reform buffoons with the opportunity for the blatant disintegration of Judaism.[117]

The report is most fascinating in its own right for the mockery it displays by a Prussian official toward the efforts of the Reformers, but it also provides his testimony of the attitudes of his Frankfurt colleagues toward Jewish religious life. Indeed, in supporting the radical Reformers, the Senators could hardly have shared the goal of *Reformverein* leader M. A. Stern to bring about the demise of all individual religious faiths. Their objective could only have been, as the Prussian representative suggested, to increase the turmoil dividing the Jewish community and to facilitate desertion from Judaism.

The Senate, of course, claimed in its responses to the petitions of Rabbi Trier that it would not become involved in an internal religious dispute, and it even scolded Trier for returning repeatedly to their forum. Yet, where should Trier have lodged his protest of the wording of a government decree if not with the government authorities themselves? Apparently the government was merely interested in covering the tracks of its interference, and historians have in such matters often followed suit.

Moral judgments are made with great frequency in the historiography of nineteenth-century Jewish religious movements, condemning one side or another, (usually the Orthodox) for involving the civil authorities in internal controversies. However, such judgments overlook two basic aspects of the dynamics of these controversies.

The first fallacy in especially attributing to the Orthodox the blame for government interference strangely overlooks the generally closer connections between government officials and the proponents of Reform. The case of Israel Jacobson demonstrates the distinction quite clearly. Successful efforts often attributed to the Orthodox of Berlin in the second and third decades of the century resulted in the closing by the Prussian government of two private Reform houses of worship. One of these services had been organized by Israel Jacobson, who had left Westphalia after the fall of Napoleon. But before Napoleon's fall, the same Israel Jacobson had headed the government-appointed *Consistoire* in Westphalia which had declared in 1810, "In general, nowhere but in the synagogue under whatever pretext, may a public worship service (minyan) take place without the special permission of the board." This and other clauses of the synagogue ordinance issued by Jacobson with the authority of the government effectively prohibited the Orthodox from organizing religious services that did not conform to Reform practice. In Berlin the Reformers were turned out ostensibly because of Orthodox petitions to the government authorities; but in the earlier case in Westphalia and later in Weimar and Mecklenburg, the Reformers effected the same result, except that they themselves represented the government authorities.[118]

There is a more fundamental fallacy in the entire approach of castigating the Jewish parties for seeking the intervention and support of the state powers. Behind such condemnations lies the tacit assumption that civil government in Germany remained apart from these disputes unless prompted by the participants to become involved. Yet, the governments of the German states, as well as those of Britain and France, still considered religion to be very much part of their legitimate concern. Only in America had church and state been separated. One need only think of Napoleon's convoluted relations with religious authorities. In fact, the Frankfurt Senate had earlier refused to grant greater autonomy to the local Lutheran church at the expense of its own power.

During the summer of 1843, as the *Reformverein* was increasing its public declarations, Trier too decided that it was time for a firm response. Assisted by two members of the Frankfurt rabbinate, Beer Marcus Adler and Aaron Moses Fuld, Trier turned to a number of his rabbinical colleagues in Germany and other lands and sought their views on the dangerous new sect that was emerging. Trier published the responses in early 1844 under the title *Rabbinische Gutachten ueber die Beschneidung*. Twenty-eight views were published, including those of S. D. Luzzato of Padua, the Reformer Samuel Hirsch of Luxemburg, the moderate Mannheimer from Vienna, and Samson Raphael Hirsch, then of Emden. In the introduction, Trier also quoted a response from Bernays of Hamburg and acknowledged contributions by both Philippson and Fuerst in their respective newspapers. Trier had astutely not hesitated to cross party lines in compiling his work.[119]

Trier submitted his request to the Senate for a ruling excluding an uncircumcised child from the Jewish community on August 4. When he submitted the same request on September 15 and October 31, he appended those views which had already been returned to him. The compiling of these views was not intended to persuade an alienated sector of the Jewish community by overwhelming them with rabbinical condemnations, but rather to persuade the Senate of the gravity and illegitimacy of the act. The arguments which Trier summarized in the introduction and which precisely repeated his own views expressed earlier reveal that the Senate was the primary audience.

Failure to perform the commandment of circumcision was

punishable in biblical law by death. A father who had not provided for his son's circumcision should be viewed as having
withdrawn from the Jewish community and indeed was to be
excluded from membership. Having shifted the focus from the
child to the father, who was the real culprit, Trier argued that
an Israelite who had so disregarded Jewish legal principles could
not be allowed to take the special oath for Jews—*more judaico*.
The argument was intended to demonstrate clearly to the Senate
the no-man's-land that was being created. If the Senate should
insist upon the special oath for the father, the rabbis still retained
the power to refuse to administer the oath to him as a Jew, and
the man was left neither as Jew nor as non-Jew.[120] The Senate,
as we have already observed, refused to issue the ruling requested by the rabbinate, referring Trier back to the community
board and to defeat. By the end of 1844, four sons remained
uncircumcised.[121]

The *Reformverein*, as such, had run the course of its influence
in the Frankfurt Jewish community. Its members remained influential, but its program and especially its tactics were unpo-
pular. After the end of 1843, little was heard of the society. In
1845, apparently dissatisfied with the innovations introduced
into the main synagogue by Leopold Stein, the *Reformverein* attempted to organize separate services. That attempt failed, and
it was the last reference I have found to its activities.[122]

By that time, the leaders of the *Reformverein* had found a new
outlet for their endeavors. The accepted opinion that the society
quickly disappeared from the communal scene has left the question of what direction its members took after its demise. In fact,
the subsequent path of its leaders can be traced.

During the winter of 1845–1846, a radical religious society was
formed in Frankfurt and became known as the *Montagskraenzchen*. It was open to members of all faiths and its purpose
was "to support spiritual progress in general." In the words of
its founder, Nikolaus Hadermann, it was open to "all true *friends
of reform* of all confessions and religious parties" (my emphasis).
Among the society's leaders were Theodore Creizenach, Heinrich Schwarzschild, and Joseph Rueter, all members of the Jewish *Reformverein*, the official title of which had been the Friends

of Reform. It is apparent that, disappointed with the response to their program within the Jewish community, these radical Reformers took a leading role in encouraging the development of a neutral religion in Germany, which became one of the objectives of the *Montagskraenzchen*.[123]

While the Senate and Trier were arguing over the circumcision question and the *Reformverein*'s influence was declining, the board sought to resolve the issues at a more fundamental level. The board's position on the circumcision question is not known. When Trier complained to the Senate, he referred to the destructive activities of the *Reformverein*, but not at all to the board.[124] The response that does emerge from the turmoil over the *Reformverein* and circumcision was the board's decision in 1843 during the height of the controversy to elect a deputy rabbi for the community. Rabbinical authority had clearly sunk to impotence, and anarchy now threatened the community's structure. The board was finally forced into action.

ELECTION OF A DEPUTY RABBI

On December 9, 1843, the board of the Frankfurt community finally acted on the long-slumbering question of a deputy rabbi and elected Leopold Stein, until then rabbi in Burgkundstadt, to the position.[125] The board had sat passively on the question of the deputy rabbi for four years. The 1839 regulation required Trier's approval of the new assistant, and perhaps this forestalled any appointment. But if in 1839 the board felt that the parties were too equally divided to act decisively or if it felt that it could afford the luxury of patience, by late 1843 the eclipse of rabbinical power and internal discord both over the *Reformverein* and the circumcision question necessitated a resolution.

In the late 1830s the dispute over the appointment of a deputy rabbi had been integrally related to renovation of the synagogue building. The interlocking of the issues was now continued by an arrangement arrived at by the community and the brothers Rothschild. The agreement, signed in May 1843, is usually referred to rather simplistically as a pledge by the Rothschilds to construct a new synagogue building at their own expense in return for a pledge by the community to appoint a second rabbi who would meet with Trier's approval. But, in fact, the contract represented a comprehensive attempt by the Rothschilds to impose a settlement, essentially by means of their financial strength, upon the divided community that could reunify the divergent contingents. In some respects, the Rothschild plan reversed the Senate's decree of 1839, in favor of the rabbinate and the Orthodox party.[126]

The contract between the parties was finalized on May 12, 1843. The Rothschilds undertook the cost of constructing a synagogue for the Frankfurt community as a memorial to their father. The community pledged to provide an "eternal light" in his memory and to observe the annual anniversary of his death. In order to ensure that the appropriate religious spirit would continue to reign, the brothers requested that both the construction and the internal design of the synagogue be placed under the rabbi's supervision. They then stipulated nine conditions intended to guarantee the continued strength of tradition in the synagogue. The contract stipulated that the new synagogue would be constructed on the location of the two existing main synagogues, "the Rabbi [Trier] having already granted his approval of their demolition." So much for Trier's previous legal objections. An interim synagogue was to be established for Sabbaths and festivals. Neither demolition of the old nor construction of the new could take place on the Sabbaths or festivals. The supervision of the construction and internal design of the new synagogue was to be entrusted to a committee divided evenly between members of the combined board and council on the one hand and a second group appointed by Trier on the other. The construction plan and the internal arrangement were to be approved by the board and council, as well as by the rabbi. The right of the rabbi to appoint an equal section of the synagogue committee surpassed by far his prerogatives as stipulated in the 1839 *Regulativ*. The agreement also conflicted with the Senate regulations on the question of reforms.[127]

The Rothschild agreement made explicit that the rabbi had the final authority in liturgical matters. He was also responsible for introducing whatever changes were possible in order to "improve and enoble" the services. The agreement claimed not to infringe upon the board's domain, but the *Regulativ* had stated that the board and Council were responsible for the religious requirements of the community. The Rothschild agreement gave that power to the rabbi.

The contract also insisted that a second rabbi be appointed to assist the aging Trier. The assistant rabbi was to function alongside Trier "in harmony and unison" and work for the welfare of the community, as well as guaranteeing its religious unity. Having stipulated that the new assistant must be able to work harmoniously with Trier, the contract then adds: "It is self-understood that the combined board and council should proceed with the selection in accordance with regulations." The interpretation later applied to this clause was that the appointment was subject to Trier's approval, a contingency that was stricter than the Senate's requirement that Trier certify the candidate's proficiency in Jewish theological matters.[128]

The agreement also stipulated certain moderate innovations. The new structure was required to contain a women's ritual bath. The public sale of honors was eliminated and a systematic distribution without regard to status or wealth introduced. A qualified cantor was to be secured.

In sum, the contract sought to maintain the authority of the rabbinate in the appropriate religious spheres and to introduce some moderate reforms. In several aspects, as we have noted, it weakened the powers of the board and council as granted by the Senate, while strengthening the position of the rabbinate. The previous controversy over the elimination of one synagogue paled in significance compared to the questions of power and authority that were emerging in the late thirties. The total settlement imposed by the Rothschilds sought to insure the authority of the rabbinate and the question of the number of synagogues disappeared. In short, the Rothschilds tried in 1843 to buy a package that could not be won in 1839 either from the municipal authorities or in the community elections. They almost succeeded.

Construction of a new synagogue was a matter of the highest priority on the community's agenda and, seemingly, a prerequisite for the introduction of meaningful reforms. But despite the claims the board had made in 1838 about the pledges already received, the fact was that without the support of the Orthodox *minority*, the project was a financial impossibility. It was for this reason that the board agreed voluntarily to surrender the powers it had fought so hard to receive from the civil authorities. As will be even clearer later in this study, whatever notions we may have from later times or different countries concerning the financial standing of the supporters of Reform must be qualified. In 1837 the Orthodox party observed that a less elaborate plan of renovating the existing structure was called for, partly because of the lack of support that had been forthcoming. The Orthodox then pledged to finance the renovation project themselves. When the Rothschild plan failed in 1844, the community proved unable to finance the project without the support of the Orthodox. No construction program was begun until 1854.[129]

The appointment of Leopold Stein was not a blatant violation of the Rothschild agreement. Stein could be classified during this period of his career as being among the moderates of the new school of rabbis. During the second Rabbinical Conference, he supported Zacharias Frankel's stance on the use of Hebrew in the synagogue service. Even the Orthodox leader Emanuel Schwarzschild later admitted that Stein's reputation at the time was that of a staunch supporter of tradition. In fact, Trier hesitated to lodge a protest when the appointment was first announced. One report indicates that a number of Orthodox actually supported Stein.[130] The board, however, had not consulted Trier in the appointment. Such an affront contradicted the underlying purpose of the Rothschild agreement. Trier eventually protested Stein's appointment to the Senate, but was reprimanded for not taking the issue directly to the board. Amschel Rothschild was not happy with the turn of events, and it was perhaps under his prodding that Trier waited for Stein's arrival for further action. Trier and Rothschild received Stein separately. Trier remained unsatisfied. The board insisted upon Stein's appointment, and when Trier refused to certify Stein's candidacy in accordance with the regulations, the Senate waived the requirement. Trier resigned his position as rabbi of the Jewish Community of Frankfurt, and the Rothschild offer to construct a new synagogue building for the community was withdrawn.[131]

The Reform takeover of the community's institutions was now complete. The school; the board, appointed by the civil authorities; the council, nominated by the community's membership; and now the rabbinate and synagogue were in the hands of those grouped together under the rubric "Reform." Although writers talk of a virtual collapse of Orthodoxy in Frankfurt, the victory for the Reformers had not come easily or suddenly. Reform controlled the institutions, but not all the people. Forty years had passed since a small group had founded the Philanthropin School with its progressive approach. Its graduates, we assume, provided a core of strength for Reform endeavors in the next generations. Its program included a service that attracted certain limited groups within the community. It brought to Frankfurt a succession of scholars, who contributed to the scope and depth of the Reform cause. Thirty years passed after the Philanthropin inaugurated its service before innovations of significance were introduced into the main community synagogue. There was nothing immediate about that victory.

It had been as long since the board was constituted by proponents of innovation. One might assume that in the intervening period they had attempted to introduce changes into the synagogue and that we merely lack the sources to document these attempts. But the constellation of forces at that time was not propitious for innovation in religion any more than in politics. Germany of the post-Napoleonic era hosted the reactionary alliance of "Throne and Altar," and the Reformers did not actively assert their programs. In Frankfurt, the Reformers used the school to fill their own needs for the present, while sowing seeds for the future. We do not know that this was a conscious strategy, but it did enable the roots to develop for the campaign ahead.

The Orthodox had, for their part, strengths of their own in reserve. But 1844 was not yet the time to use them. The Orthodox had fought hard, but they had asserted particularism in an age that prescribed democracy and unity. They would now have to wait until society learned once again to appreciate their values and strengths.

Orthodox Comeback

The period of Orthodox decline in Germany was short-lived. Only in the late 1830s did Reformers initiate an active attempt to control religious life in the communities, and by the mid-1840s, the Orthodox were responding seriously to the challenge. With the events of 1848 on the horizon, and even more in their aftermath, several governments that had previously supported the cause of Reform Judaism began to reassess their former policies. By 1850 the Orthodox resurgence was well under way. Yet a myth has been well established that Orthodoxy was on the verge of collapse at mid-century in Germany, and especially in Frankfurt. This picture of Orthodox collapse, most clearly expounded by Samson Raphael Hirsch himself, does not correspond with the historical reality of the Orthodox situation—not in Frankfurt, not in Germany.

ORTHODOXY UNDER DURESS

In an 1854 essay, *"Die Religion im Bunde mit dem Fortschritt,"* Hirsch enumerated the intrusions of the Frankfurt community board into Orthodox religious observance, portraying that board as one of the most militant and uncompromising Jewish communal authorities in Germany.[1] As we have seen, the board had actually moved at a slow pace in introducing innovations into the community's religious life, appointing a moderate Reformer as rabbi only in 1843 when at least two dozen communities were *already* being served by Reform rabbis. Hirsch constructed his very different picture by projecting some of the board's later more radical actions back into the early century. Thus while Hirsch asserted that the board's active oppression of Orthodoxy dated back to 1818, the abolition of the religious burial society, the ongoing neglect of the synagogue building and its subsequent dilapidation, and the prohibition of discourses on the weekly Torah portion were all actually issues of the period between 1837 and 1842. In fact, only one issue preceded 1837: the supposed prohibition of Orthodox education for the youth of the community, which we shall examine below. Even the later events, which we considered in the first chapter, were depicted by Hirsch out of context and with polemical hyperbole. For example, he recounted the board's refusal of an offer by the Orthodox party to renovate the main synagogue. Almost ironically, he accused the board of allowing the synagogue to sink into dilapidation, while he ignored the board's own continuous efforts to renovate the building—efforts which had been, in fact, forestalled by Orthodox opposition.[2]

The most serious charge raised by Hirsch focused on the instruction of youth in traditional subjects, which he claimed was forbidden from 1818 to 1838 by punishment enforceable by the police authorities. "The men still live," declared Hirsch, "who as youth fled with their books to study in secret." He even hinted that adults as well were hindered in their study of rabbinic texts. Later writers easily inferred that the study of Talmud had been completely forbidden. But on this point, too, Hirsch was inaccurate.[3]

Talmud study still flourished in Frankfurt, at least into the 1830s. The French author Alexander Weill recorded in his autobiography a detailed description of the teachers of Talmud in Frankfurt and of their methods of instruction. In his youth, Weill had been an Orthodox Jew and an accomplished student of rabbinics. Having surpassed the level of Talmud study in his native Alsace, Weill was sent to Frankfurt to further his education.[4] He arrived there in the late 1820s and remained until 1836.[5] Weill portrayed a vivid picture of Talmudic study in Frankfurt during this period.

There were at this time three rabbinical courses in Frankfurt. The first was conducted by Chief Rabbi Trier and only the best students were admitted. The second was conducted in the Klaus synagogue by Rabbi Jacob Posen and was composed of pious students, more pious than knowledgeable. The third class was located at the home of Rabbi Aaron Fuld, a young amateur teacher, but a gentleman, quite erudite, who married a rich heiress and attended the Bourse daily. He had a certain number of pupils, to whom he lectured on the Talmud for two hours before attending the Bourse. He translated the Talmud literally and presented it not as a religious book whose principles were law and had the force of law, but rather as an archaeological and historical science. In those two hours, he ran through some twenty pages of Talmud, only translating, without any interpretation or discussion.[6]

Superior students, however, found opportunity for their scholarly growth. Weill described the atmosphere in Trier's lesson.

After coffee, we went to Rabbi Trier's home. This was no longer a cold archaeological course about syllables and phrases, a moribund recital as at Rabbi Fuld's. This was the living word, overflowing, intoxicating, a word of fire and of faith!

Scarcely half an hour had passed, and the lesson turned into a melee, a battle of discussions, of disputes, of cries, of roars. . . . Then suddenly the bewildering cries were cut off by a deathly silence, each one meditating and searching for the proper solution, the contradiction to raise, or perhaps a new explanation of a puzzling text. . . .

Usually, the Rabbi let us sink into a labyrinth of contradictions and reserved his solution until the end, which he then gave us with a smile of satisfaction on his lips. His solution was often received with abundant hurrahs and foot stamping.

On the other hand, when his solution left us dissatisfied and our objections fell upon him from all sides, he walked about impatiently, and at times he became quite angry. Then he would raise his lectern and slam it down noisily, raising a cloud of dust which enveloped us and cut off our speech. Then it was our turn to smile, not in comfort, but in disdain. We wanted reasons and not lecterns.[7]

In addition to their formal studies, a dozen of the best students visited the home of a Rabbi Schalem each evening to study Hebrew, biblical exegesis, and Talmud.

From 8.00 p.m. on, a dozen *bachurim*, the brightest, sat at his house, where they found a superb Hebrew and Chaldean library, a plain square table, a warm room, chairs, and two candles. . . . Usually from 8.00 to 10.00 p.m., they devoted themselves to the classical study of Hebrew and exegesis. From 10.00 until midnight, to the study of Talmud. From midnight until the head of Rabbi Schalem collapsed on his old books, they threw themselves into the Aggadas, some of them studied Josephus or even a bit of secular history.[8]

To be sure, rabbinical study in Frankfurt in the 1820s and 1830s may not have reached the heights of previous decades, but neither had it collapsed or disappeared.[9]

While it was not true that Talmudic study was illegal in Frankfurt between 1818 and 1838 as claimed by Hirsch, the board did hinder attempts by the Orthodox *in* 1818 and again *in* 1838 to establish a school combining secular and religious subjects. In 1818 one Model Schuster agreed to donate the substantial sum of fifty thousand gulden for the establishment of such a school. The board, however, claiming it was acting "for the welfare of the community," successfully urged the Senate to prohibit the school from opening.[10] It thus assured an educational monopoly for its own Reform viewpoint as taught in the Philanthropin.

A second attempt to open a school with instruction in both religious and secular subjects was made in 1838. According to the account by Isaac Jost, the Orthodox at that time actually opened a school, which taught traditional subjects exclusively. The board apparently did not interfere until a petition was submitted to include secular instruction as well. The Board then responded as it had in 1818, and the Senate accepted its recommendation to prohibit the opening of the school.[11] Still another proposal for an Orthodox school was submitted in 1843. Although the school had already opened, the Senate ordered it shut down based on the 1838 decision.[12]

Thus, interference by the board in Orthodox education focused, on the whole, on attempts to establish schools which combined both religious and secular instruction. The study of Talmud *per se*, however, continued in Frankfurt as we have seen at least into the 1830s. Only by 1838 are there indications of intervention against Talmudic instruction for youth. To be sure, no extenuation can be found for the board in this revision of the picture, but what does change as a result of these revisions is the picture of the Orthodox party in Frankfurt.

In Hirsch's account, Orthodoxy had been subjected to decades of coercion in the first half of the nineteenth century and consequently had virtually ceased to exist in Frankfurt by mid-century. In fact, the coercion intensified only in the late thirties, and Orthodoxy had remained a viable force throughout the period. In 1839 the *Allgemeine Zeitung des Judenthums* reported that 500 to 700 Orthodox men attended the main synagogue alone. Various expressions of support during the years from 1838 until 1850 reveal that a stable contingent of the Frankfurt community continued to identify with the Orthodox position. In 1838, 212 members signed the Orthodox petition for revising the communal structure, and in 1845, 297 members signed an address to Zacharias Frankel upon his withdrawal from the Frankfurt Rabbinical Conference. Although in 1850 only 126 members voted for revision of the communal regulations to provide extensive concessions to the Orthodox party, by that time not all of the traditionalists still favored reaching an accord with the community board. Also, with the collapse of the democratic movements in German politics, apathy had grown in communal politics as well. The Reform side received only 302 votes on this occasion, and the Orthodox ratio of one-third of the votes had not altered significantly in twelve years.[13]

The setbacks sustained by the Orthodox between 1838 and 1844 did not, on the whole, present immediate crises as much as they foretold a gloomy future for the traditionalists' cause, for until 1844 the rabbinate and synagogue had at least remained in Orthodox hands, and the observant Jew could still fulfill his religious obligations. Once the rabbinate changed hands, however, the Orthodox Jew's situation indeed became more critical, and maintaining his religious life-style developed into a dilemma.

With the election of Leopold Stein as community rabbi, the Frankfurt Orthodox faced new problems which they shared with an increasing number of traditional Jews throughout Germany. In 1846 in an unusually open expression of personal anguish, an Orthodox Jew from an unidentified community appealed in the pages of the *Treuer Zionswaechter* to his fellow traditionalists for advice and guidance. The present rabbi of his community was not committed to the observance of Jewish law. Yet, he had the authority granted by the civil government to conduct weddings and issue divorces. Supervision of the ritual baths was in his hands. The community meat slaughterer was himself not an observer but a mocker of the dietary laws. Under such conditions, asked the writer, what should an Orthodox Jew do? The Orthodox were in the minority and lacked the financial resources for separate, additional facilities. Should they disregard their suspicions and accept the available facilities? If not, how else were they to function as observant Jews?

The anonymous author had not intended to write a polemic. He was pleading for direction. But the writer had struck at the core of the Orthodox dilemma and the guidance he sought was not forthcoming. There were but two lame attempts to respond. In one answer the writer was urged to identify both himself and his community. The author's point had been missed, for by 1846 the name of the specific community indeed did not matter. The writer could have been from Magdeburg, Schwerin, or now Frankfurt. Over twenty communities had been represented at the Rabbinical Conferences of 1844 and 1845, convoked by the Reform leadership.[14]

If in 1846 there appeared to be no solution to the problems posed by the anonymous correspondent, Orthodoxy was nevertheless beginning to struggle seriously with the precariousness of its position. The Rabbinical Conferences provided the initial stimulus for the Orthodox to begin the search for an active response to Reform encroachments. Subsequent events in Frankfurt represented a significant development in the renewed momentum of the traditionalist cause throughout Germany, but that momentum did not begin in Frankfurt.

FIRST RESPONSES

Ludwig Philippson initiated, through the pages of his *Allgemeine Zeitung des Judenthums*, the series of three annual Rabbinical Conferences held in the mid-1840s, following the initial impetus given by Abraham Geiger, who had convoked the first such meeting in Wiesbaden in 1837. Neither Geiger nor Philippson, seven years later, envisioned an authoritative role for the conference. Geiger wrote that its purpose was not "to formulate a new Judaism nor to assume synodal authority; it is to afford honest men the opportunity of discussing the best methods of conducting their office."[15] Philippson wrote in a similar vein that his purpose was to bring together the spiritual leadership of German Jews to join in "consultations on all Jewish matters of concern."[16] The participants in the conference held at Braunschweig in 1844 were, however, not to be satisfied with mere consultations. They urged that decisions be reached, which, while not binding through any authoritative system, would, nevertheless, impart moral support for the individual rabbis.[17] Samuel Holdheim, rabbi of Mecklenburg, conceded that the conference lacked the authority of a synod to reach binding decisions. Yet, Holdheim continued, rabbinical authority was based on the confidence of the communities, and the Rabbinical Conference would contribute to such confidence in the present-day rabbis. Samuel Hirsch of Luxemburg explained that a rabbi breaking with tradition would no longer be forced to stand alone, but would now have the views of his colleagues to adduce in his support.[18]

Ludwig Philippson later dated the emergence of an Orthodox party in Germany to their refusal to participate in the Braunschweig conference. Indeed, in their opposition to the conference the bonds among the Orthodox were strengthened.[19]

Leadership for the Orthodox response came from Jacob Ettlinger, since 1836 rabbi of the community of Altona. Born in Karlsruhe in southern Germany in 1798, Ettlinger later studied at the University of Wuerzburg. In 1826 he was appointed rabbi in Mannheim, and in 1836 he became rabbi and head of the *Bet Din* of Altona, where he died in 1871. Together with Isaac Bernays of Hamburg, Ettlinger provided the major rabbinical leadership for German Orthodoxy in the first half of the nineteenth century.[20]

In 1845 a declaration was issued condemning the decisions of the Braunschweig Conference. Publication of the proceedings and advance planning of a second conference to be held in Frankfurt precipitated the response. Initially, seventy-seven rabbis signed the declaration, a number that was later augmented to

116 rabbis of Germany, France, and Hungary.[21] The declaration criticized the lack of Talmudic knowledge of many of the participants in the conference and consequently protested their usage of the rabbinical title. Furthermore, they claimed that such a group, in any case only twenty-three in number, was hardly worthy of the presumptuous title of "Rabbinical Conference of Germany."

The signatories were clearly troubled over the effectiveness with which the conference had projected a rabbinical image. Their statement explained that not only were the decisions reached at the conference invalid, but they were hardly worthy of men who purported to be the teachers and protectors of Judaism. The Orthodox rabbis, for their part, would not abandon the struggle. The declaration exclaimed: "Not yet has Israel been abandoned by its God!" in a biblical phrase that became the slogan of Orthodox resistance in the later 1840s and concluded: "Israel still has its faithful guardians."[22]

The Orthodox camp had demonstrated its first major expression of opposition. To maintain the momentum Ettlinger realized that the Orthodox would require their own medium of communication. The *Treue Zionswaechter* commenced publication in 1845 on the eve of the Frankfurt Rabbinical Conference. A Hebrew literary journal, *Shomer Tzion Ha-Neeman*, appeared a year later. Ettlinger assumed responsibility for the Hebrew paper, entrusting the editorial management of the *Zionswaechter* to the principal of the Altona school, Samuel Enoch.[23]

Ettlinger, however, was not the man to spark an Orthodox counteroffensive. The *Zionswaechter* had a decade of intensive experience in the publication of Jewish papers from which to learn, and yet it failed to develop a consolidated perspective. True, as we shall see, external conditions were not yet fully ripe for an Orthodox response, but even after that time had arrived, the *Zionswaechter* ceased publication in 1854—the same year that Hirsch's *Jeschurun* first appeared.

The *Zionswaechter* failed in its attempt to follow Philippson's model of leadership as set forth on the pages of the *Allgemeine Zeitung des Judenthums*. Philippson reported on victories and setbacks; Enoch brought word of injustices and helpless dependency on goodwill.[24] Philippson grappled with the issues of his day; Enoch urged his readers not to despair.[25] Both newspapers proposed the establishment of institutions that would represent their respective viewpoints. Philippson succeeded in bringing the Rabbinical Conference to fruition, but he suffered disappointments as well. One of the greatest was the insufficient financial response to his call to establish a theological faculty and seminary. But Philippson's proposals never fell on deaf ears. He possessed a sense of his times and the strength to fight for his projects with determination. He precipitated reactions and openly printed the exchanges on his pages.[26] The *Zionswaechter* as well put forth its own share of similar proposals, but with one exception these never reached fruition. A detailed plan for the establishment of an Orthodox rabbinical seminary all but disappeared from the paper's pages after its initial debut.[27] The spirit of German Orthodoxy as manifested in the *Zionswaechter* was fragmented. There was nothing close to a coherent perspective. Questions went unanswered. Proposals received no response. Controversial conceptions remained unchallenged.[28] The *Zionswaechter's* major contribution was to assist the Orthodox in preserving the status quo.

One success did emerge from the Ettlinger-led initiative to organize the Orthodox camp of Germany. Late in 1845 the *Zionswaechter* began reporting on the activities of Talmud study circles, the first of which were established under the leadership of Seligmann Baer Bamberger, district rabbi of Wuerzburg in Bavaria.[29] The paper encouraged other communities to follow suit and subsequently reported extensively on the formation of similar groups. In Wuerzburg, the first study society had been formed around 1843. As of 1846, it met daily after morning services, and the participants themselves were responsible for preparing the lectures, which were devoted to the study of the Talmud. In nearby Heidingsfeld, a second group met several times a week for the study of the more basic Mishnah. The ten or so members of this group consisted of teachers and business people and included members of the community board, while the Wuerzburg group claimed a number of bankers within its membership.[30] Further reports on Talmud societies continued in the following weeks. Some reports told of newly formed groups, while others described the activities of those groups that had been established previously. A correspondent from Hesse, for example, reported on one town in which two new groups had been added to two older ones.[31]

The momentum gained its primary support in Bavaria, Hesse, and the Rhineland. By the end of 1846, the paper reported that forty study societies had been formed.[32] The subjects of study varied, but usually fell into one or more of three categories: Mishnah, Talmud, or traditional biblical commentaries and Midrash. The majority of groups concentrated on the study of Talmud, while, quite significantly, only two groups reported that they were studying legal codes, which in both cases were in addition to other subject matter.[33] It seems that the details of religious practices were not the highest priority at this juncture. Although Altona itself, the center of the movement, waited a full year before initiating its own group, it then formulated the most elaborate of the programs, with three teachers involved. Ettlinger taught the ethical text *Duties of the Heart*, a second rabbi taught the legal code *Chaye Adam*, and Enoch, editor of the *Zionswaechter*, lectured on Bible. Enoch reported shortly thereafter that some eighty members were participating in the lectures.[34]

The *Zionswaechter* simultaneously emphasized the theoretical significance of the renewed attention to the study of Judaism's classical sources. Only through studying the sources could Judaism be elevated and renewed.[35] Through a knowledge of the sources, Jews could learn once again to appreciate the value of their own traditions.

The flame of true and deep piety still burns in the breast of many Jewish youths and adults. Unlock its erudition for the people, initiate them into the holy places of the Torah, the Prophets, and the Writings, of the Mishnah, and the Talmud. Show them their treasures and they will no longer lust after foreign sustenance, after the possessions of others. Teach them God's word, God's spirit, and soon they will abandon the mendacious spirit, the deceptive words.[36]

While emphasizing the centrality of study to the Orthodox response, Ettlinger and the *Zionswaechter* opposed the efforts of Zacharias Frankel to convoke his proposed Conference of Theologians. Frankel had attained notoriety by his dramatic withdrawal from the Frankfurt conference of 1845 over a dispute on the extent to which Hebrew should be maintained in the synagogue service. Following the acclaim he received from traditionalists for his action, he attempted to continue the momentum by organization of a counter-conference.[37] The *Zionswaechter* opposed the initiative partly out of distrust of Frankel's leadership, but also out of wariness of the very concept of a conference. "What is it that we want? Deliberations? Resolutions? Has the Rabbinical Conference not already adequately demonstrated that the communities are not the least bit interested in deliberations and resolutions?"[38] The very notion of a conference with its "deliberations and resolutions" suggested a movement toward change. In its opposition, the *Zionswaechter* maintained its defense of the status quo in religious life. This was the path of the *Zionswaechter* and clearly of the mainstream of German Orthodoxy. Frankel's conference was at first delayed, and in the end it was never convened.[39]

In a revealing juxtaposition of articles, the *Zionswaechter* combined its opposition to the Frankel conference with a reaffirmation of the centrality of Talmud study to the Orthodox defense: "It is a generally recognized truth that the elevation of religiosity within the realm of Orthodox Judaism requires, above all, the promotion and revitalization of Jewish knowledge and scholarship."[40] In responding to the Reform attack on Talmudic authority, the Orthodox reaffirmed the centrality of the Talmud in Jewish life. In fact, adherence to "Talmudic Judaism" was suggested as the broadest definition of what constituted an Orthodox Jew. A correspondent from Pressburg, writing in the *Zionswaechter*, observed that diversified strands had emerged within Othodoxy of the period. While some authorities had prohibited secular studies completely, others were more lenient. Still another authority was himself a student of philosophy, but his Orthodoxy was confirmed by his exacting observance of ritual. Despite the diversity, the adherents of these different views were united in their acceptance of Talmudic authority: "We Orthodox believe that God revealed to Moses at one time the oral law as well as the written; that both together are only one Torah, each merely a part of the whole."[41]

Formation of Talmud societies represented the first significant step toward an Orthodox recovery. Membership in these groups demonstrated a serious commitment to the cause, as they demanded much of the time and efforts of their constituents. Some groups required the members to prepare and deliver the classes themselves. All of the groups met, if not daily, at least several times a week, and one society reported that each session lasted between three and four hours. As we might suspect, the topics of discussion were not confined to serious study. Enoch, in fact, expressed his hope that these groups would create a social meeting ground for traditional Jews and added that discussions of contemporary Jewish affairs comprised an integral aspect of their function.[42] The societies probably did not succeed in spreading Jewish knowledge among the indifferent or wavering. They did, however, temporarily fill the need for a positive identification with the Orthodox viewpoint, thus at least strengthening the traditionalist position against further erosion, while providing a social basis from which a stronger offensive could still be mounted.

The study societies, however, could not satisfy the basic ritual needs of the observant Jew. Kosher meat required a certified slaughterer, a school for children required teachers, numerous functions required a rabbi, and the civil legitimacy of weddings and divorces depended on his recognition by the state. Only a solution to these problems could ensure Orthodox survival into the next generation, but only a community with sufficient numbers and financial resources as well as state recognition could fulfill these needs.

In theory, the solution to the crisis precipitated by Reform triumphs in Frankfurt and elsewhere seemed simple. Already in the 1840s, it was proposed that Orthodox Jews withdraw from the Jewish communities and establish their own independent bodies. Separatism as espoused then was not a sophisticated ideological concept as in later decades. Both Reformers and Orthodox at least contemplated separation as long as they were in the minority of the Jewish community.[43] Yet, as we saw at the beginning of this chapter, the Orthodox Jew living in a community with a Reform rabbi, in fact, could not discern the best direction to take. Nor could the scholars and polemicists who wrote in the *Zionswaechter* provide him with a solution to the

Orthodox dilemma. The process of bringing the idea of separation into reality demanded three difficult prerequisites: a readiness to shatter the unity of the Jewish community, government approval of the existence of separate communities, and the financial resources within a limited group to bear the necessary expenses. The concept of separation was simple enough. Its realization was, at the outset, quite difficult and rarely achieved.

The concept of a unified Jewish community providing the Jew with his religious needs and coming to his support in hours of economic or personal crisis was strongly ingrained in the Jewish consciousness. Centuries of persecution had turned the community into the vehicle of Jewish existence. Nevertheless, in the 1840s the idea of separation arose frequently, and the definition of what constituted a unified community was called into question, opening the way for division. "Above all," wrote one writer, "the Jewish community is a religious association. Common goals, common means . . . are the essence of a community. External and inner agreement, at least in the primary concerns, are the *conditio sine qua non*."[44]

The implications of separation were potentially so grave that most writers passed over in silence what future relations would exist between the separated communities. Occasionally, however, these thoughts came to the fore. Another writer in the *Zionswaechter* insisted that the number of Reform Jews had so increased that Orthodoxy must learn to accept their existence and their strength, for they now constituted a sizable percentage of the Jews of Western Europe and America. On the other hand, they could not be retained within the Jewish community, for they had gone even further than the Karaites, who had at least accepted divine revelation of the written law. *De facto* separation had already occurred. An Orthodox Jew could not eat at their tables nor marry their daughters. The time had come for a *de jure* recognition of the situation: "No common religious bonds exist between us. . . . They must be viewed as any other religious confession, as our fellow-men, as our fellow citizens, and even more—as our kinsmen."[45] However, few German Orthodox leaders were prepared to take the drastic step of declaring a ban on the Reformers. When Solomon Eger moved on behalf of the rabbis of Posen to convince Ettlinger and his colleagues in Hamburg-Altona to ban the Reformers from the Jewish community, he met strong resistance. Eger later explained that the rabbis of Germany were reluctant to disclose their internal quarrels in public.[46]

Whatever the reasons for their hesitancy, Orthodox reluctance to rupture the community, combined with the financial burdens that would follow, made separation a most difficult resolution of the Orthodox dilemma. Meanwhile, the Talmud societies had provided an initial basis for organization, but even the Altona leadership realized that in the long run these groups could not satisfy the needs of the Orthodox nor provide the opportunity to regain the strength they had lost within the Jewish communities.[47]

TURNING POINT

The Reform movement had flourished during a decade of high Jewish hopes for full political emancipation. Western governments had hardly been subtle in indicating that they expected acculturation either in return for or in advance of legal equality. Nevertheless, the Orthodox insistence on maintaining traditional Jewish practices did not indicate active opposition to emancipation as much as their recalcitrance to pay for emancipation by sacrificing their religious beliefs. In Hungary, the Hatam Sofer rejected emancipation outright because of the assimilation it inherently involved, but most German Orthodox leaders seemed only to have viewed emancipation with a wary eye. Samson Raphael Hirsch had actually already advocated the cause of political equality in his *Nineteen Letters*, published in 1836.

Do I consider it desirable? I bless emancipation, when I see how excess of oppression drove Israel away from human intercourse, prevented the cultivation of the mind, limited the free development of the noble sides of character. . . . I bless emancipation when I notice that no spiritual principle . . . stands in its way, but only those passions degrading to humanity.[48]

In the view of Jacob Toury, Orthodox Jewry in Germany in the 1840s had concluded that the tension between the demands of citizenship on the one hand and religious requirements on the other could be best resolved by accepting only partial rights and not the full equality entailed by emancipation. Indeed, a Bavarian correspondent for the *Zionswaechter* expressed this view explicitly in his 1846 report of the discussions on the Jewish question in the Bavarian legislature:

We are not speaking of a general emancipation with all of its material and moral consequences. The majority of the petitioners would, in fact, not even want this. But all agreed on alleviation of the oppressive discriminatory laws, removal of the many oppressive limitations and hindrances, particularly those affecting livelihood and causing ill-will.[49]

Yet, despite the evidence for Orthodox preference for only limited rights, it should not be overlooked that by the late 1840s a more positive position on emancipation was emerging and Hirsch no longer stood isolated with the Orthodox camp. A major series of articles entitled "Religion and Emancipation" appeared in the *Zionswaechter* in 1847 and expounded the new attitude, rejecting the notion that the countries of Europe expected religious sacrifices as a prerequisite for emancipation.[50] All of the progress made in the first half of the century had been achieved "without a government of Europe thinking of demanding unconditional religious sacrifices. . . . What humane government of our time has demanded the sacrifices of the Inquisition?"[51] These misdirected efforts of Reform Jewry could not achieve the objective of emancipation: "In fact, all such accommodations will not result in emancipation, but rather in disintegration and collapse!"[52] Rather it was religious observance that would lead to emancipation: "The more religious we think and act, the sooner we shall free ourselves from the yoke of civil degradation."[53]

The Orthodox Jew who affirmed his desire for full emancipation in the 1840s was, in fact, preaching religious conservatism within an atmosphere of political liberalism. Another writer in the *Zionswaechter* felt the paradox and expounded the need to separate religion from politics, a combination which he feared played into the hands of the religious Reformers and caused the impression that the Orthodox religionists were indifferent to political freedom:

But we also desire liberation from the undeserved oppression imposed upon us; we also seek the benefits available to the other subjects of the state. But we will not buy privileges at the price of the holy and divine.[54]

The *Zionswaechter* also reported some support for this positive approach to emancipation from the side of the Bavarian legislative assembly, which affirmed in 1846 that "true adherence to positive Judaism is not only not a hindrance, but is actually a valuable security toward promoting and enjoying a high level of political independence and freedom."[55]

As Toury has well observed, even the Orthodox majority, who were politically passive and essentially apathetic to the struggle for emancipation, were quite determined to demonstrate Jewish loyalty to the state. Repeated statements emphasized that not only the religious life, but the specifics of Jewish law demanded political loyalty:

Are we religious observers not truer subjects and better citizens than the freethinkers? How often are Israelites enjoined in their holy books to render themselves reverent, true, and dutiful to their superiors?[56]

In the declaration protesting the Braunschweig conference, the seventy-seven Orthodox rabbis condemned all of the conclusions reached except those dealing with civil obligations.[57]

The Orthodox emphasis on political loyalty was well conceived for a period of increasing political unrest. Its poignancy echoed more clearly in the aftermath of the early disturbances. In 1847 Jews were not involved in the uprisings in Posen, at least not ostensibly, and one writer explained their absence as a consequence of the Orthodoxy of Posen's Jews.[58] In any event, the Orthodox strategy did not miss its mark and the growth of the revolutionary atmosphere during the late 1840s coincided with a number of legal actions in Germany favorable to the Orthodox cause. Let us examine three examples.

In 1838 the board of the Breslau community had elected Abraham Geiger as its assistant rabbi despite the protests of the Orthodox leadership and of Solomon Tiktin, the community rabbi. Both sides continued to petition the Prussian authorities for their assistance. When Tiktin died in 1843, the Orthodox sector chose his son Gedaliah Tiktin as its rabbinical leader. The state at first refused to recognize the younger Tiktin's appointment, but in 1846 direct petitions to the king and the minister of culture gained approval of the request of an autonomous Orthodox congregation to appoint Tiktin as its rabbi. There were more than twenty such private synagogues in Breslau, which were independent of community board control. Tiktin possessed no authority in community matters, but his status was enhanced in 1851 when the king bestowed upon him the title of royal state rabbi for Silesia. This honor, however, by-passed the communal troubles, which were resolved in 1856 by a new community constitution which enfranchised each party to appoint its own rabbi, with both appointees then enpowered as community rabbis.[59]

The Orthodox petition of 1846 not only attacked Geiger's lack of qualifications for a rabbinical post, but employed political strategy as well, arguing the principle of Orthodox loyalty to the state:

The history of all times teaches that those who remain steadfast and true subjects to their faith discharge their duties to their rulers no less than others. In fact, religious piety actually prepares one for the same devotion toward the civil authorities . . . who represent the position of God on earth.[60]

When the modest concession of 1846 was followed by Tiktin's appointment as state rabbi in 1851, the king declared explicitly:

He indeed has no right to the title, but I am nevertheless inclined for political reasons to confer the contemplated title upon him so that the party represented by him can gain the desired strength.[61]

Governments were grasping the Orthodox message ever more clearly. In Mecklenburg-Schwerin, benefits to the Orthodox also increased with the passing of political events. Unlike Breslau, Mecklenburg had not allowed private services since 1843, but beginning in 1846 there was a movement toward liberalizing the rules. The issue came to a head after the election in 1847 of David Einhorn to replace Samuel Holdheim as state rabbi.[62] The Orthodox of Schwerin were granted the right to conduct separate services and to engage their own meat slaughterer and teacher. These privileges were subsequently extended to a number of other communities within the state.[63]

Einhorn, in fact, enjoyed only a brief stay in Mecklenburg. Leopold Donath credited Einhorn's controversial leniency in circumcision as the main factor for his departure in 1851, but he added that Einhorn's radical stand in German politics made his departure desirable.[64] The two factors were actually not disconnected. While radicalism in religion had ruptured the unity of the Jewish community, the political thinking of the Mecklenburg authorities after 1848 sought a new cohesiveness within the community based on historical tradition. In 1853 the state *ordered* a reversal of the tendencies of the previous decade, specifically stipulating the required viewpoint of future state rabbis. Particularly disturbed by the necessity of allowing separate services for the Orthodox, the authorities concluded that:

The Ministry can no longer tolerate the schism among the Jews of the state which was caused by the synagogue ordinances and by the corresponding inclinations of the state rabbis, Dr. Holdheim and Dr. Einhorn, and which resulted in a segment of the Jews withdrawing from the services and resigning from the legal communal association. . . . Nor can the Ministry indulge in any further advancement of the rationalist Reform cause, to which both of the aforementioned rabbis were attached. . . . The Ministry has therefore determined not to allow any longer the division of its Jews into two separate bodies, but rather to bring about the reunification of the separated segments.[65]

The united community would be based on traditional practices.

To this end, it will be necessary, above all, to elect a state rabbi . . . who adheres to the position of historical Judaism, but also possesses the knowledge and talents as well as the sincere will to bring the divided Jews together and to introduce the necessary changes in the service.

In 1846 Prussian Jewry numbered 214,857 and represented by far the largest community within the German states and, after Russia and Austria, the third largest in Europe. The policies of the Prussian government were the most significant not only for its own Jews, but also for those living throughout Germany. After a decade of reevaluation of its policies toward Jewish emancipation, Prussia issued in 1847 a new comprehensive law on the status of its Jews.[66] The law proved so disappointing that Ludwig Philippson struggled in the pages of his paper to find any positive aspects, while Ismar Freund, historian of the emancipation struggle in Prussia, simply labeled the edict "regressive."[67] Yet, Orthodox sources embraced the law enthusiastically and considered it one of the major victories of the year 1847.[68]

A number of facets of the law did indeed secure the religious rights of the observant Jew. The law divided Prussian Jewry into local religious communities in which membership was compulsory, but it simultaneously provided a mechanism for coping with religious conflicts and allowed for the possibility of minority groups to organize separate synagogues *within* the communal structure.[69]

A limited form of democratic elections provided another important gain. Freely elected representatives were in turn to choose a board, which itself controlled religious affairs. The Orthodox assumed that Reform hegemony would be broken in those communities where the Orthodox majority had been governed by a government-imposed Reformist board. In Breslau, where a bitter feud between the supporters of Tiktin and of Geiger had raged for the preceding decade, the Orthodox were jubilant over the prospect of final victory. A correspondent in the *Orient* spelled out in detail the Orthodox response. The new law "has instilled much life into the people, but surely nowhere to the great extent as in our community."[70]

Orthodox response to the law went even further. The law did not merely provide structural possibilities, but was a virtual triumph for the Orthodox cause: "Prussia's wise ruler wants religious Judaism; enlightened, atheistic Reform will never supplant the revealed faith of our fathers."[71] What within the new law spoke so positively to the adherents of Orthodoxy? The edict had reenforced occupational restrictions and actually had strengthened Jewish political separation from the remaining population. The Orthodox were hardly grateful for these regressive steps. Yet, after the intensive efforts of the Reformers in the 1840s to accommodate themselves to what they saw as the demands of the age, the reversal suffered with Prussia's unsatisfying enactment vindicated the Orthodox position that emancipation would not be attained through the sacrifice of religious beliefs.

Nemesis has caught up with you too cruelly: you have been repaid measure for measure. You have insulted the laws; you have declared a war to the death against the Talmud, Sabbath, Messiah, against all of statutory Judaism and with the law of July 25, 1847, you have been punished.[72]

Near the end of 1847 the Orthodox of Germany could look back over a number of significant victories in a campaign which they had only recently entered. Just a few years before, prospects had not foretold a bright future, but at the minimum, Orthodoxy had progressed beyond its initial faltering and had now demonstrated a reservoir of strength. The legislation in Prussia, the decree in Breslau, and the dispensations in Mecklenburg-Schwerin all guaranteed the traditionalist his right to practice religious observance freely. Meanwhile, the Reformers' momentum was itself beginning to falter—and not only in Breslau and Mecklenburg. The Fourth Rabbinical Conference, originally scheduled to be held in Baden in 1847, was not held.[73]

The continuation of Orthodoxy in Germany had been secured in a defensive campaign, but neither in Breslau nor in Mecklenburg were there the makings of an Orthodox offensive. Tiktin, for example, seemed satisfied to maintain the status quo and even resisted the minimal innovations urged by his own Orthodox supporters. In Mecklenburg, the communities were too small and scattered to initiate a significant response.[74] The Orthodox Jews of Frankfurt, like those of Breslau, had never lost their right to worship in private synagogues. Unlike those in Breslau, however, they resolved to seek the appointment of an observant, but broadly educated, rabbinical leader. In short, the movement in Frankfurt determined from the outset to recast Orthodoxy in modern terms.

Resurgence in Frankfurt

The same factors that helped to strengthen Orthodoxy's position elsewhere soon came to the support of the traditionalists in Frankfurt, where political tensions were running high in the late 1840s. In the aftermath of the 1848 revolution, local political powers cast a more favorable eye toward the religious conservatives.

With government support in hand, the Orthodox began to organize an independent congregation, and they soon attracted to their cause a distinctive group of members who provided them with the financial means to go far beyond Orthodox efforts elsewhere. High motivation combined with the necessary resources made possible the renewed growth of the Orthodox community of Frankfurt.

REGAINED FAVOR

In 1844 Leopold Stein assumed his duties as rabbi of the Jewish community in Frankfurt and immediately initiated a process of reform in the synagogue. His first liturgical changes included the addition of prayers in German for the government and the community. A choir was introduced and the sale of Torah honors during the service was abolished. Before the end of his first year, additional prayers were translated into German, and some prayers were eliminated altogether. A German version with lyrics by Stein was substituted for the central Friday evening hymn *lechoh dodi*. By late 1846 a number of more fundamental reforms were introduced. The triennial cycle of Torah readings was adopted; the Haphtorah and its blessings were recited in German; the silent recital of the Musaph prayer and the prayers for restoration of sacrifices were eliminated.[1]

In 1845 only one year after Stein's arrival, the second Rabbinical Conference was convened in Frankfurt. The city's suitability for hosting the conference depended on the willingness of the Jewish community to assume the necessary financial and social responsibilities.[2] The board, apparently only too willing to demonstrate full identification with the Reform cause, fulfilled its obligations generously:

Most of the participants were lodged quite nicely in private homes; the rest stayed in public inns at the community's expense. Board was taken collectively at the Jewish restaurant, again at the expense of the community. . . . A musical evening was presented. The theater performed "Nathan the Wise" and invited the participants to sit in boxes free of charge. The Senate Commissioner Dr. Souchay guided the assembly through the Senkenberg and Staedel Museums and Herr v. Bethmann admitted them to his museum of plastic art work.[3]

The deliberations at Frankfurt concentrated on liturgical matters and devoted much time to discussing the extent to which Hebrew should be maintained as the language of prayer in the synagogue service. When Zacharias Frankel withdrew from the conference in the midst of the proceedings, the local Orthodox party seized the opportunity to express its gratitude for his dramatic gesture of support for the traditionalist cause. This demonstration simultaneously enabled the Orthodox to give public testimony to their own continued viability in Frankfurt to counter the Reformist image now projected by the community. Both the address to Frankel, signed by 297 members of the community, and an accompanying letter by Solomon Trier, the former community rabbi, referred to the continued presence in Frankfurt of a strong and committed Orthodox contingent. Wrote Trier, "There is still in my community a number who have not yet crossed over to the enemy camp and require only courageous representation in order to persist on the path designated by our forefathers as the true way to holiness and to immortality."[4]

The first response of the Frankfurt traditionalists to the Reform takeover of the synagogue was, as elsewhere, to organize a Talmud study society, which met nightly from Sunday to Thursday. Its founders took the initial steps to find a solution to the Orthodox problem and petitioned the board for the appointment of a secularly educated rabbi to serve their sector of the community. Their request was rejected, and a further and delicate incident at a burial convinced the Talmud society members that the future of Frankfurt Orthodoxy did not lie within the community. In April 1849, upon the death of the rabbinical adjudicator, Rabbi Jacob Posen, his two sons Lazarus and Solomon requested that Rabbi Benjamin Auerbach of nearby Darmstadt deliver the eulogy. The board, however, refused the request, and Auerbach spoke at the gate to the cemetery. Solomon Posen, outraged at the infringement of his individual rights, called for the formation of a new Orthodox community.[5]

Solomon Posen was probably convinced that the financial support required for an independent congregation would not prove as difficult in Frankfurt as it had elsewhere. Baron Willy von Rothschild, son of the head of the Naples branch of the family, Carl Meyer, had recently moved to Frankfurt. Willy Rothschild was an observant Jew, and immediately after his arrival in Frankfurt, Rothschild began to study Talmud under the same Solomon Posen.[6] The connection with the Rothschilds of Frankfurt later guaranteed financial independence for the Orthodox. Meanwhile, the members of the Talmud society began groping for a legal path to obtain approval for their plans. According to Emanuel Schwarzschild, chronicler of the founding of the IRG, they consulted Edouard Souchay for his advice. This took place shortly after the death of Jacob Posen in April 1849.[7]

Souchay had only a few months before resigned the position of commissioner of Jewish affairs, which he had held for ten years after replacing Friedrich Ihm in 1839. During Souchay's term, the Senate had consistently supported the board's more aggressive policies in the pursuit of reforming the community synagogue. It had even supported the radically inspired circumcision edict of 1843. But revolutionary events in 1848 and 1849 had altered Souchay's position on Frankfurt's political questions, including Jewish matters.

The democratic stirrings of 1848 placed the popular and respected Souchay, who represented the right wing of the liberal
party, in a difficult position within Frankfurt politics. What separated Souchay from the other liberals was not his position on
the nature of political reforms, nor the pace at which reform
should be achieved, but the methods to be employed in the
pursuit of change. Souchay insisted on adherence to the legal,
legislative process with its own provisions for affecting change.
Consequently, he demanded of the Senate, which possessed
those legal powers, that it hastily enact the required reforms in
order to avoid a confrontation over its own legitimate authority.
The Senate, however, dragged its feet and, as Souchay had
predicted, it subsequently bore the brunt of the liberal protest.
Souchay now found himself in the uncomfortable position of
being the target of the liberal attacks though he, in fact, agreed
with much of their position. He attempted to resolve the dilemma by resigning from the Senate early in 1849.[8]

Souchay's break with the liberals, however, could likewise not
be avoided and came to a head during the same period. Schwemer
said well of Souchay that he was one of those men "who, by
the turn of events, had been forced out of the ranks of the liberals
and into those of the conservatives." Sitting on the elected
"Committee of Thirty," he repeatedly supported the cause of
legal reform. Yet, observing that what had been instituted by
force could just as easily be removed by force, he maintained
his position that reforms should be introduced through the established procedures of the Frankfurt constitution. The committee, however, refused to relinquish final authority to the
conservative Senate. Only two of its thirty members voted with
Souchay.[9]

During the spring and summer of 1849, the Frankfurt moderates initiated their counterresponse to the radicals, and Edouard
Souchay stood at their head. In April 1849 they established a
newspaper to espouse their position. Political personalities were
joined in this effort by members of the financial aristocracy led
by Moritz Bethmann and Isaak Reiss. In July 1849 the moderates
reconstituted the Citizens Club into a new Patriotic Society. Again
Souchay was their leader.[10]

The position maintained by the "Patriotic" group should not

be confused with a reactionary one. In questions facing the National Assembly, their position was in agreement with the liberals. They favored the unification of Germany under a Prussian monarchy, while opposing the more radical demand for a republic. According to the German historian Veit Valentin, it was in the local issues that they held a more conservative position, although even in that context they favored full and equal political rights for all citizens. Their opposition was directed, therefore, not against either the men or the spirit of the National Assembly meeting in Frankfurt, but was aimed specifically at the radicals who controlled the majority of the local Constituent Assembly.[11]

Quite soon after the intensification of the political events, the board of the Jewish community requested Souchay's resignation as commissioner of Jewish affairs. The Senate decided to delay immediate changes, but Souchay himself stepped down around the turn of 1848–1849.[12] We can determine with some confidence what factors prompted Souchay by 1849 to switch his support from the liberals to the traditionalists in the religious conflict raging within the Jewish community.

Reform leaders in Frankfurt, on the whole, identified with the objectives and tactics of the revolution of 1848. This included both the rabbi, Leopold Stein, and a number of lay leaders of the community. During the prerevolution days, Stein openly expressed the anguish of the German Jew who had been denied equality. Stein's consolation to his Jewish audience amounted to a warning to the governments of Germany: Those who hold the power now "cannot maintain the upper hand for long, for their power is not grounded in the strength of justice but in the justice of strength."[13] Once the March days of 1848 had begun, bringing with them the prospect of emancipation, Stein issued a public statement of gratitude to his "Christian fellow-citizens." Reflecting back on this period, Stein later recalled how enthusiastically he had embraced the revolutionary events: "I myself was so powerfully stirred by the world-shattering ideas of that time, that the anticipation of a great metamorphosis, especially in relations to the Fatherland, took precedence over anything else around me."[14] A number of Jews serving in the democratic bodies in Frankfurt during the revolutionary period came from the ranks of Jewish communal leadership. Of the eight Jews elected to the Constituent Assembly, at least three, Gold-schmidt, Manhayn, and Schwarzschild, had been active in the community.[15] Goldschmidt and Manhayn had been members of the board, while Schwarzschild, the former *Reformverein* leader, had served on the School Committee from 1840 to 1846. Of the six Jews listed by Toury as either delegates or alternates to the Legislative Assembly, elected in late 1849, Michael Manhayn, Martin Emden, and Seligmann Rothschild had been members of the community board.[16]

More significant than the Jewish identification with the liberal cause was the role played by key individuals in the radical politics of the period. The *Montagskraenzchen* founded in 1846 under the leadership of Nikolaus Hadermann, served as the central meeting ground for adherants of radical positions. The society was initially intended as a forum for questions of religious reform, but with the momentum of the later 1840s it turned its attention to the political sphere as well. With few exceptions, like Hadermann himself, leaders of the group included converted Jews, like Alexander Friedleben and Maximillian Reinganum on the one hand, and leaders of the former *Reformverein* such as Creizenach, Schwarzschild, and Joseph Ruetter, on the other. However, Jewish participation was not limited to what could be discerned as "fringe" elements. Both Jacob Auerbach, teacher of religion and preacher at the Philanthropin, and even Leopold Stein, rabbi of the community, participated in the society's deliberations.[17]

Valentin listed three men as leaders of the radicals in the political assemblies of 1849: the converted lawyer Maximillian Reinganum; a Jewish doctor whom we met in the circumcision issue, Henrich Schwarzschild; and the leader of the *Montags-kraenzchen* and editor of the party paper, Nikolaus Hadermann. The frequent references to Schwarzschild's participation in the Assembly meetings portray him as an angry and outspoken opponent of moderation. In his outbursts he regularly attacked the Constituent Assembly for its impotence and had to be called to order by the chair.[18]

These men were the opponents of the moderate faction led by Souchay. In contrast to Souchay's position, they were demonstrating little regard for the legal processes by which reforms could be introduced into the Frankfurt constitution. During the summer of 1849, the atmosphere became more hostile as political tensions in Frankfurt became "more bitter, more ugly, and more personal."[19]

It was during this same summer of 1849 that the Orthodox Jews of Frankfurt approached Souchay and found in him a sympathetic ear. The Orthodox also had friends of longer standing in the Senate, supporters who had been outvoted in the confrontations of the preceding decade.[20] But in the new political climate, the authorities of Frankfurt, as elsewhere, were prepared to cast their support in favor of the religious party that preached observance of the law and loyalty to the state. The Reformers had cast their vote for a losing revolution and the patronage of the past was lost. In the choice between modernity and loyalty, loyalty now triumphed. The petition to appoint an Orthodox rabbi was approved.[21]

FOUNDING FATHERS

Frankfurt was not the first community where Orthodox Jews succeeded in organizing an independent congregation, but it was from the model of the *Israelitische Religionsgesellschaft* (IRG) of Frankfurt that Orthodox Jewry of Germany and beyond received inspiration for the struggle against Reform. Its founders were bucking the trend toward the Reform cause and were doing so in a city that in a short time had become reputed as a center for the new movement and had even hosted the most radical Reform society of the period.

How was the Orthodox initiative able to flourish under these conditions? The men involved were clearly not followers of the times, for the contemporary spirit moved in the opposite direction. Nor were they mere followers of charismatic leadership. All earlier commentators have reduced the success of Frankfurt Orthodoxy to the efforts of Samson Raphael Hirsch. But Hirsch did not arrive in Frankfurt until 1851 and played no role whatsoever in the establishment and early growth of the congregation. If we were to ignore the lay component of the initiative, we would, at the least, lack an understanding of the process that brought Hirsch to Frankfurt. In fact, we would also be missing a key factor that enabled the IRG to don the mantle of leadership of German Orthodoxy.[22]

The study of Jewish religious movements too often ignores the lay membership and concentrates exclusively on the movements' spokesmen. But an examination of the views and motives of the leaders does not necessarily teach us the motivation of the people who transformed those ideas into social reality. Who were the men who founded the IRG? What were their occupations? What was their social standing within the community? Finally, what caused them to identify with independent Orthodoxy? When we can answer these questions, the founding of the IRG becomes an event not only in the annals of religious movements, but in the lives of real human beings, an event of social significance for them and of broader historical significance for us.[23] Without the answers to these questions, we will fail to understand how Frankfurt became the center it did for German Orthodoxy.

The early history of the IRG has been clouded in a legend that a mere eleven men founded the congregation. The tale of the eleven founders emerged almost immediately after the event itself. Already in 1852, at the ceremony laying the cornerstone for the new synagogue building, Hirsch spoke of the eleven founders: "There were eleven men who arose to give their souls for this great and holy task."[24] He elaborated on the story in the 1854 essay "*Die Religion in Bunde mit dem Fortschritt*," when he wrote of eleven men who took advantage of the propitious moment to petition the Senate for the right to organize a religious society.[25] However, Saemy Japhet in his perceptive essay on the secession movement in Frankfurt attacked what he called "the tale of the famous eleven." Japhet observed that the eleven were merely the signatories of the petition to the government, and he correctly attributed the origins of the myth to Hirsch himself.

In sermons and in writings, when dwelling on the marvellous achievements of his young Kehilla, Rabbi Hirsch loved to emphasize that eleven men built up the Religionsgesellschaft. In their unbounded loyalty, his followers granted to his genius the privilege of publishing his own version, which was so often repeated that soon nobody doubted the correctness of the story; it became a beautiful legend. But nobody can tell anymore with certainty who all of the eleven were. The names perpetuated in the entrance hall of the synagogue on a bronze memorial tablet differ from those which came down to us from contemporaries. And yet, people who know next to nothing about Frankfurt, know the tale of the famous eleven. But it is a fallacy. The eleven were the signatories of the petition which had to be presented to the government. Behind them stood a body of many distinguished, high-minded, Orthodox, Frankfurt-born *baale batim*.[26]

Indeed, the number eleven became so sacrosanct that Emanuel Schwarzschild found it necessary to correct his list of the names with an erratum at the end of his chronicle when he discovered that he had listed thirteen founders instead of eleven!

The petition in question was submitted to the Senate to request permission to appoint a rabbi to serve the needs of a new Orthodox congregation.[27] By the processes of group formation, there obviously would have been a period when a relatively small number of men discussed the feasibility of establishing a congregation, but eleven men could not have undertaken such a project without assurances of additional financial support, and indeed, the Rothschilds and others had already been approached. There is no reality to the notion entertained by later writers that Hirsch came to Frankfurt to serve a congregation of eleven members. Schwarzschild related that Hirsch was elected rabbi of the IRG at its first general meeting, which was attended by forty-four members, and that the society actually had one hundred paying members at the time.[28]

The names of thirty-four men who were members of the IRG in the early days of its history can be derived from four separate lists. The first list consists of the eleven men who signed the petition to the Senate requesting the right to appoint a rabbi for the congregation. The second list was supplied by Japhet to prove that in contrast to the legend of the eleven, there were actually many more members, even at the outset. Japhet provided no sources for his list, leaving us with the problem of whether these additional men actually joined the IRG as early as Japhet claimed. Some confirmation can be derived from the appearance of thirteen of Japhet's twenty-one names on one or more of the other lists. The cornerstone document of the first synagogue building provides our third list, with ten signatures in addition to that of Hirsch. Finally, Emanuel Schwarzschild listed eleven additional men who were active in the IRG by the end of 1850.[29]

The various lists including duplications are as follows:

Eleven Petitioners

1. Selig Moses Schwarzschild
2. Lazarus Jacob Posen
3. Ludwig Rapp
4. Philipp Abraham Cohen
5. Adolph Dann
6. Salomon Jacob Posen
7. Moses Loeb Mainz
8. Moses Mayer Rapp
9. L. W. Schwabacher
10. Michel Loeb Mainz
11. Seligmann Moses Schwarzschild

Cornerstone

1. Selig Moses Schwarzschild
2. Wolf Jacob Bass
3. Ludwig Rapp
4. Gustav Hoflesch
5. Herz Jacob Weiller
6. Meyer Bendix Goldschmidt
7. Michel Loeb Mainz
8. Simon Israel Toeplitz
9. Bernhard Moses Hirsch
10. Moses Michel Herz Oppenheimer

Japhet

1. Wolf Bass
2. M. H. Bass
3. Meier Goldschmidt
4. Benedict Goldschmidt

5. David Rapp
6. Luder Rapp
7. Moses H. Schiff
8. Juda Kulp
9. Moses Michael Oppenheim
10. Mich. Mainz, senior
11. Meier Mainz
12. M. Is. Oppenheim
13. Baron Anselm Rothschild
14. Baron Willy Rothschild
15. M. J. Kirchheim
16. Menko Kulp
17. Nathan Marcus Oppenheim
18. M. B. Kann
19. Elias Schuster
20. Herz Weiler
21. Ph. Abraham Cohen

Schwarzschild

1. Baron Anselm von Rothschild
2. Baron Willy von Rothschild
3. M. H. Bass
4. Meyer B. Goldschmidt
5. Herz Jacob Weiller
6. Loeb Bass
7. Wolf Bass
8. Salomon Bass
9. Moritz Oppenheimer
10. Nathan Marcus Oppenheim
11. Juda Michael Kulp

Valuable social data on many of these members is contained in Alexander Dietz's *Stammbuch des Frankfurter Juden*, which traces the history of Frankfurt Jewish families from 1349 to 1849. Information provided includes date of migration into Frankfurt, the names of wives and children, occupations, and the names of family firms.[30]

The majority of the early members of the IRG came from the oldest families in Frankfurt. Of twenty-seven entries for which dates of arrival in Frankfurt could be determined, the families of twenty members dated back to the sixteenth or seventeenth centuries and one to 1740. Assuming that the members not listed by Dietz were later arrivals, twenty-one of thirty-four families had settled in Frankfurt well over a century and in most cases two or even three centuries before the founding of the IRG in 1849.

Of the twenty cases for which there is occupational data, sixteen owned firms in their own names. Included in this list were some of the most prominent names and firms of Frankfurt, such as the bankers Rothschild, the jeweler Oppenheimer, and Philipp Abraham Cohen, founder of the later Metallgesellschaft Bank.[31]

The most striking result of this examination into the social background of the congregation's early membership is the strong connection between the members and Frankfurt's renowned financial empire. Of the twenty members for which occupational data are available, eleven men were bankers, bond dealers, or money changers. Some played secondary roles, but a number stemmed from the oldest and wealthiest banking families in Frankfurt. In addition to the Rothschilds, the membership included Philipp Abraham Cohen, Juda Michael Kulp, three partners in the Bass Brothers banking house, Moses Schiff, who was associated with the Rothschilds, as well as some apparently smaller bankers, Selig and Seligmann Schwarzschild, and Herz Jacob Weiller.[32]

Not surprisingly, the men who affiliated with the IRG were also strongly interrelated by family ties. At least fourteen members had immediate relatives within the congregation, including parents, children, and siblings. Another four had uncles or nephews, and four additional members were cousins.[33]

In summary, the founding members of the *Israelitische Religionsgesellschaft* that we have been able to identify formed a close social and professional unit. The majority descended from families that had settled in Frankfurt several centuries before. Most of the founders had at least one relative within the membership, and at least one-half for which information is available had two, three, or more relatives. Most significant was the connection between the membership and Frankfurt's financial establishment. Many were members of Frankfurt's oldest Jewish families and of its financial aristocracy.

The banking element affiliated with the new congregation only over a period of time, and it is possible for us to trace that process. The initial steps toward the foundation of an independent Orthodox synagogue in Frankfurt were taken by members of the local Talmud circle. The earliest list of members we possess is indeed that of the eleven signatures to the Senate petition requesting the right to engage a rabbi. Of those eleven, only four were engaged in banking and of these only two, Selig and Seligmann Schwarzschild, had been members of the study association. Two other bankers, Philipp Abraham Cohen and Loeser Wolf Schwabacher, became involved in the effort by the time of the petition to the Senate in January 1850.

The Rothschilds were then formally approached for their support.[34] It will be recalled that links with the Rothschilds could be traced to Solomon Posen, a leader of the Talmud society, who served as Willy Rothschild's Talmud tutor. Possibly some of their associates affiliated with the Orthodox endeavor at this point if they had not done so previously. On the other hand, we know that a number of bankers did not yet join the effort to establish a separate congregation and were still committed to achieving a satisfactory arrangement within the framework of the organized Jewish community.

In 1849 the Frankfurt Senate granted the Jewish communal authorities increased autonomy, and the position of commissioner of Jewish affairs, vacant since Souchay's resignation, was abolished for the time being.[35] The increased role given to the community necessitated a reexamination of the ordinances governing communal life. Simultaneously, discussions in the Constituent Assembly on the freedom of religion induced the board to contemplate concessions to the Orthodox party. Article Thirty of the proposed constitution rejected the concept of compulsory membership in a religious society, and Jewish community leaders suddenly became concerned that members might take advantage of the clause to free themselves of the financial obligations of community membership.[36] A commission was elected by the community to propose a new set of regulations with the hope that a harmonious agreement could be achieved between the board and the Orthodox.

The commission was elected in March 1849. Of its eighteen members, five adherents of Orthodoxy were selected, Moritz Oppenheimer, Nathan Marcus Oppenheim, Herz Weiller, Salomon Bass, and M. H. Bass. The commission undertook to perform a difficult task during a period of political turbulence. Not only the Jewish community, but also the city of Frankfurt—in fact, all of Germany—were struggling at that very time to determine the principles that should govern political life. The commission's final report was issued only in December 1850.[37]

Most controversial in the proposal were the sections dealing with the problem of religious coexistence and especially the concessions extended to the Orthodox. A small synagogue, apparently the Andachtsaal used by the Philanthropin in past decades, was to be turned over to the Orthodox along with Torah scrolls, prayerbooks, and the services of a cantor and sexton—all provided for by the community budget. The congregation would have the right to appoint a rabbi or teacher, provided that his authority be limited to the congregation itself with expenses to be borne by the congregation and not by the community at large.

Publication of the report precipitated a barrage of polemics in the Frankfurt public press. The proposed regulations were attacked by both sides. Reformers objected to the recognition and restoration extended to Orthodoxy:

This measure is a malicious infringement of the basic rights of the German people [sic!], with which the commission apparently is not familiar or does not honor. . . . How can unity be achieved by a regulation that places upon the large majority of the community, which does not subscribe to Jewish Orthodoxy, the demand to organize Orthodoxy once again at their expense and to provide them with a center and to help them to restore all the influence which they had lost through their intolerance and outdated ideas?[38]

Even some Orthodox expressed dissatisfaction with the proposal for not transferring to them religious supervision of community facilities. Kitchens, for example, could be inspected by Orthodox representatives, but supervision remained with the community's rabbinate. Most Orthodox must have supported the regulations but, nevertheless, the proposal was defeated in February 1851, by a vote of 30½ to 126.[39]

With the failure of this attempt to reach accord within the community, the five Orthodox members of the commission itself as well as a number of other influential people joined the Orthodox congregation then in formation. At least five bankers were among the group that affiliated with the IRG at this juncture.[40]

By the beginning of 1851, the stature of the IRG membership had been well established. Members of the Frankfurt Jewish aristocracy would govern the IRG until the 1870s, and the affluence of its members remained characteristic until the end of the community.

Of course, Frankfurt Jewry generally was known for its banking connections and wealth. The Reformers, however, were more diversified and more professionally oriented in their occupations. The *Reformverein*, it will be recalled, included two doctors, two lawyers, and two writers among its members. Neither the community board nor the Council, both of which supported the Reform cause, were tilted toward the financial sector. The 1842 board consisted of two bankers and one currency dealer, one merchant, two shopkeepers, one professional, one vacancy, and one whose occupation was unidentifiable. The Council in 1840 included three currency dealers, two merchants, two professionals, and two shopkeepers. In 1842 it consisted of three currency dealers, two shopkeepers, one professional, and two unidentified. Noting that these men represented the leadership of the Reform camp, the contrast is even more blatant, for the IRG board was solely in banking hands for two decades.[41]

Money was not lacking for the society or for its members, but the "money aristocracy" of Frankfurt had suffered severe personal attacks in the decade prior to the establishment of the IRG.[42] The social tensions within the Jewish community shed light on the purposes for which these bankers actively affiliated with the Orthodox circle and provided the means for the Orthodox resurgence.

ARISTOCRACY IN A REVOLUTIONARY AGE

Although based on established traditions, the image of the Jew as the financial power behind royal thrones became more highly popularized in literature and political polemics after the fall of Napoleon in 1815.[43] The increased importance of the Rothschild family in the post-Napoleonic age was especially significant for growth of the belief in Jewish power. Their awesome wealth, the dispersal of the five brothers to Europe's major capitals, and their role in financing Europe's war on Napoleon all served as positive proof of Jewish power over the major states.

Two Jewish-born intellectuals, Heinrich Heine and Ludwig Boerne, formulated the basic themes of the new onslaught against Jewish bankers. Boerne credited the Rothschilds with preparing the way for popular democracy by uprooting the established right of the hereditary nobility, but he also maintained that the Rothschilds themselves would eventually have to be removed by revolutionary power. Boerne thus set the stage for aiming the future revolution in the Rothschilds' direction.[44]

With the growth of the revolutionary spirit, the anti-Rothschild motif became an intrinsic part of leftist political culture. In 1843 Bruno Bauer wrote in his essay *The Jewish Question*, referring to Amschel Rothschild living in independent Frankfurt, that "one Jew who possesses no privileges whatsoever in Germany's smallest principality determines the fate of all Europe." Alexander Weill, whom we met earlier as a yeshivah student from Alsace studying in Frankfurt, had since grown into a revolutionary opponent of Orthodoxy both in religion and in politics. In 1844 in his German pamphlet *Rothschild und die Europaischen Staaten*, Weill called for the states to liberate themselves from the Rothschild power.[45]

The bestowing of the rank of Austrian nobility upon the Rothschilds in 1822 sealed the identification of the family with an image of royalty, but probably because of the change in political atmosphere, the granting of simple Viennese citizenship to Solomon Rothschild in 1843 actually precipitated more frequent caricatures and satires on the "royal Rothschilds."[46] The language employed in the polemics sharpened as well, as slogans adopted connotations of Christian traditions: "Jews of the Kings and *Kings of the Jews*," and "The Jews are our lords and we their *Christian servants*."[47]

One could always be jealous of the Rothschilds, but in the "pre-March" decade jibes, insults, and critiques were in open season. The Rothschilds attracted the revolutionary fire magnetically, but the attacks were not meant for them alone. Alexander Weill summed it up simply: "By the name Rothschild, I have no single person in mind. Unfortunately, it has become a principle." With that name, Weill meant the entire system of private banking. Industrialization and modernization in general required a new banking system that was not based on providing loans for princes alone. Despite the major innovations supported by the Rothschilds and acknowledged by Boerne, for Weill and the polemicists of the 1840s the Rothschilds symbolized the economic system of the past that prevented the improvement of the people's lot and the development of the national state.[48]

Leaders of organized German Jewry were also highly critical of the Rothschilds during the decade prior to 1848 and especially faulted the family for not employing its good offices on behalf of Jewish emancipation efforts. Ironically, they demanded that the Rothschilds buy Jewish emancipation, while they themselves denied that Jews exerted any special influence over the European states.[49] The Jewish press frequently accused the Rothschilds of withholding funds from causes beneficial to Jewish life.[50] A particularly vehement attack was launched by Ludwig Philippson in 1839. Philippson opened by quoting one of the most recent attacks against Jewish emancipation:

It seems virtually ludicrous to speak of emancipation of the Jews from ancient Christian oppression. It would be far more appropriate and necessary to speak of how we Christians can emancipate ourselves from the hands of the "Jewish Money Kings."[51]

In fact, answered Philippson, there was no relation whatsoever between the Rothschild House and German Jewry: "Who can come forward and say that these people [the "Rothschild House and Consorts"] have done anything substantial for Judaism, for its external or inner emancipation, for its civil or spiritual elevation?" Yet, bemoaned Philippson, Jewish fate has been integrally intertwined with that of the Rothschilds. Following the improvements in the Jewish situation after the Napoleonic wars:

> The repulsive disposition toward Jews in Germany had increased once again with the growth of the Rothschild Houses. Their wealth and that of their consorts has depressed Jewish circumstances so that the higher the former rises, the lower the latter sinks.

It is because of this connection that Philippson felt that he could not remain oblivious to Rothschild conduct: "What must we feel, when for all that, one would bury us under the weight of that house and its possessions?"

The polemics against the Rothschilds often employed religious motifs to enhance the satirical style. Heine, as usual, excelled:

> The merchant everywhere has the same religion. His office is his church; his writing desk, his pew; his account book, his Bible; his warehouse, his Holy of Holies. The bell of the bourse calls him to prayer. Gold is his god; credit, the creed of his faith.[52]

The sanctification of money was a particularly successful analogy, precisely because the Rothschilds, at least the Frankfurt branch, were, in fact, renowned as observant Jews. Furthermore, at least from the liberal perspective, banking and religious orthodoxy signified common characteristics. The isolation and aloofness from society both of the wealthy Jewish banker and of the observant Jew converged in Heine's analogy. They both echoed the very traits of the Jew of the past—of the closed and traditional society—which the pursuers of emancipation sought both to deny and to expunge.

Hostility toward Rothschild power appeared in the internal polemics of the Frankfurt Jewish community as well and in forms that paralleled the charge of their power over political states. Thus, the Rothschilds were rumored to have offered bribes in the midst of the Senate's deliberations over the circumcision debate and to have asserted their influence to deny the spread of Reform in states neighboring on Frankfurt.[53]

In sum, the severe antagonism against the Rothschilds was not restricted exclusively to the economic and political domains and, in fact, the religious inclinations of the Frankfurt branch frequently served both as medium and as subject for the polemical attacks. Recalling the liberal and even radical political inclinations current within the strands of Jewish communal leadership, we can understand the extension of this hostility to the communal strife as well. Indeed, in addition to the rumors and innuendoes cited above, there is direct evidence that the general conflict was also manifested within the confines of the local Jewish community.

A number of non-Jewish families, like the Bethmanns, were prominent in the banking circle of Frankfurt,[54] but Jews were, nevertheless, so significant that old Frankfurt banking rules had allowed Jews the privilege of closing their banks on the Sabbath and festivals. Apparently under the leadership of Edouard Souchay, a new set of regulations was introduced in the mid-1840s which completely overhauled the city's banking laws. Among the innovations introduced, the special dispensation for Jews was eliminated. In other words, Jewish-owned banks would now be required to conduct business on holy days.[55]

Leopold Stein found himself in the midst of the issue immediately after his arrival in Frankfurt. When Stein called upon Amschel Rothschild to discuss the family's pledge to construct a new synagogue for the community, Rothschild turned the subject to the proposed regulations.[56] After Stein became the community rabbi, the Orthodox bankers sought his intervention. There are conflicting reports over the subsequent course of events, but the differences lie only in the question of Stein's personal stand. Stein later claimed—almost twenty years later—that he had attempted to act on behalf of the petitioners, but was prevented from doing so by the board. In any case, the board supported the bill.[57] The lawyer Goldschmidt, *Reformverein* leader, board member, and later delegate to the 1849 Constituent Assembly, publicly espoused the removal of the special Jewish privileges with the argument that the majority must be followed in matters of law.[58]

The revisions were passed on November 12, 1844.[59] A few months later an association was formed to protest the measure, but it would appear that the Rothschilds found the appropriate and most successful strategy: "The House of Rothschild feels itself sufficiently independent to take no notice of the stipulations of the new regulations." In fact, (despite the controversy at the outset) the regulation seems never to have been applied.[60]

Of all the attempts by the board and the Senate authorities to encourage integration during the decades prior to 1848, the order for Jews to conduct business on the Sabbath was the most serious and blatant interference with Jewish religious practices. At stake was nothing less than the right of the Jew to observe his Sabbath day. One report indicated that the origins of the anti-Sabbath legislation stemmed from the community board itself, but such rumors often accompanied anti-Jewish legislation. Nevertheless, the position of the board had been clearly stated. There can be no doubt that the widespread tensions between Jewish progressives and the Rothschilds were felt very close to home, within the community of Frankfurt itself. The banking laws also remind us that the hostility was not restricted to the Rothschilds alone, for the legislation infringed upon the rights of all observant bankers to practice their religion freely.[61]

The Jewish bankers of Frankfurt who were religiously observant thus had not only the means but also the motive to lend their support to the independent Orthodox cause. The IRG never represented all of the Orthodox Jews of Frankfurt. The remainder continued to worship in private synagogues, but the founders of the IRG wanted to accomplish more than merely to provide themselves with an Orthodox service. They sought, from the outset, to wage an offensive campaign on behalf of traditionalism against Reform. The effort began in Frankfurt as it had begun elsewhere—based on a nucleus of committed Orthodox Jews. But the momentum went further in Frankfurt because of the special hostility between friends of Reform and the financiers.

The affiliation of the financial aristocracy with the IRG of Frankfurt goes a long way toward explaining why that particular community became the model for European Orthodoxy. Of course, the IRG had the means to enable Samson Raphael Hirsch to carry out his full program free of financial concern, but the bankers brought more than money to the effort; they brought their names and their social status. As Fritz Stern has argued, the newly wealthy emulated the older elite and granted them their continued position. Thus, Gerson Bleichroeder's ostentatiousness "was only an exaggerated version of what most rich Germans did at the time: the plutocrats aped the impoverished aristocracy, and their willing subservience facilitated the aristocrats' continued social hegemony."[62] Yet by mid-century the notion of aristocracy had already changed. W. H. Riehl, writing in 1851, commented that the term had become a "figure of speech. . . and people speak of money aristocracy, administrative aristocracy, academic aristocracy." Thus if aristocracy had once implied only landowners, by our period it denoted more, and the financial elite was included.[63]

The Rothschilds themselves were attempting to enter the elite strata of broader society, and they were achieving some success in Frankfurt, in fact more than the Jewish professionals making the same attempt.[64] But within the context of Jewish society, the Rothschilds were strongly embedded in their elitist status, and there they invited, as we have seen, the hostility of the professionals, but also the esteem of the petty classes. In the 1840s it was the hostility that dominated. "The revolutions of 1848 were implicitly more antiaristocratic than antimonarchical; the Paulskirche debated whether to abolish the nobility not the monarchy."[65] However, in the aftermath of 1848, the esteem of the bankers grew again. Ernest Bramsted has described the various attitudes of the German middle classes toward the aristocracy as reflected in nineteenth-century literature. Of the various types of admiration he delineated, most relevant here is the first: the burghers from petty surroundings who demonstrated a "naive admiration of aristocratic glamor."[66]

The strongholds of Jewish Orthodoxy in Germany formed virtually a spiritual hinterland for the resurgence in Frankfurt, and the social stature of the IRG membership was a primary factor in shaping the relationship. A correspondent from Hamburg wrote in Hirsch's journal *Jeschurun* in 1854:

Nowhere has there accumulated the sterling wealth transmitted in growing sums from father to son, from son to grandson, as was the case in your community in so many families. . . . The consequence is that altogether we have relatively few genuinely wealthy members in our community and these few are on the whole—parvenues.[67]

Within German Jewry, the IRG symbolized not simply wealth, but aristocratic stature. In the reactionary aftermath of the debacle of 1848, that status was the proper ingredient for the building of a community that provided the example to follow for an Orthodox Jewry of Germany already in revival, and which now sought the path to renewed vitality.

THE SEARCH FOR A RABBI

Under the existing laws of Frankfurt, the leaders of the Orthodox congregation did not require Senate permission to form a religious society, or *Religionsgesellschaft*.[68] However, the society did require the Senate's approval in order to engage a rabbi, and they so petitioned the Senate on January 28, 1850. The petitioners announced unabashedly at the very outset—"The undersigned adherents of the Mosaic faith have withdrawn from the existent Jewish religious community of this city and have formed a new religious community." Yet, they did not intend the declaration to imply a full separation from the Jewish community, for they also declared that members of the new society would retain both the rights and obligations of members of the "political Jewish community," formed in accordance with the laws governing religious societies. They then requested the right to appoint an appropriate rabbi who would serve the needs of the numerous traditionalists of the city. The petition was prepared by Selig Moses Schwarzschild, Emanuel Schwarzschild, and Philipp Abraham Cohen with the professional assistance of a lawyer, who presented the petition to the Senate on behalf of the society. This was the petition signed by eleven leaders.[69]

In June 1850, the Senate granted the society the prerogative to appoint its own rabbi, but denied him the right to conduct weddings. The new group was being recognized as a society, but not as a separate community. A later entry in the protocols refers to this decision in broader terms—the rabbi "would not hold, at the present, any standing within the Jewish community as a whole."[70]

Once this permission was granted, the early leaders undertook to increase the society's membership. In the process, they formulated a public statement of their objectives and program and adopted the name *Israelitische Religionsgesellschaft*. The document they prepared provides a clear expression of their own vision of the character of the community they were founding. The founders of the IRG had a precise picture both of the man they wanted as spiritual leader and of the program they intended him to enact:

The ultimate objective and the primary goal toward which all our efforts are directed is solely "the protection and enhancement of revered Judaism, as transmitted by our fathers and as historically and traditionally developed; the care for the institutions which grew out of this soil; and the awakening and rebirth of a genuine religious temperament in the hearts of our youth." In order to achieve these high goals, we regard the following as the most effective and most powerful means:

1. *The Synagogue*: We want an orderly, worthy service, within the bounds of the law, but satisfying the progressive demands of the times, just as has long been conducted by the large pious communities of Europe, as in London, Hamburg, Berlin, etc.

2. *The Religious School*: We want an institution in which the ancient word of God, the true faith of our fathers, will be deeply impressed upon the hearts of our youth and will be taught by capable individuals, qualified in secular as well as religious studies.

3. *The Remaining Public Religious Institutions*: We want these to be established and equipped so that on the one hand, they totally satisfy the demands of our law, while, on the other hand, they offer no offence to the taste and sensitivity of our present generation.

4. *The Rabbi*: Finally, we want to choose as the head of our community, to supervise all of these institutions and to deliver religious sermons regularly in our pure, native tongue, a man who, through studies at a gymnasium and university, has attained a solid, broad education with a specialty in Jewish studies and who combines an unblemished character with a genuine religious conviction.[71]

The statement ends with the wish of the founders "that Frankfurt shall once again, as in times gone-by, become a model of true religious piety for all other Jewish communities," and it is signed "The Board of the Israelitische Religionsgesellschaft of

Frankfurt a.M." The document reveals that even before a rabbi had been appointed, the founders of the IRG had determined to establish an Orthodox congregation in Frankfurt that would provide inspiration for other communities and would signal the path for modern Orthodoxy to follow.

At the time this announcement was circulated to members of the Frankfurt Jewish community, the board was negotiating for the position of rabbi with Dr. Michael Sachs, rabbi of the Jewish community of Berlin. A scholar and renowned preacher, Sachs seemed eminently qualified for the new position. The Frankfurters realized that Sachs held a coveted position as rabbi of Germany's largest community, but it was also aware that Sachs was suffering in Berlin from the strife between Orthodox and Reform. Indeed, Sachs responded positively to the Frankfurt inquiry, explaining that the heterogeneous elements of the Berlin community were hindering his efforts and that his talents could better be employed in Frankfurt.[72]

Based on such an encouraging turn of events, the members arranged for annual subscriptions of five-year duration in order to finance Sach's salary and expenses. The pledges amounted to annual donations of 5,000 to 6,000 florin. Sachs was contracted to 3,500 florin, equal to Rthlr. 2,000, in contrast with the Rthlr. 1,500 he was receiving as rabbi of Berlin! The wealthy Orthodox of Frankfurt were opening their purses freely in support of the cause. Sachs and his wife were treated graciously during their stay in which negotiations were conducted. Servants were placed at their disposal. They were called upon by Baron Amschel Rothschild and his nephew Baron Willy and invited to use their box while attending the theater. In addition to whatever personal demands he may have made, Sachs stipulated that the society must have its own synagogue building. The Rothschilds were approached and agreed to contribute 70,000 florin provided that a sum of 30,000 florin be donated by other members of the society. Schwarzschild commented on the difficulty the members had pledging such an amount, but obviously their per capita resources were greater than those of the general community, which was still unable to construct its long-desired new building. (Almost twenty years had passed since reconstruction had been considered a matter of some urgency in 1834. Construction finally did begin in 1854.) Sach's conditions were accepted, and a contract was signed.[73]

The appointment of Sachs was announced to the Senate on November 9, 1850. A Berlin correspondent, reporting in the Jewish press, stressed the material attractions offered by Rothschild, glossing over the unsatisfactory working conditions Sachs faced in Berlin.[74] Only a short time passed, however, before Sachs requested to be released from his contract with the IRG. The Frankfurters had been quite surprised when Sachs accepted their calling, and they were now reluctant to agree to his release. Rothschild turned to his associate in Berlin, S. Bleichroeder, to intervene of their behalf. Bleichroeder answered with the explanation he had received from Sachs of the change in plans. The Berlin Board had taken steps to encourage Sachs to remain, and he now felt that his stronger obligation was to the Berlin community, which he could not leave in the lurch. Bleichroeder added that while Sachs could undoubtedly accomplish a great deal in Frankfurt, his efforts in Berlin would benefit a considerably larger number who sorely needed his leadership and would be greatly harmed by his departure.

Sachs in a new letter offered a somewhat less eloquent explanation for not fulfilling his contract. His wife now refused to move to Frankfurt, and Sachs found himself "caught between domestic unpleasantness and public obligations, his strength broken, and he unable to satisfy his obligations." Bleichroeder presented the stronger case, and it is not surprising that Schwarzschild concluded that Sachs had in any event been too weak a man to provide the necessary leadership for the new community.[75]

The IRG's attention was now directed by Rabbi Gerson Josaphat to Samson Raphael Hirsch, state rabbi of the Austrian province of Moravia. Hirsch, now forty-two, had established a reputation as spokesman and defender of German Orthodoxy with publication of his *Nineteen Letters of Ben Uziel* in 1836 and of *Horeb* the following year. As state rabbi, Hirsch had jurisdiction over a number of rabbis and over more than fifty communities.

Josaphat wrote to Hirsch, describing the state of affairs in Frankfurt and the significance of the endeavor. "A new Orthodox community has been formed," Josaphat wrote, "consisting of the most honorable and wealthiest people and with the Rothschild family at their head." He reviewed the selection of Sachs and the subsequent events and then emphasized the good qualities of the people. "The position of rabbi here is a distinguished one. The genuinely religious rabbi will find fertile ground."[76]

Hirsch apparently expressed his interest in a direct response to the society as his letter to Josaphat was merely a personal acknowledgment.[77] The Rothschilds approved Hirsch's candidacy and reaffirmed their pledge in support of a synagogue building. Forty-four members attended the first general meeting and confirmed Hirsch's appointment. A board was elected, consisting of Selig Moses Schwarzschild, Leopold Rapp, Philipp Abraham Cohen, Herz Weiller, and Wolf Jacob Bass.

Despite the difficulties and opposition Hirsch had faced in his position as state rabbi in Moravia, once he submitted his resignation, steps were taken to encourage him to remain. A delegation representing the fifty-two communities and 50,000 to 60,000 souls under Hirsch's jurisdiction agreed to a number of his requests. Most prominent among the concessions were the transfer of the rabbinate's seat from Nikolsburg to the state capital at Olmuetz, the separation of the state Rabbinate from specific responsibility to the local community of Nikolsburg, and the establishment of a seminary for teachers and rabbis. Hirsch was surprised by the sudden rapprochement on the side of the communities, and his subsequent letter to Frankfurt revealed a temptation to accept the concessions and to remain in Austria. Nevertheless, he yielded the right of decision to the board of the IRG, and in 1851, Samson Raphael Hirsch became the rabbi of the *Israelitische Religionsgesellschaft* of Frankfurt.[78]

Champion of Orthodoxy

When the second generation proponents of Reform initiated a wave of intellectual, liturgical, and communal activity in the mid-1830s, Samson Raphael Hirsch immediately appeared on the scene as defender of the Jewish legal tradition. While Michael Creizenach's *Schulchan Aruch* was initiated in 1833 and Abraham Geiger introduced his *Wissenschaftliche Zeitschrift fuer juedische Theologie* in 1835, Hirsch's first book *The Nineteen Letters of Ben Uziel* appeared as early as 1836, and his precocious response left little doubt that he was to be Orthodoxy's champion in the strife just beginning.

When Hirsch came to Frankfurt in 1851, he was known as the most progressive leader of German Orthodoxy, but he gradually emerged as its most uncompromising and militant defender. Hirsch was a puzzle for his contemporaries and has remained so for later scholars seeking to unravel the complex components of his personality.

Although Hirsch is often depicted as virtually a product of spontaneous generation, and indeed he often portrayed himself as well as his followers in that light, the preparation for his assuming the leadership of German Orthodoxy can to a great extent be traced to his family and community background. In short, the formative forces in the shaping of Hirsch's career derived from his childhood in Hamburg.

CHILDHOOD IN HAMBURG

A short but insightful biographical essay, published in 1908 in honor of the centennial of Hirsch's birth, cogently suggested that Hirsch's grandfather, Menachem Mendel Frankfurter, had exerted considerable influence upon the young Hirsch's development.[1] Born in 1742, Frankfurter studied in the yeshivah of the well-known Altona rabbi Jonathan Eibeschuetz. After a brief career as a teacher in Stuttgart and Berlin, he returned home and supported himself commercially, while he served the local Jewish community as a member of the board and, for an extended period, voluntarily as head of the Altona rabbinical court.[2] In 1805 Frankfurter founded a school for poor children in Altona and later led the directorship of the expanded Talmud Torah School that served the three sister communities of Altona, Hamburg, and Wandsbeck.[3]

The Talmud Torah School was conducted on the principle of teaching both religious studies and basic secular subjects. Frankfurter hoped to instill in the pupils that combination of religious knowledge and occupational training he deemed necessary for a man to support himself properly and skillfully. Each lad would then be equipped to choose his own source of livelihood, whether it be Torah, commerce, or a skilled profession.[4] In a report sent to the occupying French authorities in 1812, Frankfurter explained that the school instructed poor children who otherwise would be unable to attend public schools. Subjects included Hebrew grammar, the Bible with commentaries, and Talmud with commentaries, as well as writing, arithmetic, and the German and French languages. To the local community authorities, he wrote: "For the past eight years the community school has taught religion, writing, and arithmetic, and since 1810, French as well. The main objective remains the training of rabbis."[5] Religious studies concentrated on the Bible for the beginning student and Talmud for the more advanced.

Both in his capacity as head of the school and in his other roles within the community, Frankfurter played an active part in the religious controversies of the second decade of the nineteenth century. The proponents of reform succeeded in delaying for almost ten years the appointment of a chief rabbi in Hamburg, while Frankfurter was among those who realized the damage that the leadership vacuum was inflicting upon the traditionalist cause. Frankfurter himself was appointed to a commission formed in 1820 to resolve the religious differences within the community.[6] Meanwhile, the Reformers also asserted their efforts in an attempt to secularize the curriculum of the Talmud Torah School that Frankfurter headed. These efforts were resisted by the school board, which included not only Hirsch's grandfather, but also his great uncle Tobias Frankfurter, another relative, Samuel Elias Frankfurter, and his own father, Raphael Hirsch.[7]

In 1818, when Hirsch was ten years old, the controversy between the two camps in Hamburg took a new turn with the opening of the Reform temple. The establishment of an independent Reform synagogue hardly eased tensions within the broader community, since the two sides disputed the legitimacy of such a synagogue. Both camps turned beyond Germany toward Hungary for rabbinical support, and a rich contest of polemics followed. Meanwhile, powerful supporters of the Reform cause remained active in the community itself and successfully delayed the appointment of a new rabbi until 1821.[8]

These events in Hamburg during Hirsch's youth were of primary importance in the shaping of his career. In Ben Uziel's second letter, Hirsch explained to his correspondent: "It was my own inner life-plan and not external necessity that caused me to choose the rabbinate." That life plan had been fixed during the period under discussion, as Hirsch himself testified in a source related through some of those associated with him.

He himself often said that it had, in fact, been the defection from Judaism in his native city that had brought him to the path of life on which he led the exhausted holy heritage of the fathers from victory to victory. As an eleven and twelve year old lad, he witnessed the meetings in his parents' home, in which the traditionalists discussed the events of the day and the steps to be taken in order to oppose the bold, impertinent actions of the innovators. The helpless, despairing pain that these valiant men bespoke with their words and their destitute countenance, had so affected the boy, that he then vowed to dedicate his life to the Jewish heritage which had been given up by its own children.[9]

The meetings referred to may not have been as aimless as the anecdote asserted, for the traditionalists, in fact, retained control of the school and eventually succeeded in electing a rabbi to their liking, but Hirsch did remember these meetings as overcast with doubts and a sense of helplessness. The portrait of weakness does not conform to historical reality; rather that picture of the impotence of his precursors was a product of Hirsch himself.

In sum, Samson Raphael Hirsch grew up within an atmosphere charged with the tensions of the religious dispute between Orthodoxy and Reform. That helps to explain how Hirsch could emerge at what seemed like a remarkably early date for an Orthodox response against Reform. The movement for reform in Hamburg was preceded by the reforms introduced in Westphalia under the leadership of Israel Jacobsohn, but there the religious innovations were introduced under the protection of the Napoleonic government.[10] The religious controversy between Orthodox and Reform began in Hamburg, and the child Hirsch witnessed the height of strife first-hand in his own home between the ages of seven and thirteen.

FRIENDSHIP WITH GEIGER

On October 26, 1829, Hirsch registered for studies at the University of Bonn. Five days later, Abraham Geiger enrolled at the same university.[11] The relationship that soon developed between these future antagonists represents far more than the historical irony with which it is usually described. The affinities that brought them together and the tensions that separated them were both products of the rapidly changing dynamics in German Jewish life. The vicissitudes of their friendship provide an illustrative reflection of these changes.

Although Geiger and Hirsch both grew up in traditional homes, their family and especially their educational backgrounds were quite different. Of the two, it was Geiger who had been raised in an old-style religious milieu, and Geiger was the more deeply embedded in his religious studies. His father had been a cantor; his eldest brother a tradesman, teacher, and later *dayan* of the Frankfurt Jewish community. Abraham began study of the Bible at age three, Mishnah at four, and Talmud at six. Two years later his father became his Talmud tutor, but when he died, before Abraham had reached the age of thirteen, the role of teacher was assumed by his brother Solomon, who instructed him in Hebrew language, Bible, and Talmud. Since the family would not consider sending him to the Philanthropin School in Frankfurt, which was run by the proponents of Reform, Geiger's secular education was provided by private teachers. As happened so frequently in these situations, the piety of his family resulted in Geiger receiving his secular instruction from non-Jewish and irreligious personalities.[12]

With his instruction coming from such disparate sources, it is no wonder that Geiger repeatedly bemoaned the lack of a model to synthesize his traditional, religious learning with his secular studies. But it is interesting that even the leading teachers at the Philanthropin School, Josef Johlson and Michael Creizenach, who gradually came to influence the young Geiger, were also unable to provide him with the needed example. In his childhood memoir, Geiger wrote about the influence that his various teachers had had upon him. "There was, then, ample instruction and stimulation, and yet the lad's spirit and that of other beginners, could not be satisfied. What he greatly desired was a polished union of the separate spheres."[13]

Hirsch's enlightened family encouraged secular studies, and in contrast to Geiger, Hirsch received formal training in these studies when he attended the Hamburg Gymnasium.[14] His early Jewish studies have become somewhat of a mystery, but he did continue by studying at the yeshivah of Jacob Ettlinger in Mannheim for a period of one and a half years.[15] Then Hirsch came to study at Bonn.

By the time Geiger and Hirsch arrived at Bonn in 1830, the number of Jewish students attending German universities was already increasing. Of course, Jews still represented but a minuscule proportion of the general student body. Between the years 1826 and 1830, thirty-four Jews registered at Bonn, some 3 percent of the total enrollment. Yet, it cannot be said that Geiger and Hirsch were alone at Bonn. In fact, by attending a university in order to train for the rabbinate, Geiger and Hirsch were in the company of some 20 percent of all Jewish students in Germany. At least five others studying in Bonn in 1830 were pursuing that same objective.[16]

Yet, Geiger testified in his diary to the loneliness he felt at the university, a loneliness which was compounded by the lack of direction in their new endeavor and by the lack of a program at the university to prepare properly for a career in the rabbinate. A student in similar circumstances described the difficulty he faced in a letter published in 1842:

With what great difficulties must today's rabbi struggle: He is expected to be as proficient as Christian preachers in languages and sciences, while simultaneously like the rabbi of the past becoming an expert swimmer in the sea of the Talmud. . . . I am supposed to attain the heights of contemporary education, and yet combine the spirit of enlightenment, of science, and of philosophy with the embodiment of the old-style Orthodoxy! . . . Indeed, should I study my entire life in order to become a chameleon? No, this I cannot do.[17]

In order to overcome the lack of a proper program and to combat the personal loneliness they felt, Geiger and Hirsch decided to establish a homiletical society:

One evening, as we were walking home after the lecture, we spoke of Goethe's *Wahrheit und Dichtung*, which I was then reading; we told each other of our circumstances, and both of us bemoaned the isolation of Jewish theological students. We agreed to establish a preaching society.[18]

The same step was taken by rabbinical candidates at the universities of Heidelberg and Wuerzburg. These societies apparently contributed more to the social needs of the students than to their professional training, for shortly after the group at Bonn was founded, Geiger still bemoaned their lack of direction and leadership: "We lack the inspiration of a model and the support of a master." But friendships were formed, some of them lasting ones.[19]

Of course, the friendship between Geiger and Hirsch did not last, but even in 1830 their relationship was not altogether harmonious. Hirsch delivered the first speech in the society, and Geiger responded at the next meeting:

We had quite a long argument, in which I got to know and to admire his extraordinary eloquence, his discernment and his clear and quick comprehension. But this argument did not bring us any closer. We would occasionally also touch upon the religious aspect, at which point, although I always spoke only from the point of view of the Jewish religion, I must have often offended his views with mine.

Gradually, they drew closer to each other. They began to study Talmud together and continued for the remainder of the winter semester and through the summer.

And so, there gradually developed a mutual regard and affection. I respected his superior abilities, his strong virtue, and loved his good heart. He respected my glowing plans, which were not altogether objectionable to him. He loved my openness and my youthful cheerfulness. His company was for me quite useful and enjoyable.[20]

Hirsch did not remain long at Bonn. In 1830, at the age of twenty-two, he was appointed *Landrabbiner* in Oldenburg on the recommendation of the incumbent, Nathan Adler. Geiger remained at Bonn until 1832, where he achieved academic distinction in his Arabic studies. Soon after leaving Bonn he was appointed rabbi in Wiesbaden. They corresponded with each other in the next years, but only three letters, all from Geiger to Hirsch, are now available.[21]

During those years prior to the publication of *The Nineteen Letters* in 1836, their personal relationship remained somewhat strained. Geiger complained that Hirsch did not write frequently enough, and as a result, Geiger wrote, "I have often said to friends: Hirsch may do to me what he will, but I shall remain his friend." However, Geiger did clearly discern the distance between their religious positions. In an 1831 letter to his friend L. Ullmann, also a member of the Bonn preaching society, Geiger doubted that Reform rabbis would succeed in introducing innovations within the framework of the broader community, and he espoused the alternative path of schism. He argued that the strategies of the Reformers could easily be exposed by enlightened, university-trained Orthodox rabbis: "Hirsch, Frensdorff, even Hess will probably not move against us, because they trust us, but should not the other academics have such thoughts?"[22]

In 1833 Geiger complained to Hirsch of being too mistrustful. Writing after his appointment in Wiesbaden, Geiger's letter indicated the continued uneasiness in their relationship:

I wish you to consider whether this fear does not go too far with you, whether it does not lead you to an insurmountable distrust, whether you do not presume too much of your opinions, while rejecting as bad shepherds those who think otherwise.[23]

We do not know how close Hirsch perceived their relationship to be, but there did exist an interesting discrepancy between Hirsch's perception of his religious position and the perception of others, including Geiger. For Geiger, Hirsch belonged to the growing number of university-trained Orthodox rabbis. His letter to Ullmann still indicated a degree of trust and bond based on their common experience at the university. But Hirsch did not represent for Geiger an ally or partner in the cause of Reform.

The state authorities in Oldenburg also saw Hirsch as an Orthodox rabbi, an attribute that they did not particularly admire in him. When Hirsch complained to the regime of financial difficulties, the officials responded with the suggestion that perhaps funds appropriated for his office could be better spent:

The government allows itself merely to observe that the objective of bringing the Jews closer to the Christian subjects and diverting them from their peculiar manners and customs would be better fulfilled without a *Landrabbiner*, especially if he is, as is the present incumbent, a strong adherent of his faith.[24]

With the appearance of *The Nineteen Letters* in 1836, Hirsch gave explicit expression to his religious position and, while hardly identifying with the camp of Reformers, his position was equally distant from the Orthodox. "In an age when the contrasts stand so sharply against each other, and when truth is on neither side, in such an age the man who belongs to no party . . . cannot expect approval or agreement from any side."[25] But, of course, it was Hirsch himself who in the *Letters* extended approval to neither side. His references to the Orthodoxy of his day were sharply critical. His emphasis on the religious commandments made it impossible for Hirsch to identify too fully with the Reformers, but his language in describing their efforts was respectful:

Be angry with none, respect all, for they all feel the shortcomings which exist, all wish that which is good, as they conceive it; all desire sincerely the welfare of Israel, and if they have failed to recognize the good and have erred in their comprehension of the Truth, not they are chiefly to blame; the entire past bears the responsibility together with them. You should, therefore, respect their intentions, but you may well mourn and weep when you examine the aims to which their efforts are directed.

Hirsch's religious position was closer to the Orthodox, yet his universe of discourse had brought him closer to the Reformers.[26]

Geiger initially extended a warm welcome to the appearance of *The Nineteen Letters*.[27] Commenting on both Hirsch's *Letters* and a second theological work somewhat closer to his own thinking, Geiger wrote, "We have before us two works, alike in their highest aspiration to establish a holy truth." Despite the differences between the works, Geiger could conclude, "The floor on which all are standing is the same, the goal which all are pursuing is great; the arena is open; the contestants may all come forward."[28] However, shortly thereafter, Geiger issued a series of scathing reviews of *The Letters*. At the heart of his critique was what he considered to be the poor light in which the Reform movement of his day was presented.[29]

In *The Letters*, Hirsch had criticized the Reformers, but demanded respect for their intentions, but Geiger openly declared that the gap between them had become too great and that his deep, personal feelings toward Hirsch must be repressed, for at stake was nothing less than "the regeneration of our faith." Geiger began his review by recalling the past friendship between the author and himself and bemoaning the distance that had developed between them.[30]

The brunt of Geiger's critique did not fall upon the inadequacy of Hirsch's answers and explanations as transmitted in *The Letters* by the personality of Naphtali. Rather, Geiger mercilessly belittled the literary character Benjamin, Hirsch's straw man for providing the questions and doubts that provoked Naphtali's responses. In Geiger's description, Benjamin had originally maintained the same reverence for Judaism as Naphtali, and this attitude continued "as long as they lived together." But meeting again "after many years of separation, they had come to totally different views."[31] Geiger found Benjamin's questions to Naphtali unprovocative and intellectually inadequate. After a sharp critique of Benjamin's over-readiness to acquiesce to Naphtali's arguments, Geiger concluded, "We have, therefore, before us a man whose leisurely demands are satisfied, without the struggle of a more rigorous examination."[32] Geiger was not satisfied with merely criticizing Benjamin's passivity in the exchange with Naphtali, and he proceeded to construct his own list of questions that Benjamin should have posed. In other words, Geiger assumed the role of Benjamin in the dialogue with Hirsch.[33]

Geiger apparently saw himself as the model for Hirsch's Benjamin. This attitude is reflected in his opening recollection of their own personal relationship and by the description of how Benjamin and Naphtali had parted in their views over the years. It was for this reason that Geiger was more concerned with Benjamin's intellectual inadequacy than with Naphtali's. *The Nineteen Letters* represented for Geiger a continuation of the past discussions between the two, but Hirsch had failed in his portrayal of Benjamin to present Geiger's position adequately. Geiger found *The Letters* uncomplimentary both to himself personally and to the movement with which he identified, and he verbalized this dissatisfaction in a sharp critique of Benjamin's intellectual dullness and of the book as a whole.

Geiger's response to *The Nineteen Letters* ended the relationship between the two men, but the end had not come abruptly. Six years earlier, they had studied together and talked together, as students do, and over the years they had grown apart—as so often happens. They had never been close in their religious outlook, but they had been bound together by the endeavor, still new at that time, of seeking advanced training in secular studies as a prerequisite for a rabbinical career. In 1830 it had seemed valuable to build ties despite their differences; in 1836, Geiger found it necessary to bury the ties and to emphasize the differences. This was also the response Hirsch's *Letters* and later *Horeb* received from others in the Reform camp. Down the line, the reviews appearing in the liberal Jewish press rebuffed Hirsch's efforts.[34]

Hirsch, who had tried to speak in conciliatory terms to the Reformers, may well have wondered at the response he had provoked. Of course, Hirsch's tone was rarely conciliatory, whatever his intentions, and here, too, he expressed himself in such confident terms as are worthy of a religious champion, not of a conciliator. Geiger had urged him a few years before to be less sure of himself and his views, but that advice was not heeded in The Letters.[35]

Ultimately, however, the Reformers' rejection of Hirsch was due not to his self-confidence, but to his religious convictions. We do not know why Geiger's attitudes toward The Nineteen Letters changed after the appearance of his first review, but the break in the relationship between Geiger and Hirsch occurred within a changing historical setting. If Hirsch thought himself somewhat close to the Reformers in attitude, that very closeness now made it impossible for them to accept him, hence, Geiger's specific rejection of Hirsch's conception of Reform for not going far enough and his criticism that Hirsch's continued acceptance of binding Talmudic authority contradicted his very objective as a reformer.[36] By 1836 the Reformers were setting out to define themselves as a distinct movement. Geiger and Philippson were establishing their journals and in 1837 Geiger convoked the first rabbinical conference. Hirsch's commitments to rabbinic Judaism set him outside their limits at the very time when the Reformers were anxious to establish those limits as clearly as possible.

The Reformers were not mistaken in perceiving the distance between Hirsch and themselves. Despite the conciliatory terms Hirsch had tried to express in The Letters, his intentions in his early literary works were to offer a positive alternative to the Reformers' approach. These writings, including The Letters, represented Hirsch's first public efforts to continue the struggle against the Reformers that he had witnessed in his youth. He began his mission with an approach of conciliation, but the rebuff he received by the Reformers drove Hirsch on to more open opposition. His literary energy in the years immediately following was mostly spent as an active polemicist in the Orthodox camp.[37]

Hirsch's early religious position has often been misunderstood to have stood midway between Orthodoxy and Reform. This is not accurate. The change was more in tactics than in substance. Both *The Letters* and *Horeb* already represented the beginning of his active struggle against the Reformers. Despite Hirsch's flirtations both with reforms and Reformers, his commitment to the defense of the Jewish tradition had been steadfast from the outset. That commitment formed the cornerstone of his personality. Paradoxically, both his openness toward the Reformers in the early 1830s and the zeal with which Hirsch later defended the Orthodox cause derived from the same driving forces in his personality. Hirsch has puzzled those who have tried to understand him, but a great deal about his complex personality can be inferred from the literary testimony that he has left behind.

HIRSCH AND *HOREB*

By the late 1830s Samson Raphael Hirsch was established as a significant figure in the religious world of German Jewry, an achievement attained by the publication of his first two books on Jewish law and thought. In 1835 Hirsch submitted his first work, *Horeb*, for publication, but by request of the publishers he prepared the shorter, more popularly written *Nineteen Letters*, which was published under the pseudonym of Ben Uziel in 1836 and followed by *Horeb* in 1837.[38] *Horeb*, subtitled *Essays on Israel's Duties in the Dispersion*, is a compendium of Jewish laws, interspersed with Hirsch's often original interpretations of their spiritual significance. Hirsch classified the commandments into six categories, as he explained in detail in *The Nineteen Letters*.[39]

The writing of such a compendium was precipitated by the early seeds of a Reform theology that were emerging in the mid-1830s. Less known than Geiger's scholarly *Wissenschaftiche Zeitschrift*, but more related to the writing of *Horeb*, was the publication in 1833 by Michael Creizenach, leader of the Reform party in Frankfurt, of the first volume of his *Schulchan Aruch*, "a Comprehensive Presentation of Mosaic law."[40] Creizenach sought to demonstrate in this work that Talmudic Judaism had frequently strayed from its biblical origins. While these deviations were employed by Reformers as precedent for their own innovations,

Creizenach also maintained that the rituals established by the rabbis no longer bore any actual religious significance in contemporary Judaism:

Every religious system has two fundamentally different components: instruction on the most consequential questions . . . plus a collection of regulations and rules of conduct. . . . In no other religious system as in the Mosaic are these two primary components, teachings of faith and duties, so sharply separated.

Creizenach posed the question bluntly: "Should Mosaic Law be interpreted according to its spirit or to the letter of the law?"[41]

In *Horeb*, Hirsch adopted Creizenach's idea and composed his own encyclopedia of Jewish law. In contrast to his predecessor, Hirsch attempted to attain a spiritual understanding of Jewish law without infringing upon the significance of ritual practice. Even if the commandments were to be found incomprehensible, "We should have to perform them, not because there was this reason or another for any commandment, but because God had ordained it."[42] The practice of law could not be affected by the search for spiritual understanding. Hirsch, therefore, returned to a traditional distinction in Jewish learning between the study of law and of legend. But in Hirsch's formulation, *aggadah* became identified with that specific endeavor of providing legal practice with spiritual meaning:

There will accordingly be two spheres of thought engaged in the exposition of the Divine law. . . . One school will concern itself with the comprehension of the utterances regulating our practical conduct and with the lessons also concerned with practice, that can be derived from those utterances. That knowledge will be derived almost exclusively from the tradition. . . . The other school will concern itself with reflecting and pondering on the law, and its source of knowledge will be the illuminating power of insight which dwells more or less within each individual.[43]

Critical control over these subjective interpretations was to be provided by the specific details of the ritual: The more closely an interpretation corresponded to the components of the law, "the more such a view will commend itself to us."[44]

Through his emphasis on legal specifics, Hirsch sought to ensure the significance of continued practice. According to Isaac Heinemann, it was this very emphasis on details that characterized Hirsch's unique contribution to the genre of literature concerned with examining the reasons behind Jewish laws. Therefore, Hirsch's contribution resulted from his reaffirmation of ritual practice within the framework of his spiritual analysis. However, Heinemann concluded that Hirsch adopted this emphasis in order to distinguish between the abstract spirituality of Christianity and the spirituality of Judaism revealed in its practices.[45] The suggestion that the writing of *Horeb* was influenced by the appearance of Creizenach's *Schulchan Aruch* implies that at issue for Hirsch was the Reform tendency to substitute spirituality for practice.

Hirsch's selection of *Horeb* as the title of his first work reflects the role he saw both for his book and for himself as providing a constructive alternative to the path of the Reformers. It has generally been assumed that Hirsch intended the title, *Horeb*, to refer to the site of the divine revelation of the Torah to Israel. According to the book of Exodus, the theophany occurred at Sinai, but Deuteronomy referred to the site as Horeb. Indeed, it was only natural to assume that Hirsch sought to echo the revelation at Sinai in the title of a book on Jewish law. But just as obvious as the interpretation is the question of why, if Hirsch intended a reference to the revelation alone, he did not choose "Sinai" itself as his title.[46] In fact, Mount Horeb was also known for another biblical event, the dialogue between God and the prophet Elijah, and it was this event which made Horeb especially significant to Hirsch.

And he arose, and ate and drank, and went on the strength of that food forty days and forty nights to the mount of God, Horeb. And he came there to a cave and spent the night there, and behold, the word of the Lord came to him, and He said unto him, "What are you doing here, Elijah?" And he said, "I have been very jealous for the Lord, God of Hosts, for the children of Israel have forsaken Your covenant, thrown down Your altars, and slain Your prophets with the sword, and I, even I only, am left and they seek my life to take it away." (I Kings (19:8–10)

Moses had received the Torah at Sinai with all of Israel waiting at its foot. Now Elijah, too, spoke with God at that same mountain, but he stood there alone. Israel had forsaken its covenant and its God, and only Elijah remained loyal.

In 1835 Hirsch sent a copy of the *Horeb* manuscript to his cousin Z. H. May and sought his assistance in arranging for the work's publication. In an accompanying letter, Hirsch expressed some revealing attitudes of the author toward his work: "If I knew of even one person more capable than myself of pleading the true cause of Israel, my incapable and inexperienced pen would have rested for a long time yet."[47] But Hirsch dismissed the ability of all others to undertake the task. The older generation revered Judaism but treated it as an "inherited mummy," while the younger generation showed enthusiasm, but was nevertheless ignorant of "authentic Judaism." Hirsch perceived himself as the single source of strength in the midst of Judaism's crisis:

It is a duty to speak out if one is able only to hint at a route which others might valiantly follow. I must speak, mainly because no one else does so; this is the only justification for my coming forward. God will help me.

I do not ask for the prize of battle. I shall be happy to be merely the herald who utters the battle cry. But I am not afraid of the battle, even if I have to fight it on my own.

Hirsch's letter echoed Elijah's response to God at Mount Horeb with both men standing alone in defense of God and His law.

In his letter to May, Hirsch stated that he was prepared to take up the battle alone, but did he really think that a single man could be effective in spiritual warfare? In fact, Hirsch repeatedly referred to the potential efficacy of a lone Israelite arising in defense of his God. In his discussion of the Chanukkah holiday, Hirsch transformed the usual theme of the righteous few against the powerful into his own personal motif:

So long as the light remains pure within the confines of only one house or within the breast of only one man, the spiritual life of Israel is saved; God watches over it, and even by the light of one man He rekindles it anew.[48]

The spiritual plight of his own day was no different in Hirsch's view, as can be seen from his conclusion of Ben Uziel's eighteenth letter. "If only one remains—one Jew with the Book of the Law in his hand, with Israel's law in his heart, Israel's light in his spirit—that one suffices; Israel's cause will not be lost."[49] The author of *Horeb* and of *The Nineteen Letters* saw himself as the man who would undertake the battle in his generation, but even as Hirsch thought that he stood alone, he relied upon a spiritual prototype to serve as his model. We can now proceed to demonstrate that he drew his inspiration at first from the prophet Elijah and later from the biblical hero Phinehas as well.

For many years while Hirsch served as rabbi in Frankfurt, he published his own journal, *Jeschurun*. At a younger age, Hirsch had also planned to publish a periodical which never appeared, but the prospectus for this earlier journal was found among Hirsch's papers and published by his decendants and followers in their own journal *Nachalath Z'wi*. Hirsch's proposed periodical was to be called *Karmel, eine Zeitschrift fuer Leben und Wissenschaft im Judentum*. The paper's motto came from Elijah's encounter with the people at Mount Carmel:

How long will you hobble between two different opinions? If the Lord is God, follow Him; but if Baal, then follow him.

And they said, The Lord, He is God, The Lord, He is God. (I Kings, chap. 18)

The prospectus also contained the journal's first—and only—article, entitled "Karmel und Sinai," in which Hirsch contrasted the roles of the two mountains.[50]

Sinai was the source of God's law, but as centuries passed, Israel's commitment to that law weakened, until "there came a time when statesmanship itself was deemed higher than the words of Sinai." Altars were built to Baal and Israel became enveloped in darkness. It was then that Elijah arose and through his fires at Carmel, once again brightened the night. The words of Sinai returned to Israel's breast, and the people burst forth with the affirmation that "the Lord alone, He is God." But the light seen at Carmel was a mere flash in the night, for immediately thereafter, Elijah was forced to flee to Sinai (sic!) where he bemoaned to God in a passage fully quoted by Hirsch that all of Israel's sons had forsaken the covenant, and "I, even I only, am left." Hirsch then proceeded to contrast the roles of Moses and Elijah: "Moses died. Lucky Moses! Moses could die, for his mission at Sinai had been accomplished. Elijah did not die. Elijah could not die, for his mission at Carmel was unfinished." Hirsch followed with five paragraphs, all beginning rather pointedly with the recurring words—"Elijah lives":

Elijah lives. His spirit is carried on in the mouths of the prophets who followed him. . . . Elijah lives. His spirit is present in every newborn in Israel. . . . Elijah lives. Whenever the words of Sinai shall again be obliterated in Israel . . . whenever again in Israel the grandchildren do not wish to continue the building started by the fathers, but wish to lay a new foundation unknown to the fathers, whenever night falls once again on Israel, then too will Elijah rise once again with his spirit of fire and again form the bond of the fathers with the children and the bond of the children with the fathers, before the world is brought to ruin.[51]

Hirsch's selection of *Horeb* as the title of his work allowed him to combine the contributions of Carmel and Sinai, for Horeb signified the presence of both Moses and Elijah and symbolized simultaneously the revelation of the law as well as its defense. This dual interpretation is not imposed upon Hirsch, for he revealed it himself in a passage written some years later, following the juxtaposition of the two events in the book of Malachi:

Remember the Torah of My servant Moses which I commanded unto him in Horeb for all Israel, even statutes and ordinances. (Malachi 3:22) Wait for His word: Do not be alarmed by the present breakdown of society. . . . Await His word! In a similar period of upheaval He once sent you His prophet Elijah who restored the ruined altar of Israel and assembled the priests of Baal for the judgement of God on Mount Carmel. Wait for His word! "Behold, I will send to you Elijah the prophet, before the coming of the great and awful day of the Lord." (Malachi 3:23)[52]

Hirsch was more than inspired by Elijah; he fully identified with the ancient prophet and envisioned himself as the reincarnation of his spirit. "Elijah lives," emphasized Hirsch, and he will reappear whenever Israel should again be enveloped in darkness. In 1868 Hirsch returned to the Elijah theme and expanded the concept of Elijah's eternal return in Israel's hours of trouble. In an essay entitled "Phinehas—Eliyahu" Hirsch adopted the merging of these two biblical personalities as presented in the Midrashic interpretations.[53] Phinehas the priest, son of Eleazar and grandson of Aaron, was the biblical hero who had assuaged God's anger by slaying a tribal prince and his foreign mistress for transgressing God's commandments. Once again Hirsch transformed the active response of the courageous individual into a paradigm for future generations:

As long as even one man has the courage to take up the struggle openly for God's cause . . . it is not lost on earth. . . . He had demonstrated for all time that whenever the sanctity of God and His law is being mocked and trampled on, every other consideration must give way.[54]

Turning his attention from Phinehas to Elijah, Hirsch again related the encounter between God and Elijah at Mount Horeb, but now Elijah and Phinehas were presented by Hirsch as one: "The spirit of Phinehas reappeared in Elijah the Tishbite."[55] The motif of spiritual reincarnation begun by the Midrash was extended by Hirsch. As in the past, so in the present days of darkness, the spirit of Elijah will reappear. "Wait for his word! The upheaval will not last forever. The spirit of the returning Elijah is the physician."[56]

Hirsch's readers understood the title *Horeb* as an echo of the theophany at Sinai, but to Hirsch himself it captured the image of one man standing alone and spreading God's truth to the people of the covenant. That was Hirsch's self-image, and with different emphasis it remained so until the end of his days. In rabbinic tradition, Elijah is the forerunner of the Messianic coming. At the conclusion of "Phinehas—Eliyahu," Hirsch wrote: "Elijah is not Messiah, but he precedes Messiah and as long as Elijah is not here the Messiah too will not be here." Hirsch had also written to his cousin May, "I shall be happy to be merely the herald who utters the battle cry."[57]

How did it happen that Hirsch was able to envisage himself

as a spiritual reincarnation of Elijah the prophet? To answer this question, we return to Hirsch's own explanation of how he decided upon his personal life plan. As retold by his 1908 biographer, Hirsch was deeply affected as a child by the meetings held in his father's home to adopt a strategy for fighting the Reformers. The significant point in this anecdote was that Hirsch witnessed his father's helplessness in the wake of the Reform activities. Actually, Hirsch was not accurate in his evaluation of the effectiveness of those meetings, although we cannot speak specifically of his father's role. Yet the childhood picture of his father's impotence was stamped upon his mind, and his attitude toward the Reformers was shaped by this impression. One possible reaction by an individual to this constellation of personal factors would be deep hostility toward that force which had made his father appear weak before his own eyes. However, if the son who had witnessed this humiliation felt his own hostility toward his father, he could actually develop an admiration for that same opposing force. In fact, as we have already seen, Hirsch's attitude toward the Reformers was not uniform throughout his career, and there was a period in the 1830's when he sought to be close to them. Once rejected by them, he became their vehement opponent.

So little is known of Hirsch's childhood that there is room to object that a single source cannot become the basis for such an analysis. Yet, it is precisely because Hirsch himself singled out this specific information to explain the origins of his life commitments that the anecdote should be taken seriously in trying to understand him. The credibility of the source, which was related in print only through a secondary channel, can be confirmed by a reference to a different entry that does appear in Hirsch's writings, in fact, in the essay, "Phinehas—Eliyahu."

Here is Hirsch's description of the story of Phinehas as related in that essay:

The heads of the people were assembled to sit in judgement on this crime, when—before the very eyes of Moses and the gathering of the people—one of the leaders, the prince of a tribe, passed by defiantly with his alien mistress. At the sight of this depth of demoralization, . . . Moses and the heads of the people were reduced to impotent tears.

To Phinehas, one of the youngest of those present, these helpless tears spelt despair of his people's future. So he arose—alone—from the midst of the congregation, seized a spear and cut them both down, the man and the woman. Thus did he halt the plague which had already begun to smite the people. . . . Eleazar the father, Aaron the grandfather, Moses even, the great-uncle,—priests, teachers, and judges of the law—remained silent and wept—the offenders were a prince and the daughter of a prince; yet the young man who had not even been included in the priestly dedication of his father, arose and accomplished the deed which should not have had to wait his intervention.[58]

In this form, the story is quite parallel to Hirsch's personal anecdote. The elders, including the hero's father, were gathered together at a meeting to discuss an urgent problem of assimilation. They gathered with strong intention, but proved too impotent to activate a plan. In the biblical story, salvation was delivered by "one of the youngest present." In the analogue, the child Hirsch resolved to become the saving force.

Hirsch's interpretation of the story confirms that the two anecdotes were interchangeable or, better, quite identical in his mind. Based upon the biblical identification of Phinehas as "the son of Eleazar, the son of Aaron the priest," the various Midrashim did make some references to the family relationships of those gathered together at the council.[59] Hirsch expanded further upon this approach to the extent that he somewhat extraordinarily presented the assembly of the leaders of Israel in such personal terms as father, grandfather, and great-uncle Moses. Hirsch's transformation of the meeting of Israel's sages into a family conclave of Phineas's older relatives resulted from the impact of those parallel meetings in Hirsch's childhood. In fact the correlation between the two meetings goes even further. Using the history of the Talmud Torah School and E. Duckesz's summary of Hirsch's family history, we can deduce that among those on the board of the Talmud Torah at the time of these struggles with the Reformers were not only Hirsch's father but of course his grandfather and also Mendel Frankfurter's brother, Tobias Frankfurter, Hirsch's great-uncle.[60]

Hirsch's interpretation of the Phinehas story includes a completely irrelevant detail that Phinehas had been rejected by his father and not included in his priestly dedication. This element of narrative can be understood only if we assume that it was Hirsch himself who had suffered such a rejection and was projecting his own feelings back into the Phinehas story.[61] The sense of rejection by his family implied by this superfluous comment would help explain his later deep desire to prove himself in a realm of paternal impotence. It also helps to explain why Hirsch emphasized so often that he had been left alone to battle on behalf of God's cause.[62]

In sum, the striking similarity of Hirsch's childhood anecdote with his rendition of the Phinehas story leads to the conclusion that Hirsch decided at a young age to find his own identity within that sphere in which he considered his father to have been proven impotent. He apparently reached that decision as a consequence of a feeling of rejection by his family. He later recognized first in Elijah and then in Phinehas a complete reflection of his personality, his biography, and his ambitions, and he identified himself as the continuation of their spirit. He shared with them the image of a lone, isolated figure serving the cause of God and His law, and he began his battle alongside Elijah at Mount Horeb.

MOVE TO FRANKFURT

In 1851 Hirsch accepted the calling of the *Israelistische Religionsgesellschaft* of Frankfurt to become its rabbi. The reasons for doing so were many, even if it meant resigning his prestigious and powerful position in Nikolsburg to become the rabbi of a small, splinter group. The problems faced in Nikolsburg undoubtedly contributed to his decision to leave that post, but the position in Frankfurt also provided a number of attractive elements for Hirsch: a return to Germany, a return to the religious struggles of the day, and the leadership of a small group of true adherents of traditional Judaism.

Hirsch's deeply felt attachment to German culture and his political loyalty to the German land must have accentuated the alienation he felt from his surroundings in Nikolsburg. Josaphat's invitation to Frankfurt referred to Hirsch's isolation and suggested how much happier he would be "as a German" in Frankfurt. The distance between Hirsch and Germany increased after the events of 1849 virtually precluded the possibility of Austrian participation in a unified Germany.[63]

Further, the conflict between Orthodoxy and Reform had played a pivotal role in Hirsch's formative years, and to date, Hirsch's participation in this conflict had been peripheral. True, his philosophical and polemical works derived from the controversies of the time, but not his communal activities—and least of all, in traditionalist Moravia. The position in Frankfurt, however, threw Hirsch into the very midst of the battle and revived those inner emotions that had so moved him in his formative years. At the groundbreaking of the IRG's synagogue building, Hirsch reviewed Frankfurt's historical importance as a center of Jewish learning and contrasted the fervent religiosity of the past with the tragic reversal of the present.[64]

In that same cornerstone ceremony, Hirsch revealed something of his own perception of the significance of his move to Frankfurt. The establishment of the IRG marked a major stride toward reversing the Orthodox decline in Frankfurt. Hirsch's account of the formation of the IRG on that occasion already emphasized the role of the eleven founders, and depicted their accomplishment as a return to strength of those who had been weak and downtrodden. As we have seen, Hirsch's rendition of those events was historically inaccurate, but it provides an indication of Hirsch's thinking as he accepted the position in Frankfurt. For Hirsch, the founding of the IRG and his move to Frankfurt realized the basic elements of his own self-image. The vast majority of Frankfurt Jewry had abandoned God's word, but a small remnant had remained true and Hirsch now became their spokesman. Hirsch's decision to move to Frankfurt derived from his own self-image as the champion of Judaism in the midst of the crisis of his day.

That self-image had additional significance for our understanding of the history of Orthodox Judaism in Germany. We have already seen two examples of how Hirsch created historical images that described German Orthodoxy as being on the verge of collapse in the first half of the nineteenth century. Thus, Hirsch not only created the myth of the eleven founders of the Frankfurt IRG, but he also portrayed the traditionalist leaders in Hamburg as helpless during the struggles of the second decade. In other places Hirsch commented on the weakness of the Orthodox rabbinical leadership during that period.

These historical descriptions have been accepted at face value in the literature dealing with Germany Orthodoxy. Taken together, they portray an Orthodox leadership that was too paralyzed to oppose Reform initiatives and Orthodox teachers who were incapable of finding even the seeds of a response to the challenges of the day. In fact, I suggest that these descriptions by Hirsch do not warrant historical credibility. They are merely the literary projections of Hirsch's self-image as we have come to understand it: the image of a man alone. To project that image onto German Orthodoxy, to accept the description of isolation and weakness, is to ignore the material accumulated here and by others that Orthodoxy in Hamburg, Altona, Mecklenburg, Breslau, the Rhineland, Hesse, Bavaria, and Berlin—as well as Frankfurt—had maintained the strong remnants of their previous position and had begun the process of Orthodox renewal. When the Orthodox of Frankfurt succeeded in building a model community, they did so on the foundations laid by others and with a vast hinterland of supporters for whom the community in Frankfurt was indeed a model.

1. Portrait of the synagogue of the *Israelitische Religionsgesellschaft* from the *Illustrierte Zeitung*, October 7, 1854. Courtesy of the Leo Baeck Institute, New York.

2. Interior of the IRG's second synagogue building, dedicated in 1907 and located at the Friedberger Anlage. Courtesy of the Leo Baeck Institute, New York.

3. Samson Raphael Hirsch, rabbi of the IRG, and his family, circa 1855. Mendel Hirsch, later principal of the IRG school, is in the center. Courtesy of the Leo Baeck Institute, New York.

4. Fire in the Jewish Ghetto caused by French bombardment in 1795. The ghetto gate is in the right corner. Courtesy of the Leo Baeck Institute, New York.

5. The old *Judengasse*. The Main Synagogue, built in its midst in 1860, is on the left. Courtesy of the Leo Baeck Institute, New York.

Model Community

Until Hirsch's arrival in Frankfurt, his accomplishments as a communal leader had paled beside his intellectual achievements, but the thirty-seven years he served in Frankfurt marked the period in which a new communal structure for German Orthodoxy was created. That structure can be called Independent Orthodoxy, referring to an autonomous congregation, self-contained and self-ruled. It was primarily within that framework that Orthodoxy survived and even flourished in Germany. When, later in the century, Orthodoxy gained a stronger position within the Jewish community, it was able to do so partly because of the sustained strength it had revealed in the network of independent congregations established between 1850 and 1877. The IRG of Frankfurt was the model for those congregations. It was within its framework that Hirsch perpetuated his name as a communal leader and, as such, made his most lasting contributions to the defense and survival of Orthodoxy in Germany.

BUILDING A SYNAGOGUE

When Hirsch arrived in Frankfurt in August 1851 and moved into an apartment overlooking the Main River, he was more settled than the congregation, which still had no facilities. It was suggested to Hirsch that he temporarily attend services conducted under the auspices of the *Krankenkasse*. Even prior to Stein's appointment as community rabbi, many worshipers had attended smaller synagogues, both because of the poor physical appearance of the main synagogue and in order to support the societies to which they belonged. After Stein's arrival, there was little choice for the Orthodox but to attend one of the other synagogues.

For whatever reason the *Krankenkasse* synagogue was recommended to Hirsch, the society itself was not grateful for the honor bestowed upon them, as it failed to extend to Hirsch the respect due him as a rabbi. As a result, the IRG decided to rent an apartment in order to begin conducting its own services immediately. Hirsch's sermons highlighted the Sabbath services, and Schwarzschild attributed to the quality of the speeches both a growth in membership and consolidation of the diversified membership into a unified community.[1]

The location selected for the synagogue building was at the corner of Rechneigrabenstrasse and Schuetzenstrasse, well situated within the second area of settlement of Frankfurt Jewry. The site chosen was in the Fischerfeld area, bounded by the old ghetto on the north and the Main River on the south. The synagogue was located in the northern tip of the quarter, opposite the ghetto and less than four blocks from the community synagogue. It remained in that location for almost sixty years, when it moved to its final home in the Friedberger Anlage. Synagogue location was not a matter of dispute between the various parties in Frankfurt as it was in other communities. There was no movement by the Reform to choose a more central and integrated location. In fact, when the Reform party did finally succeed in constructing a new synagogue, it did so—as it had always planned to do—precisely where the community synagogue constructed in 1711 had stood, in the midst of the old Jewish ghetto.[2]

The Fischerfeld area, in which many of the IRG members resided, had special attractions for the Jews of Frankfurt. The Fischerfeld was a new settlement area, completed in 1811, on the outskirts of the city. In order to encourage settlement, businesses, churches, schools, and public gathering places were prohibited. The endeavor succeeded in enticing a prosperous population, including tradesmen, bankers, brokers, and diplomats. The Jewish population, just recently liberated from the narrow confines of the ghetto, took advantage of the opportunity "to exchange their small, dark homes for better accommodations—to be able to live as the other citizens of the city, and at the same time, in the most modern . . . of houses." Traditional Jews especially could benefit from the area's proximity to the ghetto, which housed the existing Jewish communal institutions, as well as the remaining Jewish population.[3]

Soon after construction of the synagogue commenced, a ceremony for laying the cornerstone marked the first public festivity under the IRG's auspices. Local notables were present, including both the mayor and deputy mayor of Frankfurt. A parchment document commemorating the occasion was placed in the cornerstone. When expansion of the building was begun twenty-two years later, a second document was added to the cornerstone.

The newer student of German Jewish history frequently bemoans the wealth of historical documents destroyed during the Second World War. But after one has become accustomed to the loss, there emerges an appreciation of the even greater value of those documents that have survived those turbulent years. Sometime after the conclusion of the war, Max Kreutzberger, formerly executive director of the Leo Baeck Institute, New York, procured two parchment documents of the IRG, one dated 1852, the second 1874.

The 1852 document placed the role of the IRG in the perspective of Frankfurt's historical traditions.[4] The text indicated how Frankfurt had been a well-established seat of Jewish religious life, a model and light for other Jewish communities in Germany. The legacy of centuries legitimated a traditional Jewish community in Frankfurt, and in the future, the IRG polemics would continue to argue that they, and not the legally recognized Jewish community, were the worthy continuation of the Frankfurt tradition. The new spirit of reform that had entered Frankfurt in the last thirty to forty years was intruding upon the centuries of traditionalism that had flourished in the city. Nevertheless, the founding of the IRG foretold a reversal of fortune that echoed the changes of fate depicted in the Psalms: Those that were once weak would now be strengthened. It is in that imagery that the humble society, with a mere eleven founders, was emphasized in the document and in IRG polemics from then on.

After the historical narrative, the document paid homage to Hirsch and to Baron Rothschild for his donation of 70 percent of the building costs. It also emphasized the importance for the future of the opening of a school to instruct the children in traditional Jewish life.

The synagogue building was dedicated on September 29, 1853. Designed to seat 250 men and 200 women, its interior followed the dimensions of a square with a three-sided ladies' gallery above the traditional platform in the center of the synagogue.[5] Schwarzschild described the dedication festivities in his memoir:

The Rabbi and members of the Board removed the Torah scrolls from the temporary location, in which the afternoon service had earlier been conducted, and they were carried in a festive procession into the synagogue. The synagogue committee welcomed them at the doors and joined the procession. The cantor chanted "Blessed is he who enters." After circling the platform seven times, the Torah scrolls were placed in the ark, and the Rabbi ascended to the pulpit and delivered the dedication address. Hymns and the evening service concluded the festivities.[6]

The Frankfurter Journal reported: "In addition to both mayors, the vast majority of Senate members participated in the celebration, as well as representatives of both Christian confessions, and very many from all stations who had been especially invited."[7] A small, but prestigious, congregation was demonstrating in 1853 to Christian observers from civil and religious circles that Orthodox Jews could construct an architecturally pleasing edifice and conduct a service as dignified and moving as that of the Reformers.

THE RELIGIOUS SERVICE

As the Reform movement gained control of one German community after another in the first half of the nineteenth century, policy guidelines were often laid down by a synagogue ordinance imposing a set of behavioral norms upon the constituent members. Often these ordinances stipulated liturgical reforms as well. Despite the integral connection between synagogue ordinances and Reformist tendencies, the IRG issued precisely such a code upon the dedication of its own synagogue building in 1853, and a revised edition was occasioned by the physical expansion of the synagogue in 1874.[8]

A number of the rules in the IRG ordinance were similar to those contained in the prototypes issued by Reform communities. Entry into the synagogue and departure from it were to be done without noise. No conversation was to be conducted during the services and no gathering together before or after the service. Children under the age of five were not to be admitted, while older children had to be accompanied by a parent. The strict procedures enforced in these external matters governed the actual conducting of worship as well. The principle was stated explicitly: "Prayers, as well as all aspects of the service must be recited with dignity and propriety." Practical aspects were elaborated on in great detail, leaving the clear impression of an emotionally placid service more typical of a Reform synagogue than an Orthodox one. Chanting or reading along with the cantor or Torah reader was forbidden, and only the rabbi could correct errors committed by either of them.

The removal of shoes in the synagogue at certain times was a sore point for the Reformers, and many forbade that practice on the fast day of the Ninth of Av and even on Yom Kippur. In this and other points there was great similarity between the ordinances of the IRG and the code issued in 1843 under Samuel Holdheim, then rabbi of Mecklenburg-Schwerin and later of the radical Reform community of Berlin. Holdheim stipulated that those wishing to abstain from leather shoes in the synagogue on fast days were required to wear felt shoes even prior to entering. *Kohanim*, who had to remove their shoes for the priestly blessing, were to do so in the vestibule and not in the synagogue proper. Likewise, the IRG stipulated that all changing of clothes was to be done in a specified room.[9]

Similar to the Reform codes in many respects, the IRG version, nevertheless, differed from its predecessors by using this medium to affirm traditional practices. While Reform ordinances included dress requirements, the IRG stipulated head covering and prayer shawls. On fast days, felt or cloth shoes were to replace leather ones.

Torah honors at the IRG were distributed in three stages,

reflecting both the influence of traditional commitments and the demand for decorum. Highest priority was given to those who, because of an event in their personal lives, traditionally received an honor to mark the occasion. These, as specified in the 1874 code, included bridegrooms, new fathers, those observing the anniversary of a parent's death, and those who had survived a dangerous experience. Remaining honors were then auctioned to the community. The sale of these honors to the highest bidder is an old custom, conducted during the service itself, just prior to the time of the honor. Because they saw this practice as an impediment to the religious atmosphere, the IRG conducted the auction following the Friday morning weekday service. Unsold honors were then distributed to those who had not received an honor in the previous four weeks. The methods employed enabled the IRG to fulfill traditional obligations, receive voluntary donations, and honor its members without marring the effect of the service itself.[10]

In practice, there apparently was much discontent concerning the distribution of Torah honors. The financing of the IRG was dependent upon voluntary contributions, and the sale of Torah honors was a leading source of income. Herman Schwab interpreted the regular purchase of these honors by certain wealthy families as a reflection of their commitment to the IRG, but he noted the jealousy and discontent of the less affluent, who received far fewer honors.[11]

Using a diversified selection of historical materials, it is possible to reconstruct the atmosphere inside the synagogue in Hirsch's time although no explicit, detailed description has actually come down to us. The synagogue ordinance has transmitted a strong emphasis on decorum, as we have seen in the examples above. Two innovative additions to the traditional service, Hirsch's preaching and the participation of a choir, added to the sense that this was a traditional service in a reform framework. The reports we have agree that Hirsch was an outstanding orator, though there was some complaint that he did not fully prepare his sermons in advance.[12]

Throughout the period of our study, the choir was under the direction of I. M. Japhet, who himself composed and arranged many of the melodies used in the IRG service. Japhet was born in Kassel in 1818 and educated at a teachers' seminary. In 1852 he came to Frankfurt to help Hirsch plan for the new school and to direct the choir. The strength of Japhet's music lay in the expression he gave to Jewish motifs, or as one music critic put it, "the Jewish soul," but the introduction of a choir could quite easily have destroyed the Jewish character of the service. In arranging his music, Japhet had to take heed of the strict rules prohibiting worshipers from chanting along.[13] The Jewish texture of Japhet's music may well have contrasted sharply with the Germanic tones of the melodies adopted in more liberal congregations; yet this custom of silent accompaniment led to numerous criticisms of sterility within the IRG services. Although substitution of a choir for congregational singing had become quite common in Reform circles, the silencing of the congregation was still an alien element in a traditional service.[14]

Japhet was not among the most important of the nineteenth-century synagogue composers, but his music was available and adopted by other communities. He published his music in a series known as *Schire Jeschurun*; a first edition was issued in 1856, a second in 1864, and an enlarged edition of both works was published in 1881. In the second series, Japhet reported on the success of the earlier volume, which had been used in nearly 180 larger and smaller communities. In the 1881 edition, Japhet indicated which melodies had been used by the IRG itself. From this unlikely source it is possible to deduce a great deal of information concerning the structure of the IRG service.[15]

On Friday evenings, the choir was active during *Kabbalas Shabbos*, a service which welcomes the Sabbath, was quiet during the *Maariv* evening service, and participated once again at the conclusion of the service. Japhet published ten versions of *Lechoh Dodi*, the central hymn of *Kabbalas Shabbos*, as well as versions of three other prayers from that part of the service. All sixteen compositions had been sung in the IRG synagogue. But, although Japhet had also composed eight melodies for parts of *Maariv*, none were used by the IRG; that part of the service presumably being conducted by the cantor alone. Several hymns were sung by the choir in the latter part of the service for which

Japhet published nine selections. They included two versions of *Shalom Rav*, which may have followed the silent devotion, and four versions of *Yigdal*, which concluded the service.

The choir played a considerably smaller role in the Sabbath morning service. Although Japhet published thirty-seven pieces for morning worship, sixteen of the twenty-six sung in the IRG were designated for festival services. Of the ten remaining pieces used on regular Sabbath mornings, five were for the Torah-reading service, two for one hymn near the end of the service, and three compositions for the priestly benediction. In total, the choir sang no more than four prayers during the morning service (*Hotzzaah, Hachnasah, Ein Keloheinu, Birkat Kohanim*). The morning service with the weekly Torah reading and Hirsch's sermon must have been considered too long to allow for any greater involvement by the choir. As it was, the early edition of the synagogue's ordinance had called for a break in the service in order to maintain decorum.

The choir did play a significant role in the evening service marking the conclusion of the Sabbath. Japhet indicated two versions of Psalm 128 and one other hymn that were part of the IRG liturgy. Herman Schwab recalled the Saturday evening service in his memoirs:

The same festive tranquility which was spread over the arrival of the Sabbath returned at the hour of its departure with the singing of Shir Hamaalot [Psalm 128] composed by I. M. Japhet. . . . Friedlaender [the cantor] stood in his Sabbath robes on the platform just as on Friday evening, his singing accompanied by the synagogue choir, conducted by Japhet himself.[16]

Schwab's memoirs, which began with the last years of Hirsch's life, also provide information on the weekday services:

There were few empty seats when the service started. There was no difference between Monday [when the Torah is read] or Tuesday morning and none between Sunday afternoon or any other. On *Rosh Chodesh, Chanukah, Purim* or *Chol-ha-Moed* only back seats were available. That there was no vacant seat on the festivals was accepted as a matter of course.[17]

Laymen did not participate in conducting even the weekday service, as was common practice. Rather, the weekday services were conducted by the assistant cantors, and in the event they were unavailable, the cantor himself, Julius Friedlaender, took over. The fact that Friedlaender substituted for his own assistants implies that the noninvolvement of laymen was virtually a principle. The synagogue ordinances support this interpretation. While mourners (*Avelim*) were not allowed to conduct services, although this was their traditional role, those observing the anniversary of the death of a parent (*Yahrzeit*) could be granted this privilege on most weekdays, provided they were qualified and the appropriate committee raised no objections. The ruling underscores the fact that laymen had only a minimal number of opportunities to conduct services, a task which primarily remained in the hands of the professional clergy. This policy ensured the dignity and regulated the format of the services. Reform ordinances had insisted upon services being conducted by cantors only—even at the exclusion of itinerant cantors—since the Westphalia code of 1810. This was one case where the borrowing of Reform policy in order to enhance worship at the IRG resulted in a tension between tradition and dignity, and victory went to the latter.[18]

The service designed by Hirsch did not strictly follow the local customs of the Frankfurt community, and Saemy Japhet recorded in his memoirs that there was some discontent within the IRG over this slight of local pride. Local traditions, known as *Minhag Frankfurt*, affected the form and content of the services with occasional deviations from the more widely accepted *German Ritus*. Hirsch included the Frankfurt traditions, but added to and modified them. In so doing, he offered his opponents a political opportunity that was not lost. When, in the aftermath of the separatist controversy, an Orthodox service was established within the community structure, the local customs were followed more strictly. Marcus Horovitz, rabbi of the community Orthodox synagogue, may have felt compelled to justify the establishment of a second Orthodox congregation in Frankfurt by legitimating himself and his congregation as successors of the historical legacy; but the contrast underscores the fact that despite Hirsch's insistence that the IRG reincarnated the Frankfurt past, his vision was not limited to restoring the community to its position as a citadel of Jewish tradition. Rather, while harnessing the strengths offered to him by his notable membership, he set forth to build a model for all of German Orthodoxy, a model untainted and unrestricted by local nuances.[19]

Hirsch adopted from the Reformers at least the form of their service, if not the substance of their liturgical changes. He had actually dabbled with extensive reforms himself in his first two communities, eliminating certain prayers and ceremonies from which he felt estranged. Most notorious of these acts was the striking of the *Kol Nidre* prayer from the Yom Kippur service.[20] However, by the time Hirsch came to Frankfurt, he had adopted a more moderate stance.

The conservative constituency that awaited Hirsch in Frankfurt, of course, proved conducive for a more moderate path than Hirsch's early communities, but it would be more than reductionist to suggest that Hirsch merely towed the congregation's line—it would, in fact, be a misconception of the dynamics of his leadership. Hirsch's reign in Frankfurt marked a period of creative and productive communal leadership which reached a level of accomplishment that implies not an opportunist turnabout but a mutual sharing of outlook between rabbi and congregation.

Even prior to Hirsch's appointment, the congregation had concluded that Orthodoxy must come to grips with the forces of modernity. When, in the 1840s, the Orthodox party still had hopes of finding a *modus vivendi* within the organized community, they petitioned the board for the appointment of a traditional rabbi endowed with a secular education. Furthermore, the full program published by the founders in 1850 clearly indicated that they were determined to construct a positive symbiosis between Orthodoxy and contemporary culture.

On the other hand, if the congregation had vague notions of a future direction, a coherently defined and integrated conception was the product of Hirsch's endeavors. For example, Schwab recalled the origins of the participation of the choir in the service concluding the Sabbath. In the early years of the congregation the worshipers had often pushed out toward the door—before the conclusion of the service. Hirsch was displeased and sought a solution that would encourage the people to remain until the end. Schwab informs us that it was for this reason that Hirsch asked Japhet to arrange the choral version of Psalm 128, *Shir Hamalaus*. In Schwab's brief report, the choir was not introduced into the Saturday evening service as a concession to communal pressures, but as an act of strength resulting from a clear vision of the course that the Orthodox service should take. That clear vision was Hirsch's contribution.

The individual elements of the new Orthodox service originated before Hirsch. Bernays had introduced sermons into the Orthodox service in Hamburg three decades prior to Hirsch's arrival in Frankfurt, and Michael Sachs conducted a service in Berlin with both preaching and a choir. And yet, these men had failed to cast a new image for Orthodoxy. They were the rabbis of communities divided by the conflicts between Reform and Orthodox. Hence their actions communicated nothing more than concessions introduced in order to maintain peace and a fragile unity. Most revealing is the fact that when the Orthodox party in Berlin later formed a separate congregation under Ezriel Hildesheimer, it discarded Sachs's innovations, which apparently were seen as resulting from communal politics and not as a positive program for Orthodoxy.[21] It was precisely in this area that the IRG under Hirsch's leadership had succeeded.

Isaac Heinemann described the attitude in Frankfurt in such a way that the contrast with the other communities is clear.

The new was not tolerated in a spirit of weak compromise, nor was it indiscriminately placed next to the old. Modern pedagogy, oratory, and aesthetics were to be harnessed in the service of tradition. The weapons forged by the Reform Movement were to be instrumental in its defeat.[22]

Samson Raphael Hirsch's aristocratic mannerisms had been out of place in Nikolsburg, but he held to them for they were an integral part of his personality.

It seemed quite incomprehensible that a *Landrabbiner* should trouble himself about the rabbi's attire. And when he himself arrived on the Sabbath in a frock coat and white tie, some of the gentlemen present simply could not understand it.[23]

In Frankfurt, Hirsch found his natural constituency, but they required a mentor to translate their social status into stature. The rabbi who taught them not to bolt for the door before worship was completed became that mentor.

THE COMMUNITY MEMBERSHIP

By the time Hirsch arrived in Frankfurt, one hundred families had affiliated with the IRG. In 1853 it reported a membership of 180 families, and by 1860 it had reached 250. Sources indicate that at the time of the separatist controversy in 1877, membership was between 300 and 355 families. Jacob Rosenheim estimated in his memoirs, written years later, that around 1885, the membership had stood about 400 families. The period of most rapid growth, however, followed Hirsch's death in 1888, since the same source estimates the 1899 membership at greater than 1,000 families.[24]

Emanuel Schwarzschild, whose memoirs have been referred to previously, was the long-standing president of the congregation, and he executed this position with a strong hand. The financial aristocracy, who had come to the IRG's support soon after its founding, fully dominated the lay control of the community. Rosenheim, long-time leader of the Orthodox *Agudas Jisroel* movement, reported in his memoirs, "The management was concentrated in his [Schwarzschild's] hands. Like him, all the members of the Board were members of the Exchange, and therefore community matters could be handled daily during trading hours."[25] The memoirs of both Rosenheim and Herman Schwab, based on Hirsch's last years and the period following, describe the board and council of the IRG as aloof and independent of the membership as a whole. Except for the controversy over secession, there were only rare attempts to dispute the board's power. Discontent surfaced only over the distribution of Torah honors, which were often purchased and monopolized by the richest of the members.[26] The implication of these sources is not that the IRG was a congregation of the wealthy alone, but that the wealthy dominated its internal politics.

One may suspect that Rosenheim's recollections could easily have been slanted in favor of recalling only the most influential personalities who served as members of the board, but a check of the board's membership based on an annual city handbook between 1855 and 1866 confirms once again the dominance of the financial circle. Of the thirteen persons who were on the board during this period, eight can be identified with banking, investments, and currency trading; two were prominent jewelers; and three cannot be located in Dietz's *Stammbuch*. The bankers listed include Philipp Abraham Cohen, Wolf Jacob Bass, Heinz Jacob Weiller, and Emanuel Schwarzschild. Several other bankers served on the school and financial committees. These included Wilhelm Carl Frhr v. Rothschild (on the school committee!), Juda Michael Kulp, and Philipp Ellinger. Old, prominent, and successful Frankfurt families, although not directly or totally involved in the banking circle, were also board members. These included the jewelers, Moses Michael Herz Oppenheimer and Nathan Marcus Oppenheim, as well as Meyer Benedict Goldschmidt.[27]

The information we have gathered here concerning the board corresponds to a description of the membership as a whole during our period, by Meier Schueler, long-time teacher at the IRG school and its last principal:

Almost all of the members were businessmen. Many were involved in banking and in the bourse. Only a few members were craftsmen, and . . . none were academically oriented other than Hirsch's own sons and a few teachers who had migrated from outside Frankfurt.[28]

To emphasize the low academic profile of the membership, Schueler added that only in the 1870s did a second doctor affiliate with the IRG. The first was one of Hirsch's sons.

There are no published lists of the IRG's leadership during the first years of the Prussian annexation. When the lists reappear in 1871, the social cohesiveness of the IRG board had begun to break down. An increasing number of names are unidentifiable in Dietz's *Stammbuch*, implying in most cases that they were newcomers to Frankfurt. A separate document furthermore confirms the origins of a number of these men from outside Frankfurt.[29] In 1871 one of the board's five members had moved to Frankfurt from Karlsruhe and by 1874 the Board included three non-Frankfurters. The constituency of the IRG's leadership was changing.

How religiously committed were the members and lay leadership of the IRG? Obviously, the level of observance is difficult to determine with precision; yet, the myths that have emerged implying that the members of the citadel of German Orthodoxy were themselves far removed from traditional practice can be dismissed. Strikingly, a primary source for these assumptions was Emanuel Schwarzschild's comment in his memoirs that by the late 1840s there were no native Frankfurt contemporaries of his age who continued to perform the commandment of *Tephilin*. Schwarzschild himself immediately qualified this statement by adding that there were a few observant lads, but these were either a few years younger or older than he.[30] Other sources indicate, however, that religious observance had not deteriorated so completely. We know that a group of adults, albeit a limited one, formed a Talmud study circle in the 1840s. Another source indicates that when Hirsch first began to recruit pupils for the new school of the IRG in the early 1850s, some parents resisted because secular studies were to be included. Had these same parents not encouraged the older siblings of the new pupils to put on *Tephilin*? When Gerson Josphat wrote Hirsch in 1851 to inform him of the position with the IRG, he commented that he himself was instructing a number of young people in Frankfurt in the holy Torah and that he had the hope of increasing the number. He went on to express his desire to open a yeshivah in Frankfurt. Had Josphat no realistic basis for thinking that there were families who would send their own children or support visiting students? Were none of his students fulfilling the commandment of *Tephilin*?[31] Whatever the validity of Schwarzchild's particular claim, it should not be concluded that traditional life had come to a complete standstill. But why should an Orthodox source have been so misleading? By so doing, Schwarzschild effectively increased the dimension of Hirsch's and of the IRG's accomplishments in their building of an Orthodox community. Schwarzschild's comment is similar, then, to the mythology that evolved of the eleven founders of the IRG: The level of success attained by the community was enhanced by drawing an even more negative picture of the initial conditions.

When we proceed to the later period and discuss the decades following Hirsch's arrival in Frankfurt, a much clearer picture exists of the serious religious commitment of the members of the IRG. The essential clue is found in the community's by-laws, approved and published in 1875, which stipulated explicit requirements for membership in the IRG and for serving on the board.[32] Membership was closed to Jews who had not been circumcised, who had refused to have circumcision performed on their sons, or who had not been married in accordance with Jewish religious law and with a religious ceremony. Stricter requirements were placed on officers and employees, who were expected to observe the Sabbath and festivals, as well as the laws of Kashruth.[33] Although the by-laws specifically forbade public violations of these laws, there should be no question that the officers of the community were expected to be observant Jews in private as well. An individual who had been disqualified from office would be eligible once again "only after living a number of years as a traditionally observant Jew," implying that his observance was not to be limited to the public spotlight alone.

In fact, the IRG actively sought to discourage discrepancies between the public and private attitudes of those involved in communal life. Bakers seeking IRG approval were instructed that "a Jewish baker requires the same trust as a kosher meat slaughterer or butcher," while restauranteurs were informed that they were to show themselves to be trustworthy in religious laws as much in their private lives as in the conducting of their business.[34]

The IRG at least attempted to affect the private lives of those connected with it, and there is some indirect evidence that it succeeded. A number of firms were prepared to fulfill the strict requirements imposed on food enterprises in order to obtain certification of Kashruth, implying that a sufficient number of community members actually dealt with these kosher firms. In 1877 we know that there were three meat slaughterers, three kosher butchers, two bakeries, and two food stores affiliated with the IRG.[35] Since the community was then between 300 and 350 families, we may conclude that Kashruth observance must have been the norm. In 1876 in response to a critique of the newly established requirements for officers, Emanuel Schwarzschild commented that he knew of no member who openly violated the Sabbath day by opening his business or by smoking publicly and that a large number, if not the majority of members, did not carry on the Sabbath.[36] A suggestive comment comes from a memoir dealing with a period several decades later. Around 1900, a boy from a nonreligious family who was sent to study in the IRG school found himself quite out of place, for while other children came from families that were not affiliated with the IRG, he alone came from a nonreligious family.[37] Undoubtedly, the IRG had nonobservant members, but they were certainly not officers of the community and perhaps, in general, not deeply involved in communal life. By 1876 they apparently were a limited percentage of the total membership.

Conversely, not all Orthodox Jews of Frankfurt were members of the IRG. A number of small, neighborhood synagogues had been active in the 1840s prior to the founding of the IRG and they continued to function afterwards. In 1858 the community board, in opposing the IRG's efforts to win legal separation from the community, referred to a number of these synagogues still conducting Orthodox services and being supported primarily by endowments and private donations.[38] Solomon Geiger, for one, the Orthodox brother of Abraham Geiger, who rebuked Hirsch for his disregard of local customs, is never mentioned in connection with the IRG.[39]

THE SCHOOL

Both Hirsch and the founders of the IRG placed high priority on the establishment of a school that would provide instruction in both religious and secular subjects. All writers depicting the early history of the IRG school trace its development to Hirsch's letter to the IRG board in August 1851 in which he proposed that instruction be provided a few hours weekly for advanced students in Jewish teachings and commandments. Hirsch also suggested lessons in Bible for the older youth. A year later, Hirsch urged the founding of a school that would combine "the basics of religious life with general social education."[40] Of course, the board needed little convincing to adopt Hirsch's proposal, since the lay leadership had already called for the establishment of precisely such a school a year before Hirsch's first memorandum.[41]

In 1852 the IRG board petitioned the Frankfurt Senate for the right to establish a school. The board expressed its conviction that their endeavors to establish a solid basis for Orthodox life would be successful only if their youth were instructed in accordance with the religious principles by which the IRG was governed. The objective of the school would be to train its pupils as "human beings, Jews, and citizens." To accomplish this goal, the school would provide instruction in both social and religious "knowledge and experience." Superior students would be directed to advanced work, presumably in Talmudic studies, but the plan stipulated explicitly: "We need not teach all our children to become theologians, yet none may remain ignorant of religious subjects."[42] The curriculum proposed in the petition to the Senate called for instruction in German language, natural history, geography, world history, mathematics, writing, French, English, music, and art. Religious subjects included Hebrew language and literature, religious faith and commandments, and biblical history.[43]

The school's orientation was toward preparation for a career in business; it was not an academic *gymnasium*. There was no instruction in Latin or Greek, and the curriculum was not designed as preparation for the highest school examinations. Jacob Rosenheim observed in his memoirs that the commercial emphasis was neither an accident nor a compromise. The school program reflected the objective of establishing a class of educated and committed Orthodox laymen, and it set out to do so in a city highly oriented toward finance and commerce.[44]

The school was opened in 1853 with eighty-four pupils, fifty-five boys and twenty-nine girls. Enrollment grew steadily:[45]

1853	84
1857	193
1862	259
1885	ca. 500

The curriculum fulfilled the objective of combining religious and secular instruction, but the educational impact of the IRG school did not derive from its course of studies. In fact, the historical significance often attributed to the school's program of study has been exaggerated. The IRG school had initiated neither the combined study of religious and secular subjects, nor even the contemporary adaptation of the ancient rabbinic saying *Torah im derech Erez*, which served as the school's motto and became strongly identified as the hallmark of Hirsch's thinking. The Talmud Torah school in Altona, opened by Hirsch's grandfather a half-century before, provided precisely the same educational orientation as the school of the IRG, as did the school in Halberstadt.[46]

The educational strength of the IRG school lay in the community framework that provided the structural basis on which the school program was built. Although the objective of the school was envisioned as educating future generations in the ways of Orthodox Judaism, and although both Hirsch and the founding leadership of the IRG were convinced that the community could not flourish without such a school, the evidence indicates that the long-term effectiveness of the school in educating its pupils depended on the success and strength of the community itself.

Former students in the school differed widely in their evaluations. Herman Schwab, whose family was actively involved in the IRG, testified in his memoir to the thorough preparation received in the school for later becoming a worthy layman in an Orthodox synagogue. Yet Selmar Spier put forth a totally negative evaluation of the school: its buildings, its program, and its teachers. Significantly, Spier disclosed that he was the only pupil he knew of in the school who did not come from a religious home. He demonstrated little attachment to the community itself and did not even mention the IRG synagogue in his memoir.

A far more sober evaluation of the school's achievements than either of these examples comes from Jacob Rosenheim in a lengthy discussion in his memoir. Rosenheim, who entered the school in 1878, observed that during Hirsch's period, on the whole, only those graduates of the school who remained "within the milieu of the Frankfurt community" continued to practice as Orthodox Jews. However, those who left Frankfurt soon after completing their studies tended to stray from the traditional path.

Despite the differences in their judgments of the school, the three accounts all support the conclusion that the positive influence of the school program depended upon the broader foundation and continued support of the community framework. Without that support the school's effectiveness proved temporary at best, but with those pupils whose school experience was combined with an active communal role in their family life, the school succeeded in its objective of training an Orthodox lay leadership for the next generation.[47]

EXPANSION AND SELF-DEFINITION

The growth of the IRG's membership necessitated an enlargement of its physical facilities, which was begun in the summer of 1874 and completed but three days prior to Rosh Hashanah, one year later. The occasion was marked with two celebrations quite similar to the cornerstone laying and dedication of the original building. Yet, while the earlier festivities had been attended by officials and prominent personalities of Frankfurt, both the cornerstone laying in 1874 and the dedication of the enlarged facilities in 1875 were limited to members of the community only, with local officials not invited.[48] Much had happened in the two decades between 1852 and 1874. Bismarck had succeeded in unifying Germany under Prussian hegemony, but not with the voluntary approval of all Germans. Frankfurt, one of the independent free states of the old empire, had lost its autonomy, to the dismay of many of its citizens.[49] The absence of public officials, who would now represent the new order, may have resulted from a desire to avoid an affront to still strong sensibilities, loyal to the autonomy of the past. It certainly reflected, however, the new priorities in Hirsch's objectives.

The presence of public notables at the earlier founding ceremonies had seemed to announce that the IRG enjoyed an official relationship with the authorities, as well as their protection. But by the mid-1870s, Hirsch was prepared to act in accordance with his political philosophy, in which he conceived of autonomous religious communities that were no longer extensions of the civil political structure. Full political emancipation of German Jews ended any need for a political intermediary between Jew and nation. Consequently, a political presence at the ceremonies in the 1870s was no longer required; nor was it relevant. In fact, the opening paragraphs of the by-laws, adopted during this very same period, refer to a Judaism strong enough to support itself "without state coercion."[50]

As at the earlier celebration, a document was placed in the cornerstone, and this document, as well, is now in the possession of the Leo Baeck Institute, New York. In contrast to the first document, the second makes no reference to the IRG's position in the sequence of Frankfurt Jewish history and virtually no reference to its Reform opponents. Rather, it recounts the growth of the IRG and its adjunct facilities, describing the congregation as a model community for Orthodox Jews elsewhere. The intervening years had not been quiet years but "years of war and world shattering events; kingdoms were overthrown and elevated, and the political and social conditions of the world were in flux." Indeed, as we have noted, Frankfurt itself had, during this period, ceased to be a free city. In the midst of this turmoil, the IRG had remained unaffected by the flow of events, and the progress in the development of its institutions was continuing. Theologically, Hirsch often spoke of the constancy of Jewish law in contrast to the upheaval of the outside world. In this document the IRG was depicted with that same sense of continuity within, while the world outside was struck by confusion.

At the first cornerstone ceremony, Hirsch had called attention to the need for a school to provide the proper religious education for the children of the community. At the 1874 ceremony, Hirsch applauded the accomplishments of the school that had long since been established and then turned his attention to the one task that remained—separation from the Frankfurt Jewish community. He hoped that passage of legislation that would enable separation would come soon, and perhaps by the time of the dedication of the enlarged building the following year, the community could stand before God as a *"Fully free independent Jewish community"* (his emphasis).[51]

It was during this period of reconstruction that the IRG undertook to compose and ratify a set of by-laws to govern the congregation. In Schwarzschild's words, this had not been done earlier "in order to obtain more experience," but by 1874, he continued, the need could no longer be deferred.[52] The adoption of a constitution did not take place at an arbitrary moment in the community's development but, rather, indicates that the community was going through a period of self-definition. The most significant sections of the statutes reflect that broader process.

Membership in the IRG was limited to Jews who themselves and whose sons were properly circumcised and who had been married in accordance with Jewish law. In addition, officers of the IRG were restricted from publicly transgressing the laws of the Sabbath and Kashruth.[53]

The regulations affirmed that the community's life was based on traditional Judaism as expressed in the Torah, the Talmud, and the *Shulchan Aruch*. The society's objectives were to advance the three bases of Judaism: *Torah*, *Avodah*, and *Gemiluth Chassadim*: study, worship, and loving-kindness. All decisions made by the society must be in accordance with Jewish law, and it was the prerogative of the rabbi to determine the religious suitability of any decision.[54]

A proposed text for the statutes was issued on December 21, 1874. The extensive powers given to Hirsch in that version were criticized in the Jewish press, and the general membership meeting of February 21, 1875, revised several of the sections dealing with questions of rabbinical authority. The proposed version had declared that "the rabbi's word is the decisive authority for the community," and that "all decisions of the General Meeting, of the Board and Council, and of the various commissions are invalid and void, if the rabbi declares them to be in violation of religious law." However, the membership struck this entire clause from the statute and emphasized that "the authority of the rabbi is also limited by religious fundamentals." In a related matter, another revision restricted the rabbi's authority to specifically religious questions, excluding his legitimate leadership from nonreligious, that is, political, matters.[55]

The members also separated the two positions of rabbi and

school director. Their concern was apparently not so much with Hirsch, the father, but with Mendel Hirsch, the son and heir apparent. While Hirsch had served as director from the time the school was established in 1853, the members added clauses to the by-laws expressing the possibility that the positions of rabbi and school director would not always be united. Hirsch's grooming of his son as successor was already being criticized within the community, and it was feared that if Mendel Hirsch were to become school principal, the basis would be established for his eventual succession to the rabbinical post as well. In fact, the son became principal in 1877 but did not succeed his father as rabbi of the IRG after Hirsch's death in 1888.[56]

In 1876 S. Sueskind, Reform rabbi in Wiesbaden from 1844 to 1884, issued a sharp critique of the statutes in which he primarily charged that the IRG had trespassed the limits of a private society and had declared itself in these statutes to constitute a full-fledged Jewish community. Indeed, Sueskind's attack and the response it generated must be understood in the light of the controversy of that time over the proposed law of secession, which we shall discuss in subsequent chapters.[57]

Sueskind challenged the right of the IRG to single out the laws of circumcision and marriage as prerequisites for membership or those of the Sabbath and Kashruth for holding office, especially since the IRG had recognized the *Shulchan Aruch* as its ultimate authority and that code treated numerous other commandments with equal significance.[58] Sueskind admitted that a *chebra*, or private society, had the right to determine—even arbitrarily—its requirements for membership, but the IRG had declared itself in the by-laws to be "the old Frankfurt Jewish community, the embodiment of its objectives; the guardian of its principles and tasks; the heiress of its religious right." As such it no longer had the right to exclude Jews from membership. According to Sueskind, it was Hirsch himself who was responsible for this grandiose vision, the members of the IRG being totally satisfied with their present status as a society.[59]

Sueskind mocked the claim that the IRG constituted the legitimate successor to the old Frankfurt community. The growth in membership over the years had not derived from native Frankfurters but rather was due to the affiliation by the increasing number of rural Jews who were moving into the city. Sueskind referred to the newcomer from the hinterlands as an *Am Haarez*, thus playing on the Hebrew term which literally means "people of the land" and idiomatically refers to an ignoramus.[60] Isaac Hirsch responded to Sueskind's attack in lieu of his father, who was ill at the time. He opened by examining Sueskind's motives in becoming involved in an internal matter of the IRG and explained that in Wiesbaden, where Sueskind served, a group of Orthodox Jews was likewise petitioning for the right to separate from the Reform-dominated community. Hence, Sueskind's attack was against the separatist cause as a whole.[61]

Hirsch then turned immediately to the relationship between society and community. The IRG was certainly not a *chebra*, a society, "within the Jewish community" in the traditional sense. Rather, the IRG was a society diametrically opposed to the present Jewish community of Frankfurt. According to Hirsch, the disagreements between Sueskind and the IRG over the role of the rabbi reflected broader differences between Reform and Orthodox Judaism. While Orthodoxy emphasized ritual practice, Reform spoke in the abstract categories of "Religion," "Belief," and "Dogma." For the Orthodox, real authority lay not with the rabbi, but with religious law as presented in the codes. The rabbi's task was to spread knowledge of the law to all members of his community and, in turn, any member of the community could dispute a rabbi's decision, basing his argument on the rabbinical codes. Thus, argued Hirsch, the *Shulchan Aruch* hardly constituted a "paper pope" as it was referred to by Sueskind, but a medium toward independence and freedom within Jewish communal life. In the Orthodox realm, knowledge of the Torah is not limited to the professional "Jewish theologian," but is accessible to all men coming together voluntarily to study. Hirsch charged that it was the Reform rabbinate that discouraged the study of Jewish sources by "laymen," leaving the rabbi as the sole "theologian" qualified as an authority in Jewish matters. Which side, indeed, was responsible for creating a class of Jewish pagans, of "Am-Haarzthim"? retorted Hirsch—that term would best fit the laiety created in Reform circles.[62]

With regard to the prerequisites for membership in the IRG, Hirsch stated that these requirements had been adopted by the

IRG from the very outset. These matters were of urgency to the founders themselves, precisely at a time when Reform circles were agitating for laxity in their fulfillment. Emanuel Schwarzschild, writing his own response to the Sueskind attack, commented in a similar vein, "At the founding of the Religionsgesellschaft in 1850, before a rabbi had been chosen, before a service had been conducted, in order to ensure the religious position for all time and make it independent of a changing majority, four clauses were adopted as fundamentals."[63] Schwarzschild denied that the refusal of the IRG to accept as members those who failed to fulfill the minimal requirements could be termed an "excommunication." The difference in perspective reflected once again the changing status and structure of the Jewish community. Under existing German law, a Jew was still required either to hold membership in a Jewish community or to relinquish, at least civilly, his identification as a Jew. Sueskind had therefore remarked that while a society could well adopt prerequisites for membership, a corporation claiming to be a Jewish community could not, for if it rejected an applicant for membership, it ostensibly denied his very Jewishness. Schwarzschild, however, saw the matter from a perspective that reflected more closely the legal situation they envisioned for the future. Separate communities could bind the Orthodox together, while the Reformers would be free to maintain their own communities as well. The rejected applicant had recourse either to affiliate with the alternative body, or, for that matter, under the proposed separatist legislation to remain a Jew without *any* formal community identity.

There actually was no disagreement between the two sides that the adoption of the statutes was integrally related to the current campaign for separation rights. Sueskind's arguments were not chosen arbitrarily, but to reflect his opposition in the broader battle. The IRG could not be legally recognized as a Jewish community, traditionally all-encompassing, because it was, in fact, no more than a closed society. Its spirit violated the interests and attitudes of the modern state, especially because of the authoritative power given to the rabbi. Sueskind thus echoed one of the earliest concerns of the modern state in dealing with traditional Jewish communities—the power of the rabbis to influence Jewish behavior and attitudes.

However else the IRG leaders may have perceived its need for a full constitution at that time, it is apparent that Hirsch indeed did see it as a prerequisite for future separation. Already twenty years earlier, Hirsch had proposed a set of by-laws to the congregation, and he had stipulated explicitly that each member of *Kehillath Jeshurun* was to affiliate only with that community and provide material and spiritual assistance to it alone.[64] No positive action had been taken on the earlier proposal, and the later version made no such demands of the members. Yet we can still deduce from the first statutes that Hirsch understood the adoption of a set of governing laws as a necessary demonstration of the congregation's readiness to assume the total responsibility of a separate and independent Jewish community and that he thought it necessary for the IRG to declare openly how a community based on the ideals of the Torah would be governed.

The IRG had grown in size and stature. In two decades it had developed the complete facilities of a community dedicated to the fulfillment of traditional Jewish law. The early 1870s were years of renewed activity in the IRG. Physical expansion, a new synagogue ordinance, and adoption of a constitution are tangible signs of the energetic efforts being extended. But these are not simply signs of progress and growth. In fact, after the IRG's first decade, continued growth was slow. Membership had stood at 250 families in 1860 and 355 families in 1877. The fervent activity of the 1870s did not indicate that the IRG was further establishing its position. Actually it was risking that position as it cast aside self-complacency and prepared for a new battle on the road toward Orthodox revival. A changing constituency from within and a new political atmosphere outside had brought the IRG to the crossroads. At the outset, the IRG did not stand unified behind the change. In fact, the sharpening of tactics, especially the fight over withdrawing from the Jewish community, alienated a large proportion of the membership. But we might be more precise in suggesting that disunity had already appeared within the IRG with the influx of new arrivals to Frankfurt. Sueskind asserted that it was these newcomers who had swelled the ranks, a contention not denied by Schwarzschild, and our own examination indicated that these men were, by the early 1870s, appearing regularly on the board in combination with natives of Frankfurt. Meier Schueler commented on the growth in his survey of the IRG's early history:

Until 1866 immigration to Frankfurt was difficult, but still a number of Jews, especially from Kurhessen, Hessen, Darmstadt, and Bavaria, were permitted entry into the free city. A high proportion of these migrants placed great value on religious institutions and affiliated with Hirsch's congregation.[65]

The statistics show that the Jewish population increased during the first half of the century, but only at a slow rate. Between 1823 and 1847, the number of Jews grew from 4,530 to approximately 5,000; by 1871, the figure stood at 10,009. The sharpest increases occurred in 1858 to 1864 and 1867 to 1871 (see Table 5.1).[66] On the whole, the Jewish population increased at the same pace as the general population and remained between 9 and 11 percent of the general population throughout our period (see Table 5.2).[67] What did change during this period was the percentage of non-Frankfurters in Frankfurt within the Jewish community (see Table 5.3).[68] With the Prussian annexation of Frankfurt, this distinction was no longer considered in the statistics, but, of course, the continued growth of the total number of Jews due to free migration after 1866 indicates the continued decrease of the percentage of old Frankfurt families.

Table 5.1. Jewish Population in Frankfurt am Main, 1823–1875

Year	Total Jewish Population
1823	4,530
1847	ca. 5,000
1858	5,730
1864	7,620
1867	8,238
1871	10,009
1875	11,887

Table 5.2. Jews as a Percentage of General Population, 1823–1880

Year	Percentage of General Population
1823	10
1858	9
1864	10
1867	10
1871	11
1875	11.5
1880	10.1

Table 5.3. Percentage of Adult Natives (N) and Outsiders (O), 1823–1864

Year	N	O
1823	71.65	28.44
1858	56.35	43.65
1864	54.59	45.41

The IRG had served for two decades as a last point of contact with traditional society for a number of interrelated families with common objectives and interests. But continued industrialization, the unification of Germany, and urbanization had quickly reduced the existence of a kin society to an anachronism. The characteristics of the community had not yet, however, outlived their usefulness. Migrants had good motivations for affiliating with the IRG, being attracted both because it, and it alone at that time, could fill their still strong religious needs, while simultaneously bringing them in contact and organizational affiliation with the oldest and wealthiest families of Frankfurt Jewry.

The new members did not overrun the older element, but they did strain the nature of the IRG, forcing it to reexamine its position within the community. The IRG made room for its new arrivals by expanding its facilities. The social ties that had served as cohesive bonds gave way, and in their place the Orthodox principles that had governed the congregation from its outset were now concretized and adopted as the connecting tie.

By the time these transformations occurred, the IRG had gained a position of commanding influence within German Orthodoxy, which, as a whole, had benefited from many of the same factors that had supported the IRG in its growth. The movement that stemmed from Frankfurt did not cause this stabilization, but it did contribute to the morale of traditionalists elsewhere, as poorer communities could draw strength from the Frankfurt phenomenon that combined Orthodox practice with worldly success.

The Politics of Separatism

Even in earlier centuries, religious controversy posed a difficult challenge to the unified Jewish community, which was, at the most, capable of absorbing into its midst legitimate and established alternative rituals such as that of Sephardim and Ashkenazim. But the nineteenth century challenged the very core of Jewish communal existence, as the religious strife between Reform and Orthodox arose within a political context which itself questioned the continued organization of Jewry into a separate corporative entity. The concept of community survived in the nineteenth century in Europe because virtually all of the parties involved, including the civil authorities, sought its continuation. The exception, almost the sole party that sought an end to the compulsory community, was the group of Orthodox separatists in Germany led by Samson Raphael Hirsch. While separatism in its elementary form comprised little more than the response of a minority actively searching for a legal medium which guaranteed its right to practice religion in accordance with its own dictates, Hirsch's sophisticated formulation of the separatist ideology was derived from the various forces acting against the community concept. Yet, separatism did not begin in the 1870s, nor did it begin with Hirsch—nor with Orthodoxy.

REFORM ATTITUDES TOWARD SCHISM AND COMMUNITY

In 1831 when Reformers were just beginning to emerge after a decade of inactivity, Abraham Geiger, still a student at Bonn, in a letter to his friend L. Ullmann, examined two possible strategies for the Reform party to follow. The first path called for working within the framework of the entire Jewish community, which would allow, however, only moderate changes, and even these at only a gradual pace. Under such circumstances, the Reform rabbi could only present a platform somewhat inconsistent with his own true position. He would be allowed to introduce positive reforms, but he would be denied the right to attack and destroy that which must be removed. This inconsistency endangered both his own position and the cause of Reform as well. Geiger, therefore, preferred the second path, which endowed the Reformer with total freedom:

I believe, however, that there is an alternative, and if my convictions remain unchanged, it will be my life's task to pursue it. This alternative is that of separation. Simply stated, the issue is as follows: All the Jews in any one country, who have rejected the Talmud in their hearts, should proclaim this fact openly and obtain permission from the State in which they reside to form a religious community of their own.[1]

For the next decade, Geiger wavered in his commitment to separatism. In 1839 he wrote to M. A. Stern: "Schism is out of the question, for there would not be the slightest historical support for the seceders. Since every development is possible only within the framework of history, he who wishes to exert influence on such development within Judaism must cleave to that history even if it is against his will."[2] The following year, he abandoned his esteem for the historical process:

Of what avail, then, are all our petty reforms? . . . What good is a program which only passes in silence over that which should be fought articulately? . . . I therefore feel that even schism, the whole means of salvation, recedes from possibility, and hence all I can see is a slow languishing that spreads from the heart of culture outwards to the extremities.[3]

By 1841 he had returned to his position of a decade earlier. In a letter to Leopold Zunz, he wrote: "What could possibly save us in our present state of inner confusion? The only course I can think of is schism."[4]

These were the years of Geiger's critical struggle for recognition as assistant rabbi of the community of Breslau. The drawn-out battle apparently caused Geiger to rethink his position frequently. In the end, Geiger determined that his place must be within the community and not on its periphery. The Reform congregation of Berlin twice invited Geiger to serve as its rabbi, once in 1846, when the congregation first decided to organize regular Sabbath and festival services and again in 1861, after the death of Samuel Holdheim. On both occasions, Geiger answered that he was unwilling to become the rabbi of a private association.[5]

Geiger's refusal to abdicate his communal position in Breslau in favor of the independent Reformers of Berlin marked the last stage in his thinking on community and schism. Meanwhile, the decision by the Berlin Reformers to reconstitute their society from a pressure group into a functioning religious congregation provided, aside from the Hamburg temple, the lone case in Germany that realized Geiger's original notion of Reform separation.[6]

Initial permission for conducting the Reform services was extended to the congregation in 1846.[7] With the appearance of the Prussian Law of 1847, the Reformers were confronted by the stipulation that Prussia's Jews would henceforth be organized into unified communities defined by geographical region. Membership in these communities was now obligatory, and the law posed a dilemma for the Reformers who wanted to avoid interference by the community in their congregational services. On March 21, 1848, the congregation voted to petition the Prussian authorities for the right to establish a second and independent synagogue community in Berlin. Yet, not intending a complete break in the community, they stipulated that they sought the separation "without thereby abolishing the unity of the Jewish community with regard to humanitarian institutions." By the latter they meant the cemetery and agencies that cared for the poor, the sick, and the aged. Because of the political events of 1848 and 1849, consideration of the petition was delayed until it was resubmitted in March 1850.[8]

In response to the petition of the Reform congregation to establish a separate synagogue community in Berlin, the authorities requested that the Reformers submit an explanation of the creed of their faith. The state's question precipitated an extensive debate between some of the laymen under the leadership of Sigismund Stern and the congregation's rabbi, Samuel Holdheim. Despite Holdheim's objections, the congregation responded that a definite creed contradicted their very position as reformers and that, furthermore, Judaism itself did not profess such a creed of faith. Nor did Judaism recognize, according to the lay position, a unified, hierarchical church structure. Communities as well as individuals enjoyed religious freedom and were subject neither to compulsory beliefs nor to mandatory commandments.[9]

The Prussian authorities were unmoved by the Reformers' declarations. In the eyes of the state, separation from the Jewish community amounted to nothing less than separation from the religion practiced by the community. However, the state claimed that a religious community could be defined only by a specific set of positive dogmas, and if the Reformers lacked such a creed, that was to be viewed as positive proof that they had not yet amalgamated themselves into a solidified and identifiable community.[10] The state contended that a common creed of faith was the force that united and stabilized a religious community, guaranteeing that the community would not readily be dissolved. Rather than imposing a Christian conception of religion on Judaism, the state's preoccupation with dogmas stemmed from a political concern that religion alone should be the binding force of a religious community. In fact, the congregation soon came under the jurisdiction of an 1851 law which placed all societies lacking corporative recognition under police supervision. According to Holdheim, this supervision guaranteed that religious associations were fulfilling only religious functions and had no other "political or social intentions."[11]

Because of the government's refusal to recognize two independent Jewish communities in Berlin, members of the Reform congregation were compelled to maintain their membership in the larger community as well. It is to this compulsory double taxation that David Philipson attributed the lack of growth of the Berlin congregation. But that explanation will not suffice. According to Holdheim, as well as to a report in the *Allgemeine Zeitung des Judenthums*, an internal agreement was reached in the 1850s between the Reform congregation and a newly elected and sympathetic Berlin community board which enabled the Reform Jews to deduct congregational dues from their community taxes. If the Reform community of Berlin did not grow, the explanation does not lie in the financial burden of double membership.[12]

The young Abraham Geiger contemplated schism and the Reform congregation of Berlin attempted it, but the fact remains that separatism never fully blossomed as a strategy or as a principle in the German Reform camp. This is a more precise formulation than David Philipson's bemoaning in 1907 that even in his day, the Berlin Reform congregation and the Hamburg temple were "the only official reform congregations in Germany."[13] In the nineteenth century, *community* remained a higher priority for the Reformers of Germany than *movement*. Nevertheless, a number of communities equaled, if not surpassed, the Hamburg temple in the reform of their services.[14] Clearly, the Reform triumphs in those communities represented at the Rabbinical Conferences of the 1840s negated the need for the development of autonomous Reform congregations. But Reformers did not always win the communal struggles, and yet they almost always chose not to separate. Why did the supporters of reform in Mecklenburg, who lost control of the community by state dictate in 1853, not organize independent synagogues? Why did Geiger refuse the rabbinate of the Reform congregation of Berlin that would have freed his hands for a more consistent—and more radical—reformation?

Philipson was correct that the state often insisted upon the unity of the Jewish community. In fact, this was the case in Mecklenburg where the state demanded an end to the separate Orthodox services and guaranteed a traditional course for the community in order to preserve unity. This was also the intent of the 1847 Prussian law which stipulated compulsory membership in the local community. But the establishment in Cologne, Mainz, Darmstadt, and Karlsruhe of independent Orthodox congregations similar to the IRG of Frankfurt indicates that the authorities were not always opposed to religious autonomy.

For the young Geiger, schism had offered the prospect of theological consistency. Yet, the lack of interest in autonomous

Reform congregations demonstrates the extent to which supporters of reform in Germany were quite satisfied with aesthetic
changes. If these innovations could be attained within the communal framework, there was little reason for schism.

Finally, as I suggested in the opening chapter, neither separation nor autonomy would contribute to the emancipation
struggle that motivated so much of the Reformers' endeavors.
When Abraham Geiger discussed schism with an acquaintance
in 1831, he found him disinterested in the cause of secession
unless "he could be convinced that these separated Jews would
have well-grounded hopes of attaining civil equality, in which
case he would work energetically on its behalf."[15] While Geiger's
acquaintance was sympathetic to those Jews who had converted
to Christianity, Geiger was not. The acquaintance's doubts about
the value of separation imply that he saw little purpose for a
stop-gap on the way to conversion. For Geiger, for the leaders
of Reform Judaism, there indeed was a purpose—the retention
of Jewish identity.

It is sometimes thought that the interpretation which empha-
sizes the importance of the emancipation struggle in the rise of
the Reform movement offers only a derogatory comment on that
endeavor. The opposite is true. These men could readily have
attained emancipation as Christians, but the Reformers of Judaism in Germany sought it as Jews. In contrast to what they
themselves often claimed, the Reform Jew of the mid-nineteenth
century gave full expression to his Jewish ethnicity. In fact, he
was one of its strongest champions. Given his integration into
gentile values, his laxity in religious practice, and his commitment to emancipation, the refusal of the Reformer to surrender
his Jewish identity demonstrates an active historical and social
consciousness of being a Jew. For men like Ludwig Philippson
and Abraham Geiger, that identity was demonstrated within the
context of community, and in consequence, Reform Judaism
presented little challenge to the integrity of the Jewish
community.[16]

REVOLUTION AND COMMUNITY

The calls for separation increased as the community relationships reversed and the Orthodox were relegated to the minority

position.[17] But if the religious strife between Reformers and Orthodox had, by the late 1840s, already severely taxed the unity of the Jewish community, the revolution of 1848 brought the trials of the community to a head. Religious coercion contradicted the principles of freedom enunciated by the revolutionary program, specifically in the frequent appeals for the divorce of church and state.

Ludwig Philippson astutely analyzed the impact of the revolutionary events upon the Jewish community and expressed grave doubts over the community's capacity to survive. Troubled by a number of reports of lack of financial support, Philippson warned that Jews would not voluntarily contribute to the upkeep of communities once taxes that were formerly compulsory became optional. Inner strife had weakened attachment to the community, while the political revolution had provided a new outlet for a growing sense of religious indifference. Nor were the two factors disconnected, for if Jews had been willing in the past to join together despite their religious differences, the spirit of 1848 encouraged the camps to affirm their right for independence:

Both parties let themselves be held together during the reign of absolutism; but now that the consciousness of freedom permeates all—and the gospel of the "Separation of Church and State" has become accepted everywhere—the parties will no longer remain together.[18]

The impact of 1848 can be seen in the petition of the Berlin Reform community for recognition as a separate community. Though necessitated by the law of July 1847, the resolution was passed by the congregation on March 21, 1848, at the very height of the revolutionary enthusiasm.[19]

Philippson envisioned the conglomeration of forces that could easily bring about the dissolution of the Jewish community. If Jews received their freedom within the framework of a separation of church and state that exposed the community to the whims of voluntarism, Philippson feared that the community would not survive. The state might assume responsibility for the community's social institutions, but then only a religious structure would be left intact. The likely hesitation by the state within the revolutionary atmosphere to assert its authority and protection over a purely religious community would thus still leave the community sentenced to extinction. In sum, Philippson was convinced that the synagogue could survive only if protected by a layer of social functions and state support.[20]

The collapse of the revolution brought about a renewal of the compulsory community. On July 1, 1851, the Frankfurt Senate reaffirmed, "it is not the prerogative of a Jewish citizen to sever himself from the obligations of the Jewish community."[21] In Prussia, it was only after the revolution that the 1847 law that strengthened the community's bonds could first go into effect. The Jewish community survived primarily because the revolution did not, but a lesson had been taught that the Jewish communities would be endangered if abandoned by state support or if their unity was ruptured by secession. In the future, most community leaders envisioned the emancipation they sought within the context of a continuing Jewish community organization. Perhaps because the modernization of Germany and, with it, Jewish emancipation, were henceforth promoted by conservative regimes, Jewish communal leaders eventually attained both of these objectives.[22]

THE STRUCTURES OF ACCORD

In the early years of the conflict, the Reform Jews of Frankfurt had assumed that the Orthodox party would soon disappear.[23] Traditionalists apparently thought at first that the Reform movement represented merely a passing fad. But Reform had grown in strength and Orthodoxy had proved its sustaining power. In most communities where religious freedom was tolerated, both parties found substantial support. Whatever the initial expectations of the two sides, after 1848 it became clear in most major German communities that a *modus vivendi* had to be found in which both Reform and Orthodox Jews could remain within the same community.[24] As the majority of these communities searched for a harmonious accord, three general patterns of communal structure emerged.

In a few communities, the institutions were in Orthodox hands, while a Reform minority remained members of the main community but formed an independent congregation. In Hamburg, this arrangement dated back to 1819 and lasted until 1865, when the overall Jewish community was dissolved. Members of the Reform congregation of Berlin were compelled to hold double membership between 1847 and 1858.[25]

In a number of communities, the reverse situation developed, in which an Orthodox minority maintained membership in both the Reform-dominated community as well as in their own independent congregations. This, of course, was the case in Frankfurt, as well as later in Mainz, Cologne, Darmstadt, Karlsruhe, and Wiesbaden.

The third type of communal structure, often confused as the "Hamburg program," actually originated in Breslau, where it evolved during the decade 1846–1856. It restored the Orthodox to equal status within the community by allowing the individual member to select between an Orthodox and a Reform association, each of which had its own rabbinical leader and provided both synagogue and schools. All members continued to support and benefit from the community's social and welfare institutions.[26]

The first type, in which a Reform minority held a double membership, soon disappeared. In Berlin the first elections held in compliance with the 1847 law returned a board friendly to the Reform cause. A new arrangement was reached in 1854 and implemented in 1858, in which members of the Reform congregation were exempted from that part of the community dues designated for religious purposes. In Hamburg the Jewish community was actually dissolved after emancipation was granted in 1864. This new and unique procedure enabled Jews to choose a synagogue community in accordance with their personal preference, while the welfare functions were absorbed by the government.[27] Thus, by 1865, nowhere in Germany did Reformers suffer from double taxation.

The *Israelitische Religionsgesellschaft* of Frankfurt was the archetype of the second pattern, that of an autonomous Orthodox minority. When the attempt of 1849–1850 to reach an accord within the Frankfurt community failed, most Orthodox in Frankfurt became convinced that independent Orthodoxy provided the only viable solution to their problems. The relationship between the autonomous congregation and the Jewish community was a matter of controversy and confusion from the outset.

CONGREGATION AND COMMUNITY IN FRANKFURT

While Prussia's Jewry struggled to decode the implications of the 1847 law governing its political rights and community obligations, the Jews of Frankfurt, untouched by the Prussian legislation but deeply affected by the revolutionary presence in their city, sought to unravel what remained for them in the legacy of the 1848 revolution.[28] With regard to communal structure, the abolition of the position of Senate commissioner for Jewish affairs widened the sphere of independence of the Jewish community; yet, the increasing political integration of the Frankfurt Jew into burgher society meant that the significance of the Jewish community as a political institution was on the wane. Thus, paradoxically, the parameters of power of the community in Frankfurt were being diminished precisely as its independence was growing.

Because the communal bonds in Prussia were strengthened by the 1847 legislation, the democratic challenge to the notion of compulsory membership was felt more keenly in Frankfurt, where the countervailing effect from the 1847 Prussian law was absent. The prospect of religious freedom and an end to compulsory membership in the religious community had virtually intimidated Frankfurt's community board into considering concessions to the Orthodox sector with the hope of preserving their presence on the membership rolls. The commission responsible for revising the community's ordinances proposed that Orthodox Jews receive access to the smaller community synagogue and be entitled to conduct services within the community framework and at the community's expense. The Orthodox could even engage their own rabbi, a request they had previously been denied, although only at their own expense and provided that the rabbi expect no authority within the community.[29]

Despite the gesture intended by the board, a number of the Orthodox took their cue from the doubts that had been raised over compulsory membership. In the petition to the Frankfurt

Senate of January 18, 1850, requesting the right to appoint a rabbi to serve the newly formed autonomous Orthodox congregation, the founders declared in their opening paragraph, "The undersigned adherents of the Mosaic faith have dissociated themselves from the existing Jewish religious community and have formed a new religious community."[30] But complete separation between the two communities was not their intention, and the potential seceders themselves prescribed that their secession from the religious community would cause "no detriment to those rights and privileges which they enjoy as members of the political Jewish community."

Defeat of the commission's proposed revisions in February 1850 underscored for the Orthodox the impossibility of a solution dependent upon the community's goodwill. As we have seen, the new autonomous congregation now benefited from an influx of members. The attitude of the congregation's leadership toward the community was certainly shaped by the recalcitrance of the community to reach an accord. Both in Breslau and in Hamburg, concessions were already being extended to the respective minority segments. In Berlin concessions were offered in 1854. In Frankfurt the weakest proposal of all had been defeated and no further offers were extended until after the law of separation was passed in 1876.

Defeat of the proposed ordinance left the Jewish community in a legislative vacuum, as no relevant legislation regulated the community's affairs. Meanwhile, several members of the IRG openly challenged the concept of compulsory membership by refusing to pay their community taxes. The Senate responded to complaints lodged by the board in July 1851 and affirmed that the payment of taxes was in fact obligatory.

The presentation of Adolph Dann and Consorts assumes ... that it is at the discretion of each individual Jewish citizen to decide whether he will continue to be a member of the Jewish community or sever his ties. [This] is both an error and an impossibility. ... The relations between the Frankfurt citizen of the Jewish religion and the Jewish community are a matter self-evident according to both the word and the spirit of the existing stipulations. Just as one who has been granted citizenship does not make a special declaration that he is entering the Jewish community and that he is willing to participate in its obligations, so is it hardly in the power of a native Jewish citizen to sever his obligations toward the community.[31]

In sum, the religious strife of the previous decade had divided the community membership, but only after the events of 1848 did the organic integrity of the community structure come into question. Moreover, the pre-1848 acknowledgment of communal unity was not to be fully restored. Once the Senate had bequeathed autonomy to the board, it could not simultaneously enforce its desire for a harmonious and unified community, and the community itself proved incapable of doing so.

Other major communities in Germany had succeeded by the late 1850s in reaching an accord, but in Frankfurt, the Reformers' fear of an Orthodox restoration after the decades required to unseat the traditionalist control of the synagogue and the deep social tensions between the parties maintained the conflict at a high pitch. The Orthodox in Frankfurt had no alternative but to follow the path of autonomy, for which they indeed did possess the financial means. Notwithstanding that their wealth and social standing implied the appropriateness of an independent Orthodoxy, it should be recalled that a number of bankers had actually endeavored arduously to pass the new ordinance and to preserve communal unity. But the Reformers refused and the social forces were free to propel the Orthodox of Frankfurt to prominence. Controversy within the community, however, did not subside, but now centered on the relationship between the autonomous congregation and the larger Jewish community.

Soon after the election of Samson Raphael Hirsch as rabbi of the IRG, its board petitioned the Senate to transfer jurisdiction over kosher meat slaughtering to its own rabbi.[32] The Senate understood the request as a challenge by the IRG to the powers of the established community and responded with an explicit delineation of the limits of the IRG's license to organize a separate congregation and, more pointedly, to secure the services of its own rabbi:

1. Both the petitioners and the Board of the Jewish community are agreed that the kosher slaughtering facilities are subject to the religious regulations of this community, so that the examination, su-

pervision, and consultation with those responsible for the slaughtering are within the domain of the community rabbi.

2. The rabbi, chosen by the petitioners to fulfill their religious needs . . . has no standing at the present time within the Jewish community.

3. The community Board reported that it will satisfactorily supply the needs in question as it has done in the past.

4. The Senate cannot become involved in determining which of the two kosher slaughtering supervisors possesses the greater competence.

5. The Senate expects the community Board not only to maintain the relevant institution so that it satisfies the religious requirements of the community members, but, moreover, to comply with the wish of that segment of the community for which the institution appears to be of primary importance that they be given proper consideration. All this lies within the well understood interests of the community itself, precisely so that there will be no necessity to impose arrangements in another way.

In the sixth and final section, the Senate expressed concern that not all of the petitioners were paying the obligatory taxes to the community and reconfirmed their decision that membership in the community was compulsory for Jewish citizens of Frankfurt.[33]

The Senate's response reveals the countervailing stresses acting on its position. The establishment of an autonomous congregation with Senate approval conflicted with the unified structure of the community, still cherished by the Senate.[34] Like the Orthodox, the Senate was finding it difficult to value both unity and religiosity. A comparison with the Senate's actions during the circumcision debate a decade earlier demonstrates again the new favor enjoyed by the Orthodox camp. The Senate was no more interested in testing the religious piety of meat slaughterers than it had been in determining the relationship between circumcision and admission to the Jewish community, but whereas in the 1843 dispute, the Orthodox party had been faulted for repeatedly bringing petitions on internal religious matters before the Senate, it was now the community board's responsibility to maintain harmony. The Senate's message makes it clear that it was the board's obligation to compromise *its* position to appease the Orthodox.

The IRG petition that its own rabbi assume responsibility for supervising meat slaughtering indicated their desire to define for themselves an integral role within the community structure. However, the board's unwillingness to weaken either its authority or that of its rabbi; the Senate's unwillingness to intervene in a religious matter or to violate community autonomy; and the unique circumstance that Frankfurt Orthodoxy possessed considerable financial means resulted in the IRG's development of institutions duplicating those of the community. Two parallel communities were emerging, but members who subscribed to the IRG by choice were required to support the main community by law.

In 1854 the board of the Frankfurt Jewish community renewed its long-standing attempt to construct a new synagogue building. Faced with the obligation of community members to finance the new edifice, the board of the IRG petitioned the Senate to exempt its members from those communal taxes designed for ritual and educational purposes. The petition was repeated frequently in the 1850s, but unsuccessfully, with the most extensive argument rendered in 1858 in a forty-four-page memorandum.[35]

The board asserted that financial considerations were the sole cause behind the IRG claims. "A question of money is to be restamped as a question of conscience." The IRG effectively rebutted that the amount involved was minimal. Within the IRG's budget of 25,000 florin, some 19,000 florin were allocated for ritual and educational functions parallel to those performed by the community. The community board itself claimed that the total annual taxes of the petitioners amounted to 2,300 florin, of which only about one-half was allocated for these purposes. Based on a membership of 140, the average IRG member was paying 9 florin to the community in addition to the 135 florin he had already paid to the IRG for the same purposes.[36] Indeed, the difference was not worth the legal efforts involved, but the community's demand that the IRG membership contribute toward construction of the new synagogue reopened an old and sensitive wound. Precisely because the board had insisted upon innovations in the service and the appointment of a Reform rabbi, the Rothschilds had withdrawn their pledge to pay for the new building themselves. The IRG had then undertaken to build and maintain its own synagogue, "and now we should in addition be required to help balance their school and synagogue debts!!"[37]

The Orthodox denied that they were secessionists. "We are not the separators, . . . but the last remnant that has remained true to the traditional shrines of Judaism." Their case was not one of theological truth, but of historical continuity. "Not because ours is the true Judaism, but because ours is the old Judaism, the only legitimate one for centuries even here in Frankfurt."[38]

The board countered the IRG petition with the argument that at stake was nothing less than the continuation of the organized Jewish community, for accepting their request would establish the principle that withdrawal from the community was a legitimate option. "There will be no end to the sectarianism if every tiny faction which does not agree with the forms recognized by the majority, has the right, on that account, to withdraw from the whole."[39] Fully realizing that the Senate would balk at the idea of filling the role of arbitrator, the board made it clear that the onus would fall upon the Senate to determine which of these groups represented the true Judaism. Furthermore, even if the Senate tried to avoid the theological selection, the board argued that it would prove still more difficult to refuse some groups the exemptions it had granted to others. The board's solution was to recognize the path of the majority as representing true Judaism. "The religion of the majority alone, according to the principles of Judaism, is the true and legitimate religion."[40] With regard to toleration, there was nothing "liberal" about the Reformers' position.

The communal structure proposed in the IRG petitions approximated that adopted in Breslau in 1856. Each member of the community would affiliate with one or the other of two religious societies responsible for providing ritual and educational facilities. The costs of maintaining the societies would be borne exclusively by their memberships. They would be governed as autonomous bodies with the IRG filling the role of the Orthodox society and the existing community institutions assuming the functions of the Reform sector. As in Breslau, a unified community board would be responsible for social institutions dealing with the poor, the sick, and the cemetery.[41]

The IRG proposal reflected the tripartite division of community functions formulated by Hirsch in his 1854 essay, "Jewish Communal Life." According to Hirsch, the model community was responsible for *Torah, Avodah,* and *Gemilut Hasadim*—Study, Worship, and Welfare. The IRG proposal echoed Hirsch's ideas and his language.[42] Considering that the IRG board would hardly have composed an ideological document without Hirsch's approval, it seems clear that in the 1850s, prior to the full emancipation of the Jews of Frankfurt, Hirsch was willing to accept a community structure that left Orthodox and Reform, despite their religious differences, as members of a single Jewish community. The board, in the course of its opposition to the IRG plan, quibbled over the distribution of functions designated by the IRG. They insisted that the cemetery belonged to the ritual category and not to welfare, while the rabbi's salary was a general community obligation and not a specifically religious matter. These revisions of the distribution of functions reduced the IRG proposal to a state of absurdity. The Orthodox would remain responsible for contributing to the salary of the Reform rabbi, but would be denied burial rights in the community cemetery. Clearly, the board was not taking the IRG plan very seriously, but their response also reflects their overall strategy. The board was in some difficulty to explain why a compromise could not be reached in Frankfurt, but they knew that if a debate should arise over the religious classification of community institutions, the Senate would hesitate to become involved.

The Orthodox plan and the Reform rejection demonstrate how the two parties held significantly different views of the nature of community and of the relation between the community and the individual. Traditionally, the community provided a general framework and fulfilled certain functions, but many needs fell upon a cluster of private societies that contributed perhaps just one specific function to the community and yet filled a spectrum of needs for its own members. It was through such societies that the poor, the sick, and burials were tended to. Most societies guaranteed their members throughout their lives a synagogue in which they could feel they played an important part and provided them with insurance that they would not be left alone in times of sorrow and not forgotten after their death.[43] In contrast, in the Reform view, the community represented a totality, a single unified organization which directly controlled all activities. Under their aegis, societies were dissolved and their functions turned over to committees. For example, Frankfurt's Burial Society, whose membership consisted of a number of older families of the community, was disbanded in 1841 and its duties turned over to paid employees of the community. This rationalization of the community was a product of the nineteenth century, originating in France under Napoleon and exported to Germany during the French occupation. It effectively reduced the number of options available to the community membership and allowed the Reformers to dislodge secondary levels of power within the community that often resisted the Reform program of innovation.[44] Although the IRG's own proposal also reflected a degree of this rationalization by placing the social institutions under community control, it retained the traditional sense of private societies fulfilling the religious needs of their members.

Based on their perspective of the totality of community, the Reform board of Frankfurt argued that the establishment of a synagogue by a private society hardly relieved the community of its responsibility to maintain a public synagogue open to all. Furthermore, only the community could guarantee the permanence of a synagogue. More important, the board argued that individual members could not contribute less to the common treasury because they used certain facilities less frequently than others: The community and therefore its members were responsible for maintaining all of the facilities. In fact, Orthodox Jews often used the same argument that the entire community shared responsibility for religious facilities. In Prussia in the earlier years of the century, there were a number of complaints to the authorities from those who made no use of the ritual bath but were required to support its upkeep. In those cases, Orthodox rabbis insisted that such facilities could be maintained only with communal assistance.[45] In Frankfurt, however, the Orthodox found the communal institutions unacceptable, and they were perfectly capable of supporting their own facilities.

The two parties disagreed on the fundamental nature of the Jewish community in another sense as well. For the Reform board, the community's functions were still defined by the broad parameters of the political organism that had traditionally characterized the Jewish community:

We consider our community exclusively as a religious community; but because of the duress and strain of earlier times, whose tragic legacy we have not yet swept away, our community is also a political community.[46]

The Board pointed out that it was still responsible for the supervision of funds and institutions, for the care of the sick, and for maintaining schools. The IRG rejected the contention that the Jewish community was a political organization.

Since Jews have been accepted into the general corpus of citizens and subject to the general jurisdiction of the police and civil authorities, there is no longer a political Jewish community. The last trace of a political character has been removed and only a Jewish religious communal life still truly exists.

The IRG did not dispute that the board fulfilled the tasks listed, but it claimed that these did not characterize a political community, for any other religious community was responsible for no less. Here, the IRG's argument was weak, for it was unable to deny that the community filled functions beyond the realm of a religious society, while the parallel with other religions did not hold. Christians received their social and welfare services through the government, not by way of their church. Put differently, this part of their argument was premature. It was based on a notion of Jewish emancipation that was still incomplete, and for the time being the IRG petition represented a combination of progressive planning and wishful thinking.[47] Again in 1858 the Senate advised the two sides to reach an accord on their own. "An understanding between the parties could with good will easily be attained and is certainly to be recommended."[48]

In 1861 Leopold Stein resigned as rabbi of the Frankfurt Jewish community after a prolonged struggle with the board and the leadership of the Philanthropin School over the limits imposed on his authority. Stein protested continuous inroads into his independence and the successful efforts of the school's directors to curtail his involvement in the educational process.[49]

Stein's resignation raised Orthodox hopes that a reconciliation between the camps under Orthodox hegemony would now be possible. The IRG submitted a proposal to the Senate that apparently suggested that the community engage a preacher to replace Stein, but entrust full rabbinical responsibilities to Hirsch.[50] However, the community board imported the leading Reform spokesman Abraham Geiger to replace Stein.[51] The subsequent few years were relatively insignificant in the chapters of Geiger's illustrious biography, but they bore heavy meaning for the history of Frankfurt Jewry and for the city of Frankfurt itself.

EMANCIPATION AND SEPARATION

With a single paragraph passed in October 1864, the Frankfurt Senate completed the emancipation process of Frankfurt Jewry: "Those limitations on the political rights of Jewish citizens ... currently still in force are hereby eliminated."[52] Jewish emancipation was attained together with the granting of equal rights to the inhabitants of several villages legally tied to Frankfurt. The joint edict followed by only a few months a law which gave almost complete freedom to Frankfurt's citizens to earn their livelihood in the occupations of their choice. Richard Schwemer wrote of this period with specific reference to the new occupational freedom: "The last remnant of the medieval bulwark has disappeared. Frankfurt now truly became a modern city."[53]

However, the IRG did not agree that the last of the medieval restrictions had been removed. Two months after the emancipation law was passed, a full campaign was underway both in the general press and in the city's assembly to free the Orthodox from compulsory membership in the Jewish community. Emanuel Schwarzschild summarized the Orthodox position in the *Israelit*. The new law had indeed lifted all restrictions for Jewish citizens, except the requirement to hold membership in the Jewish community.

As a result of emancipation, the state has become nondenominational. It is unconcerned, nor has it reason to be concerned, with the religion of those who wish to become its citizens. The state has nothing to do with Christians or Jews or Turks, but deals only with citizens.

It follows, argued Schwarzschild, that the state had no business interfering in the religious beliefs of the Jewish citizens.[54] The debate on compulsory membership in the Jewish community was carried over to the floor of the Legislative Assembly.[55]

The argument that complete equality was still lacking was correct in more ways than the Orthodox cared to admit. Christian citizens of Frankfurt were not compelled to belong to any particular religious community. Regardless of denomination, they were entitled to benefit from the city's social and welfare services. Yet, a major factor behind the government's continued insistence on membership in the Jewish community was precisely to prevent Jews from becoming a burden on the general welfare facilities. In fact, a memo had been issued with the emancipation law assuring Christian citizens that the new law did not release the Jewish community from its obligations to care for its sick and for its schools and religious institutions.[56]

The traditional Jewish practice of assuming total responsibility for the welfare of fellow Jews was both efficient and thrifty for the state, but it contradicted the basic assumption of emancipation that legal differences between citizens were to be eliminated. The Prussian emancipation act of 1812 and subsequent judicial decisions had clearly stipulated that Jewish citizens of the old provinces were entitled to equal benefits and that Jews could not be compelled to pay additional taxes to the Jewish community in order to provide parallel welfare services. According to the Prussian jurists, Jews were, in consequence of the 1812 law, members of the "general community of citizens" and therefore had the right to expect the general community to provide for the Jewish poor and sick.[57] Frankfurt Jewry was informed by the very text of the law of 1864 not to expect similar considerations. The Orthodox glossed over this aspect of inequality and turned to Hamburg as a model for their claims of religious freedom.

Hamburg, an independent city like Frankfurt, adopted a new

constitution in 1860 which granted political emancipation to its Jewish citizens. There, too, a protest arose that the supposed equality was *de facto* incomplete because of the continued obligation to hold membership in the Jewish community, but in Hamburg the move to end compulsory membership and, in fact, to dissolve Hamburg's Jewish communal structure came from the community board itself. Calls for dissolving the community dated back to the short-lived emancipation of 1849, when Gabriel Riesser argued that emancipation under condition of membership in a religious community was incomplete. Both the arguments of 1850 and of the 1860s emphasized the discrimination practiced in the sphere of welfare, where Jews suffered double indemnity. The Jewish leadership protested both the discrimination involved and the heavier financial burden.[58]

The Jewish community of Hamburg possessed a unique set of circumstances that strengthened the case for repeal of compulsory membership. Sephardic and Ashkenazic communities had long existed side by side. Hence, there were no illusions in Hamburg of a unified Jewry, even in the political sense. Religious disunity was even more blatant, as by 1862 the Reform temple was more than forty years old. Over the decades, the board of the Ashkenazic community had been forced to mediate between the Orthodox and Reform camps and often found itself in the midst of controversy and personal discomfort. This provided one of the major causes for the board's own activity in petitioning the civil authorities to relieve it of the burden of religious responsibility.[59]

In accordance with these arguments, the board proposed, as Riesser had done earlier, that the present functions filled by the community be redistributed. The state should assume those social and welfare obligations which it filled for Christian citizens, while religious needs would be filled by private societies chosen by the individual in accordance with his own personal preferences. The board's proposal is what became known as the "Hamburg program": dissolution of the organized community, voluntary membership in private religious associations, and state responsibility for welfare.[60] The model differed from the structure adopted in Breslau, where social and welfare obligations remained the responsibility of the community and community membership was obligatory. But in fact, the law passed in Hamburg in 1864 was different from the board's proposal, and the "Hamburg program" never actually existed in Hamburg.

Traditionalists in Hamburg opposed the board's plan and obtained 459 signatures on a petition in response to the board's petition with 169 names. Helga Krohn has suggested that the traditionalists hoped to retain a broader base of financial support for the community's religious facilities.[61] In addition, it must be noted that German Orthodoxy consistently affirmed the traditional responsibility to tend to the needs of Jewish brethren regardless of the alternative sources of welfare available as a result of emancipation. This had been the reaction of Prussian Jewry to the 1812 law, when Jewish communities continued to provide these services and to tax their members, with but a handful turning to the courts for exemption.[62] Samson Raphael Hirsch also maintained that Jews should retain these responsibilities in postemancipation society.[63]

In accordance with the law passed in 1864, the newly constituted communities were responsible for the schools, cemeteries, and care for the poor and sick, as well as matters of general concern. Little of the community's social functions had changed, and only 1.2 percent of the members resigned. The major difference effected in Hamburg was the separation between religious and social interests. The community board was liberated from its thankless tasks of mediation, and each religious group now enjoyed complete autonomy.[64] Discrimination in welfare had been legally terminated, but Hamburg Jewry demonstrated that it fully intended to retain the responsibility of caring for its own. The first community board elected after the 1864 law consisted of nine liberals and six traditionalists, guaranteeing contact and joint endeavors by the two camps.

The Protocols of the Frankfurt Senate record that on January 23, 1866, the Senate ordered the board of the Jewish community to report within a short period on the ways and conditions in which the IRG was to be separated from the community in matters of school and religion. According to the Senate, the matter could no longer be delayed.[65] It is apparent that emancipation had dictated the legal necessity of separation. But by the summer of 1866, Frankfurt was no longer an independent free city, the Senate was no longer autonomous, and for the time being Germans of all religions were faced by matters of greater urgency.

Unification and Separation

In 1872 Marcus Lehmann, editor of the *Israelit*, opposed the formation of a German counterpart to the French *Alliance Israelite*. "Is it advisable for German Jewry to separate from the general union of Jews in order to form a special organization?" Lehmann's concern went further than the question of political effectiveness. "As far as Judaism is concerned, there exists for us and all our rational co-religionists no difference between German, French, Italian, Dutch, English, American, and Oriental Jews. They are all our religious brothers, if they respect our faith and wish to live as Jews."[1] The unification of Germany under Bismarck encouraged the leaders of the German Jewish communities to make their own attempts at unification, but the Orthodox were wary of these efforts out of fear that underlying the attempt to unify German Jewry lay an effort to establish a German Judaism heavily influenced by the thinking and approach of the Reform movement. The resistance to the union of German Jewry was strongest precisely where the resistance to the union of Germany was greatest.

ANNEXATION OF FRANKFURT

During the 1860s, Prussia initiated a process that soon culminated in the establishment of a North German Federation in 1867 and in the further unification of Germany in 1871. For the citizens of Frankfurt, these events signified the demise of Frankfurt's independent sovereignty, and nationalist sentiments in Frankfurt were shadowed by a marked reserve toward Prussia's intentions.[2] The *Neue Frankfurter Zeitung* emerged as the leading forum for opposition toward Prussia's increasing role. In 1864 the paper spoke of the Prussian state proving itself ever more clearly as a union of "Absolutism, Junkerism, and Militarism," a combination totally incompatible with the cause of freedom.[3] The *Frankfurter Zeitung* pursued its attacks on Prussia, and in 1865 distribution of the paper in Prussia was forbidden.[4] Other papers joined the *Zeitung*, making Frankfurt the focal point for a democratically oriented opposition to Prussian leadership.[5]

The opposition to Prussia soon extended into the mainstream of Frankfurt's political thought. Even Edouard Souchay, who had cultivated a pro-Prussian policy in Frankfurt since the 1830s, now addressed himself to the recent developments involving the succession to the Danish throne and the annexation of the provinces of Schleswig-Holstein. Souchay warned that Bismarck was leading Germany into a war that was incompatible with its democratic hopes.[6] Of course, Frankfurt, was not alone in its opposition and concern over the likelihood that Prussia was about to impose a unification on Germany on its own terms. The neighboring states, Hannover, Kurhessen, and Nassau, all took steps to resist the coming confrontation. But in each of these states, opposition parties existed which favored a stronger Prussian connection, while in Frankfurt all but a few shared the extensive hostility towards Prussia.[7]

According to Richard Schwemer, the causes for Frankfurt's attitudes lay in differences between the political cultures of the two states. Frankfurt was a republic; Prussia, a monarchy and an absolutist monarchy at that. In Frankfurt, the citizen was sovereign; in Prussia he was the king's subject. The middle class wielded influence in Frankfurt; in Prussia, influence belonged to the nobility and ranking officials of the state. Prussia's interests were agrarian; Frankfurt's were commercial. Frankfurt's power was economic, while it lacked a militarist tradition. Prussia had the tradition and now threatened with the power.[8]

Prussia's occupation of Frankfurt in July 1866 came as no surprise, but nevertheless raised the anxieties of different sectors of the population. A number of citizens left the city, while others arranged for Swiss citizenship. Jewish bankers were reportedly prominently represented in both groups, but the *Allgemeine Zeitung des Judenthums* claimed that disproportionate attention was being given to the Jewish flight.[9] The tensions in negotiating a dignified transition from sovereignty to subservience proved too severe for Frankfurt's ruling mayor Fellner, whose suicide symbolized the turn in Frankfurt's history.[10]

Postwar controversy between Prussia and Frankfurt centered predominantly on Frankfurt's position within the new Prussian realm and on a severe war indemnity imposed on Frankfurt by Bismarck. Local leaders were particularly incensed over the financial penalties and dispatched a delegation to Berlin under Baron Carl Meyer Rothschild to negotiate the amount involved. Protest from abroad, Rothschild's influence, and the intervention of Bismarck's personal financial advisor Gerson Bleichroeder resulted in a relaxation of the indemnity.[11]

Carl Rothschild continued to play an important role in the first years of Prussian rule in Frankfurt. Bismarck and Rothschild had met during the 1850s, when Bismarck served as Prussian ambassador to the German Confederation. Since then, the Frankfurt Rothschilds, first Amschel and then Carl, had served as Bismarck's personal bankers. Only in 1866–1867 with the emergence of a Prussian empire, did Bismarck switch his account to Berlin and to Bleichroeder, a Rothschild agent.[12] Actually the Rothschilds had good reason to side with Austria in the current rivalry. Vienna had hosted one of the family's principal houses, and Austria had granted the brothers the status of nobility. But Carl Meyer remained closer to Prussia. In 1867 Frankfurt elected him by a vast majority as its representative to the North German Parliament. The choice of Rothschild, a symbol of Frankfurt's international importance as a financial center, seemed an astute one. In sending Rothschild to Berlin, Frankfurt hoped to enter the Prussian realm with a position of strength.[13]

The majority of Frankfurt Jewry did not share Rothschild's positive inclinations toward Prussia. Indeed, they had their particular reasons for concern in the aftermath of annexation.

Signs of tension emerged within the first year of Prussian rule when the community's Philanthropin School and the IRG's Realschule applied for recognition by the Prussian authorities that would entitle their graduates to register for one year of military service in lieu of a longer term of duty. The otherwise affirmative response stipulated that the schools could no longer accept Christian pupils. The condition did not affect the Orthodox school, but the Philanthropin had proudly included a number of Christians on its rolls, and the community leaders were enraged at the insult hurled at the positive strides taken toward integration. A Frankfurt correspondent for the *Allgemeine Zeitung* remarked of the conflict: "So it happened in the month of July, one thousand eight hundred and sixty-seven, during the first year of the Prussian regime in Frankfurt a.M." Frankfurt Jewry was concerned.[14]

By 1870 the press had reported a number of other incidents of anti-Jewish attitudes by Prussian officials. Two arrest warrants appearing in an official publication declared the suspects to be Jewish—information not provided in the case of other religions. More seriously, one of the warrants described the suspect as possessing "a Jewish Physiognomie." The Frankfurt correspondent to the *Israelit* referring to the incident declared that "at the most one might have thought it possible in 1770, but it was totally unexpected in 1870."[15] In 1867, the *Frankfurter Journal* reported an attack on Jewish political rights appearing in a Berlin paper.[16]

In sum, the sharpest opposition to the establishment of Prussian hegemony in Germany arose in Frankfurt; while Frankfurt Jewry, having their own grievances, felt the current anxiety even more keenly.

The chain of events provoked quite different responses from Frankfurt's two rabbis, Abraham Geiger and Samson Raphael Hirsch. Despite the occasional setbacks Geiger had suffered from the Prussian authorities during his long tenure in Breslau, he deemed German unification under Prussian rule as a meaningful step for full Jewish liberty. Objectively, the Jewish situation in Frankfurt had surpassed the advances attained by Prussian Jewry during the early part of the century. Even excluding the revolutionary interlude, successive legislation in 1833, 1853, and 1864 had progressively cleared away Jewish disabilities in Frankfurt, while Prussian Jewry had actually regressed as a result of the 1847 law still in effect. But Geiger's vision of German Jewry and its welfare went far beyond the limits of Frankfurt, and it is only this broader scope that can explain Geiger's sympathy for the Prussian conquest. In early November 1865, Geiger wrote to M. A. Levy:

Germany's disunion and the ineffectiveness of the attempts at unification will place the power of government in Bismarck's hands. I wish it were already his, and that I would have my pleasure at the dissolution of the wretched enterprise of the small states with their altogether unintelligible arrogance. Freedom would then arise despite him. Should we be surprised that the same disorganization reigns in Jewish matters?[17]

Opposed to the provincialism of the smaller states, Geiger was convinced that the unification of Germany would enhance the general cause of freedom, but Geiger also perceived the events in Prussia as significant for Jewish life in Germany. In his letters to Levy, Geiger followed his political remarks with references to the Jewish situation. The second of the letters struck a more responsive chord:

Berlin now appears to have embraced the course of progress in its last election. . . . This belongs at once to Prussian, to German, to European affairs. . . . This much is certain. When the times are once again aroused, Judaism will occupy an entirely different position both scientifically and practically than in the days when Reform efforts were first asserted in the years of the 30's and 40's. The tasks it has to perform will also be far nobler. Then too will the means and the strength be found.[18]

Frankfurt's hostility toward Prussia did not dissipate in the years following the occupation. In fact, the opposite is indicated by the results of the first Reichstag elections held in 1871 following the declaration of the German empire in Versailles. Carl Meyer Rothschild, who had represented Frankfurt's hopes for a dignified entry into the Prussian realm, was defeated by Leopold Sonnemann, editor of the *Frankfurter Zeitung* and leading spokesman of anti-Prussianism. Sonnemann ran on a platform calling for a democratic Germany in accordance with the vision of the National Assembly of 1848–1849 and opposing the absolutism and militarism that were now characteristic of Prussia.[19] Abraham Geiger could not make his peace with the provincialism that reigned in the city. Already in August 1866, he expressed his "homesickness" for Breslau and noted that since early July he and his family had isolated themselves. In 1870 Geiger left Frankfurt to become rabbi of the Jewish community of Berlin.[20]

In contrast to Geiger's virtually isolated position as supporter of Prussia, Samson Raphael Hirsch seems to have shared the concerns and anxieties of most Frankfurters for the future of their democratic traditions. Specifically, there is evidence that Hirsch was greatly troubled over the implications of the Prussian occupation for Frankfurt Jewry. To my knowledge, Hirsch did not state these views directly, but they are reflected in the major work which he was writing at that time—the volume of Exodus of his *The Pentateuch, Translated and Explained*, published in 1869.[21] The passages in question were written in relation to the biblical verses: "Now a new king arose over Egypt who did not know Joseph. And he said to his people: 'Look, the Israelite people are much too numerous for us.'" (Exodus 1:8–9)

In the Midrashic explanation of the verse, Rav and Samuel debated whether a new king had, in fact, arisen or the identical king of Joseph's time had reversed his policies and issued new decrees. Since the twelfth-century exegete Abraham Ibn Ezra, a consensus had grown at least among Jewish commentators that the new king did not stem from the reigning house but had overthrown one dynasty and established his own. Some commentators specified that the new king descended from a native Egyptian dynasty and succeeded in overthrowing an outside usurper of the throne. Hirsch's immediate predecessors in Orthodox interpretation glossed over the verse, adding nothing different to its understanding.[22]

In his commentary, Hirsch agreed with the consensus that the verse indicates the establishment of a new dynasty, but while other writers suggested that the descendants of a native house had expelled a foreign intruder, Hirsch maintained the opposite position. For Hirsch, the new king was the outside invader. To my knowledge, Hirsch's interpretation of the verse has no echo in earlier or even later Jewish exegesis:

Vayakom melekh Khadash al by no means designates an ordinary lawful change of dynasty. *Kum al* is always an overthrow by force. So it seems that the old dynasty was overthrown and Egypt fell under the power of an invading dynasty from outside, hence also *asher lo yadah et yosef*; to a fresh native dynasty Joseph would not be unknown. It is quite characteristic that the motive given for the whole subsequent enmity against the Jews is that the new king did not know about Joseph. The people did know of him and did not look askance at the Jewish province and at the Jewish people growing in it. They considered the Jews as benefactors and not as intruders, and did not feel their own security threatened by their growth.[23]

It was not the indigenous local population that was responsible for the new wave of anti-semitism. They, in fact, demonstrated a positive appreciation of the Jews living in Goshen. Rather, the conquerors invading from the outside and who "knew not the Jews" implanted the new policies. They did so in order to strengthen their own position.

This first act of anti-Semitism was engineered from above. It did not spring from the people. They were incited from above. Jew-hatred was a political measure which the new dynasty used to strengthen their own position of force and violence. There is little new under the sun and historical events at large are as old as history itself.[24]

Hirsch imposed the events of his day onto the story of the Egyptian enslavement of the Jewish people in Egypt. For Hirsch, the rise of the new king became the submission of the native regime to an outside conqueror. Responsibility for the growth of anti-semitism in Prussian-occupied Frankfurt was transferred both from the local population and from Frankfurt Jewry, who had in Hirsch's projection interacted with their neighbors with a "high standard of social behavior." There is no reason to assume that this interpretation of biblical anti-semitism was intended as a specific warning to Hirsch's congregation or to his readers, but the attitudes expressed reveal to his later audience the fear Frankfurt Jewry held for their security and freedom in the first years after Prussian occupation.

ORTHODOXY AND JEWISH UNIFICATION

The movement toward German unification was echoed by German Jewry in the strides taken toward the founding of a confederation of Jewish communities. Dresden lawyer Emil Lehmann proposed the idea of a council of communities in an 1869 essay, "Hear, O Israel!", a far-ranging work which amounted to a full agenda for German Jewry in the wake of complete political emancipation. Lehmann, who later served in the leadership ranks of the *Gemeindebund*, did not distinguish between religious and communal reforms. Among his proposals for religious reform were the abolition of circumcision and the encouragement of intermarriages between Jews and Christians.[25]

Lehmann's proposal for a confederation of communities won a quick response from the community board of Leipzig, which was already scheduled to host a synod of Reform rabbis and lay leaders in the summer of 1869. The Leipzig Board decided to convoke a separate meeting of community leaders to discuss matters not of a religious or theological nature. Abraham Geiger, then still rabbi of Frankfurt, urged that the two bodies be combined, but the host board insisted on distinguishing between the religious synod and the communal *Gemeindetag* in order to enable communities leaning toward Orthodox or traditional directions to participate in the forthcoming conference.[26]

After the successful conclusion of the conference in July 1869, the actual establishment of the *Gemeindebund* was delayed in order to gather a minimum of one hundred communities ready to affiliate. A further delay was caused by the Franco-Prussian War of 1870. With the conclusion of the war and the declaration of the German empire, the Jewish communities took stock of their new circumstances and now responded more readily to the idea of a confederation. The *Gemeindebund* was formally established in April 1872.[27]

Between 1869 and 1872, Moritz Kohner, chairman of the Leipzig community board and provisional chairman of the *Gemeindebund*, actively solicited the entry of Orthodox communities into the confederation. In explaining the organization to Orthodox leaders, Kohner insisted that it would take no interest in matters pertaining to religion.

First responses from Orthodox circles were sympathetic, though not totally supportive. Marcus Lehmann, rabbi of the IRG in Mainz and founding editor of the Orthodox *Israelit*, found it appropriate to publish a lengthy report of the *Gemeindebund's* activities.[28] In April 1871 Kohner visited Ezriel Hildesheimer, rabbi of Congregation Adass Jisroel in Berlin and rector of the new Orthodox rabbinical seminary. Hildesheimer published a report on his meeting with Kohner in both the *Israelit* and the *Juedische Presse.*

Should it turn out to be true, and I have after meeting with Herr Kohner not the least reason to doubt the matter, that the Gemeindebund places above all the unfortunate condition of world Jewish welfare . . . , then every true friend of humanity, every noble Jewish heart can only happily praise many times those, who succeeded in finding the right way.[29]

During their meeting, Hildesheimer explained to Kohner the nature of Orthodox concern over the proposed community confederation and emphasized Orthodox distrust of the *Gemeindebund* as a "central organ representing the interests of German Jewry." But, in fact, Hildesheimer was not fundamentally opposed to centralized Jewish organization and concluded his discussion with tentative approval.[30]

The two editors of the *Juedische Presse* picked up the discussion begun by Hildesheimer. Samuel Enoch expressed the most cautious of the positions, but other articles joined Hildesheimer's positive tendency. The second editor, J. Hollander, sided with the fictitious Hungarian layman who, in arguing with a German rabbi, declared:

You maintain that association with the Gemeindebund is unnatural. On this point, I cannot agree. All of us belong together to the province of Jewish humanity. If the specific life of the Orthodox party is not to become extinct, the religious differences must be constrained to religious questions. *As human beings, nothing separates us.*[31]

Shortly thereafter, the paper published still another series supporting Orthodox cooperation.[32] However, despite the apparent openness of Marcus Lehmann and Hildesheimer and his followers, the Orthodox, in practice, made no positive gestures toward the *Gemeindebund*; by 1872, even the sympathetic understanding expressed earlier had disappeared.

According to one report, the Orthodox were poorly represented at the founding meeting of the *Gemeindebund* in April

1872; according to another account, they were not present at all.[33] Hildesheimer had used the word "mistrust" to describe the Orthodox attitude toward the new organization and that notion would seem to summarize the reasons for Orthodox reluctance to participate in the opening session. Ismar Schorsch has delineated the factors contributing to that mistrust. Despite Kohner's insistence that the *Gemeindebund* would remain outside the religious sphere, the Orthodox could hardly overlook the organization's origin within the program of radical reform espoused by Emil Lehmann. Nor could they ignore the connection between the *Gemeindebund* and the synod of Reform leaders. Furthermore, the provisional leadership of the *Gemeindebund* was comprised of men openly identified with the Reform cause, including Emil Lehmann and Ludwig Philippson.[34] In practice the Orthodox mistrust was not misplaced.

However good the intentions of the *Gemeindebund*'s leadership may have been, they did not maintain their pledge to remain outside the sphere of religious matters. The founding constitution called for the *Gemeindebund* to take steps toward establishing institutions of higher learning "to cultivate Jewish *Wissenschaft* and to educate rabbis, preachers, teachers, and cantors respectively, with the appropriate participation of the Gemeindebund in the management of these institutions."[35] In 1871 a pamphlet was published under their auspices which denied belief in a personal Messiah.[36] Hildesheimer, an active leader in collecting support for the Jews of the land of Israel, demanded an explanation from Kohner for a pamphlet on that subject published by the *Gemeindebund*.[37] Between 1872 and 1875, the organization placed the quality and content of Jewish education in Germany high on its list of priorities. In 1872 it delegated responsibility to prepare a program for Jewish education to Emil Lehmann and invited other Reform leaders to serve as consultants. Among these were Philippson and Aron Horwitz, rector of the *Hochschule*, the new Reform rabbinical seminary in Berlin.[38] Clearly, the *Gemeindebund* had either abandoned its self-imposed limitations to avoid religious matters or never properly understood the boundaries of activity that those limitations implied. Orthodox doubts were being confirmed.[39]

Furthermore, at its founding meeting in April 1872, the *Ge-*

meindebund acted on several important matters in a way perceived by the Orthodox as counter to their own interests. Marcus
Lehmann was especially incensed at the vote of approval extended to Bismarck for his struggle against the Catholic Church.
The conference in its letter of support to Bismarck declared that
the Church, after all, had been responsible in history for much
Jewish suffering. Lehmann, in turn, raged at the inappropriate-
ness of the *Gemeindebund*'s action and at the lack of concern for
Jews living in Catholic states.[40]

The *Gemeindebund* also passed a resolution by Ludwig Philippson opposing legislation granting Jews the right to secede
from the Jewish communities. This brought the confederation
into direct conflict with Orthodox aspirations to pass precisely
such a law. Lehmann drew his conclusion—"no Orthodox community may affiliate with the *Gemeindebund* and those few who
have already done so must secede."[41]

In contrast to Lehmann and Hildesheimer, Samson Raphael
Hirsch had not vacillated in his rejection of Orthodox participation in a national community organization. In 1871 Isaac Hirsch,
substituting for his ill father, wrote on the *Gemeindebund* question
in the pages of the *Israelit*. The analysis echoed his father's pen.
It was not the Orthodox who had sought the strife that was
tearing communities apart. The Orthodox had not caused the
separation between the parties, and the Orthodox could not now
be expected to take any stride in the direction of the Reformers.

Your position is out of reach for us. In order to participate with you,
we should first have to burden our consciences with desertion and
treason toward the Most Holy. Therefore, you can easily come toward
us and we shall welcome you with warm brotherly affection,—but we
can take no steps toward you.

What of Kohner's continued insistence that the *Gemeindebund*
would not penetrate into religious matters? Hirsch responded
directly and pointedly that the declaration that the *Gemeindebund*
would have nothing to do with religion could come only from
those "who do not understand Jewish religious law."[42]

The Orthodox rejected the Reform bid for cooperation in the
Gemeindebund but why were the founding leaders of the *Ge-*

meindebund, who were all identified with the Reform movement, so interested in Orthodox cooperation? Obviously, those who favored communal cooperation must have been prepared to relax the level of religious strife. For Ludwig Philippson, we can go further: Philippson was fully prepared to call a truce ending the forty-year strife between the parties. His views on the future of politics within the Jewish community were the same as his perspective on the politics of his times.

The important events then unfolding in German history precipitated a series of articles by Philippson in 1870 dealing with contemporary political conditions in Europe. Philippson's analysis was hardly complimentary to European leadership which, he thought, lacked the strength and ability to effect significant changes. Party strife had dominated European history since the French Revolution, but, looking back, Philippson concluded that no party had proven capable of establishing anything permanent. No party had represented entire nations, or, in fact, anything more than a sizable minority. A continuation of a nearly century-long struggle would bring neither peace nor stability to Europe. Nor would further party strife accomplish meaningful results. "It becomes more and more clear that political and social circumstances cannot be changed by a single party, especially a radical party."[43]

Philippson wrote his analysis in the context of the political atmosphere outside Jewish life, but his conclusions applied no less, and perhaps even primarily, to the political dynamics within the Jewish community. German Jewry had also set out to safeguard the existence of the Jewish community in a postemancipation age by uniting the fragmented forces of German Jewry. Ludwig Philippson placed the preservation of the communities at the top of his priorities.[44]

An increasing number of Jews were abandoning any notion of religious life whatsoever, and this crisis drove Reformers like Philippson and Kohner to envision an alliance with the Orthodox as the natural step to continue the fight for Jewish survival. In fact, Philippson responded far more positively to the formation of the *Gemeindebund* than to the renewal of Reform conferences in the form of synods. "For nearly forty years our efforts have been directed to awakening a sense of solidarity, which the Jews lost as a result of the splintering and isolation of their communities."[45]

In sociological terms, Reform Judaism was becoming a denomination. The readiness of moderate Reformers to accept a bipartisan status quo represented a change in the Reform outlook that formerly had anticipated the complete disappearance of Orthodoxy in Germany. The change in perspective was an explicit comment on the Orthodox success in strengthening its position.

Philippson's analysis of the general political scene and its implications for the Jewish community was, as usual, essentially correct. The two parties were almost ready for cooperation, but Jewish communal politics lagged behind the general scene by one phase. When modernity in Germany took the form of a new state, it was introduced not by the liberals, but by the conservative Bismarck. Creation of the modern state required coalitions; so did the postemancipation Jewish community in order to survive the pressures of the new milieu. Bismarck's alliance with the liberals only strengthened the notion that this was a time for modern conservatism, but the Orthodox leadership did not yet perceive their position as sufficiently strong to relax the conflict and work toward unity. They enjoyed an ace in hand to strengthen their position further, and they chose to use it. This was not Hirsch's objective in pursuing the fight for the right of separation, but it was, as it turned out, the position of most of his colleagues in the Orthodox party.

TOWARD A LAW OF SEPARATION

The Prussian law of 1876 enabling Jews to secede from membership in their local Jewish communities has usually been identified as an offspring of the *Kulturkampf* legislation of 1873. Undoubtedly, passage of the law was influenced by the need to extend to Jewish citizens the right of separation offered to Christians in 1873, but this should not be confused as historical cause for the wave of activity by the leadership of Orthodox Jewry in pursuit of that right. The board of the IRG in Frankfurt had been petitioning for a form of separation since 1854, and in 1864 the Jewish community of Hamburg reconstituted itself with a complete separation of religious and social functions. Meanwhile, even in Prussia, the drive for the right to separate did not wait for Bismarck's *Kulturkampf*.

The first legal decision in Germany upholding the rights of Jews to sever ties with the local Jewish community was issued in the southern state of Baden in 1869, following a long dispute in Karlsruhe between Reformers and Orthodox over the familiar issues of a new synagogue building and liturgical reforms. When, in 1868, a Reform-inclined majority voted to introduce an organ into the Sabbath services and to contract a loan of up to 60,000 gulden for a new synagogue, twenty-five Orthodox members announced that they were breaking away from the community and would, henceforth, refuse to contribute to its expenses. In December 1869 the Baden government upheld the legality of their withdrawal and even agreed that the secessionists would no longer be affiliated with the Oberrat, the central organ of Baden Jewry.[46]

The Oberrat issued a public condemnation of the division within the community caused by the secession. They argued that never before had the unity of the Jewish community been divided in the name of Orthodoxy: "Our history knows no other example of Jews in the name of Orthodoxy publicly and solemnly dissociating themselves from the Judaism and Jewry of an entire land."[47] Samson Raphael Hirsch responded to the Oberrat in a pamphlet published in 1870, in which he attacked the assumption that Jews and Judaism were still united. "Religious unity has not existed for some time and wherever it is missing, the enforced unity of the community . . . is nothing but an empty, meaningless form."[48] While few joined the original twenty-five in taking advantage of their new legal freedom,[49] the Oberrat's argument that such an event was new in Jewish history clearly indicated that the community authorities had been confused and placed on the defensive by the Orthodox stroke. The threat of separation was no longer a theory, and the leaders of Prussia's Jewish communities began to weigh its dangers; while the Orthodox spokesmen actively considered its potential value.

The year 1870 saw the rise of two conflicting tendencies within German Jewry. As a strong and unified Prussia went off to war with France, German Jewry too began to seek its own unity and strength, and enthusiasm for the proposed *Gemeindebund* grew in the aftermath of the war.[50] But the precedent of the Baden decision and the immediate responses among Prussia's own Orthodox to attain similar rights weighed heavily as a counterforce against Jewish unity.

Both tendencies, the one toward unity, the second toward renewed strife, were reflected in Ludwig Philippson's leading articles of 1870. Philippson placed full responsibility for the divisions within the community upon the Orthodox. In the 1840s, they had refused to attend the rabbinical conferences, and now in the 1870s the New Orthodox, as Philippson referred to them, represented the major current threat to communal unity. Armed with secular education and fluency in German, these new-style rabbis used the most despicable and, in Philippson's word, "irreligious" techniques to espouse their cause.[51] Reform leadership apparently was finding the new-style Orthodox more difficult to cope with and to challenge than the old, but Philippson's hostility represented more than the wounds of struggle. Already in 1870, the Orthodox were busy agitating for the rights of separation, and Philippson feared that their success would prove the undoing of the Jewish community.

In his discussion on the *Gemeindebund*, Philippson emphasized the need for unity and the threat posed by the separatist question.[52] The continued strife and the growth of religious indifference had already weakened the Jewish community. The legal right for both groups, the dissenters and the indifferent, to withhold financial support would signal the community's demise despite the many nonreligious functions it fulfilled. Actually, Philippson thought that the establishment of the principle of separation of church and state in modern Germany was inevitable. Ironically, he even thought that a law of separation would be passed first for the Jews and only later for Christians—"perhaps first for the Jewish communities for which the legislators and rulers of the state bear the least concern." Philippson, in fact, declared that he himself was not opposed to a voluntary system of religious affiliation. Previous experience elsewhere had already shown that religious attachments were strong enough to overcome the difficulties that would be caused. The communities, however, must first prepare themselves, and this could not be accomplished by each community individually, but rather was a task for the *Gemeindebund*.[53]

Meanwhile, Samuel Enoch, close associate of Jacob Ettlinger in Altona and formerly the editor of the *Treuer Zionswaechter*, now rabbi in Fulda and co-editor of the *Juedische Presse*, maintained the same cautious path that had characterized the Altona approach in the 1840s. Enoch doubted the value of separation for the Orthodox and, writing in the *Juedische Presse*, openly expressed his doubts that the Orthodox minority would have the moral and, presumably, the financial resources to carry it through. Yet he concluded that the very threat of separatism would serve as a powerful weapon for the Orthodox to employ.[54]

Following the lifting of all Jewish disabilities in 1869 and the establishment of the empire at Versailles in 1871, all parties within the Jewish community concurred that a serious revision of the 1847 Prussian Jewry law was necessary. That law was still the most recent comprehensive statement on the legal status of the Jews and the Jewish community in Prussia. During the years 1871–1872, Orthodox activity increased on behalf of totally revoking the law, which included the stipulation of compulsory membership in the local community. In many respects, the 1847 law had been superseded, especially in recent years, by the lifting of political and occupational restrictions. The vast expansion of Prussian territory also necessitated a new comprehensive statement, since in the meantime Jews were still subject to the different laws of the various states annexed by Prussia. The situation was comparable to that prior to 1847, when Prussia had maintained numerous and contradictory Jewry laws on its books.[55]

While Philippson and other Reform spokesmen called for modifications in the 1847 law, Orthodox writers urged revocation of a law so steeped in its preemancipation origins. Marcus Lehmann attacked the law *in toto* for what he called its medieval content. In this way, he associated the remaining requirement of community membership with various outdated limitations that had since been removed.[56] Another writer, in a series of articles appearing in the *Juedische Presse*, maintained that in the aftermath of emancipation and the establishment of the modern state, there should be no special Jewry laws at all:

The state must advocate equal rights for all and dissociate itself from any particular faith or confession. In other words, all citizens in the modern state should be considered and judged without regard to their religious views, as long as they do not offend those principles which comprise the foundation of the modern state.[57]

In 1871 Philippson reported in his paper that legislative activity had already begun and that a new Jewry law was expected by the following year. Hoping to influence the nature of the new law, Philippson sent his proposals to the boards of the Jewish communities in the old Prussian provinces. Except for striking those clauses in the 1847 law related to political and occupational restrictions that had since been annulled, Philippson proposed few changes in the preemancipation legislation. He sought to continue compulsory membership in the local Jewish community and to maintain special facilities for the Jewish poor and sick at the community's expense.[58]

A critique of the Philippson proposals appearing in the *Juedische Presse* took exception to a number of key points in addition to the question of compulsory membership. The 1847 law had discriminated against the Jews of Posen and, in fact, preserved a totally separate compilation of ordinances. Philippson had merely glossed over the existing distinctions between Posen and the rest of Prussia, but his critic objected that the continuation of this discrimination in the contemporary circumstances was "neither understandable nor justified." Posen was still one of Germany's strongest bastions of Orthodoxy.

The question of whether Jews required or desired special social and welfare agencies other than those provided by the government for other citizens necessarily arose in the last stages of the emancipation discussion. Philippson called for maintaining separate Jewish institutions. The Orthodox correspondent disagreed only in principle:

As long as the local general community demands the same contributions from us as from other religions for the civil care of the poor and the sick, they have not the least right to also demand of us to establish our own special institutions.[59]

In fact, the Orthodox were certainly not less committed to maintaining separate Jewish institutions in accordance with religious law. They objected to discrimination by the civil law more forcefully than the Reformers because they also objected to control of these legally compulsory institutions by a Reform community.

For all its shortcomings, especially in the aftermath of emancipation, the 1847 law included a clause that in theory could have sufficed for the Orthodox claims for religious independence. Section 53 of the 1847 law provided that in the event of a dispute over religious matters within a local Jewish community, the minister for spiritual affairs and of the interior would appoint a commission to attempt to settle the dispute. However, this procedure was never employed. A ministerial memorandum of 1853 that reinstated the 1847 law after the revolutionary interlude had, in fact, revoked the above clause. In addition, by 1873, both the Reform Makower and the Orthodox Hirsch agreed that such direct intervention in the internal matters of the community would no longer be desirable.[60]

In January 1873, Adelbert Falk, minister of education and public worship, placed before the legislature four laws generally intended to define the limits of the Catholic Church's jurisdiction and to weaken the influence of its hierarchy on German Catholics.[61] The fourth of these "May Laws," passed by the legislature in that month of 1873, facilitated the path for Christians of all denominations to secede from their churches. The wording of the law's section 8 extended the right of separation to the members of all religious bodies recognized as legal corporations and theoretically, therefore, to members of the Jewish communities as well. However, a memorandum prepared by the ministry explained that the law was intended only to allow Jews to withdraw from Judaism altogether and not from local Jewish communities without surrendering one's Jewish identity. The memorandum explained that resignation from a Jewish community would be equivalent to a Christian resigning from his parish without seceding from membership in his church, and this, the memorandum stated, was not allowed by the new law.[62]

From this point on, once the government had announced its secession law of 1873, the Orthodox campaign for the legal right to separate from Reform-dominated communities was recast as an attempt to extend the provisions of the 1873 law. Nevertheless, as we have seen, 1873 in no way marks the beginning of Orthodox efforts on behalf of such legislation. The law that was eventually passed in 1876 should be seen as an additional act of emancipation legislation and not as a foster child of the *Kulturkampf*.

Soon after the government proposed its law, an amendment to grant Jews the right of secession from their communities was defeated by the Chamber of Deputies. A number of speakers in opposition to the amendment claimed that the Jewish case was both unique and complicated and that a totally separate law was required. On the other side, Moritz Warburg, a Jewish member of the chamber, protested the continual reliance on special legislation for Jews: "Today, Jews sit in all of the legislative bodies of Germany, but within civil society, a great deal still remains to be desired, primarily because of such special laws."[63] The government's representative responded that the present law did entitle a Jew to leave his community by leaving Judaism, but "rightly and legally, Orthodox and Reform Jews are members of one and the same religious society." He concluded that Jewish religious communities must continue to be governed by special legislation, and announced that the regime was then working on a new law.[64]

Edouard Lasker, the leading spokesman for the Orthodox cause, proposed that the chamber pass a resolution calling upon the government to introduce new legislation as soon as possible that would grant Jews throughout the monarchy the right to secede from their local Jewish communities out of religious motivations. The resolution also called for the revocation of any remaining restrictions on Jews in different parts of the country. Lasker admitted that an extension of the separatist law to include the Jewish communities could harm the ability of the communities to function, but failure to do so would be an infringement of the individual rights of the Jews. Furthermore, the harm to be caused to the Jewish community was no different than the potential weakening of the Lutheran and Catholic communities already included in the existing legislation.[65]

The chamber passed Lasker's motion, and the government spokesman assured the representatives that new Jewish legislation would be proposed at the next session of the legislature. Both parties now came forth with proposals for the nature of the new legislation.

The Orthodox position was put forth in an anonymous pamphlet addressed to the legislative chamber. The pamphlet is generally attributed to Hirsch and seems to represent a unified Orthodox stance on the importance of the right of secession from the Jewish community.[66] Hirsch congratulated the Prussian government on passage of the general separatist law, for it granted most citizens freedom of conscience in religious matters. Only Jews were not entitled to benefit from the new legislation. He maintained that Christian legislators did not appreciate the great differences that separated the two parties, while they were also concerned over the continued ability of the communities to fulfill their financial obligations. According to Hirsch, the lack of denominations within Judaism led Christians to assume that Jews could easily be unified within the same community, but, in fact, the differences within the Jewish religious parties were greater than within any Christian church.

Within none of the Christian churches is there a deeper cleavage than between Reform Judaism . . . and Orthodox, traditional Judaism. Indeed, the differences between old Catholics and new Catholics, as well as between the Evangelicals and the Reform churches, do not match the differences in the Judaism of today.[67]

Despite the great differences within the community, Hirsch assured the legislature that no mass movement of resignations would follow passage of the proposed law. In the smaller communities the bonds between the members were too strong and the mutual dependence of one Jew upon the other too great to allow a significant division of the community. Only in the larger cities would a substantial number of resignations be forthcoming, for there a sufficient number of Jews who shared common religious views would be able to organize their own independent communities. Yet, Hirsch, like Lasker, questioned why the danger of dissolving of the Jewish communities was any greater than the threat posed to other religious communities.[68]

The Reform camp also took advantage of the government's delay in submitting new legislation, and two of its spokesmen issued their own proposals. Hermann Makower, Berlin lawyer and president of its Jewish community, issued a treatise in 1873 which provided a comprehensive examination of the current laws regulating Jewish communal life in old Prussia and in the newly acquired provinces and proposed new legislation to unify the various regulations. A similar proposal was also put forth by Ludwig Philippson.[69]

Both Makower and Philippson took the position that Jews who would prefer a different type of service than that conducted by the general community should receive a portion of their community taxes as an allocation for the expenses involved in maintaining a separate synagogue.[70] Unlike the Breslau system, this concession took cognizance of separate Orthodox services not under communal sponsorship. Nevertheless, from the Orthodox perspective, some of the basic problems involved in remaining part of a Reform community with a Reform rabbi remained unresolved.

The two Hirsches, father and son, responded to the proposals. S. R. Hirsch answered Makower's contention that a voluntary community structure would prove ineffective. Hirsch maintained that Jewish communities had existed long before states had decided to intervene in religious matters. These communities had provided all of the services provided by the contemporary community, but had been organized and maintained voluntarily by the local Jewish population. Hirsch pointed to the IRG of Frankfurt itself as proof of what could be achieved by a voluntary religious community. In 1873 the congregation boasted of 325 members, a synagogue with 1,000 places, two schoolhouses used to instruct 408 pupils, and a special fund for orphans, widows, and poorer students. No government coercion had been necessary for these achievements, only a community of committed and like-minded individuals.[71]

One of the factors that characterized Hirsch's approach to separation can be detected in these essays. While the other Orthodox proponents of separatist legislation admitted that they were striving for equal rights for a weakened minority, the Hirsches made it clear that in a certain sense Orthodoxy was now combatting the Reformers from a position of strength. The IRG of Frankfurt served as positive proof that Orthodoxy would survive the challenge of religious freedom. In fact, it could prosper in such a setting. But the great concern expressed by the Reform leadership over the end of compulsory membership in the Jewish community revealed for Isaac Hirsch the naked truth of Reform weakness in the present circumstances.

This then is admittedly the result of forty years of Reform activity of Herr Philippson and his associates! . . . The strength claimed by Reform has proven itself so weak that the communities can be maintained only through coercion.[72]

The government hesitated in putting forth new Jewish legislation, probably out of concern for the future of the Jewish community if compulsory membership were eliminated, and because the active opposition of the *Gemeindebund* also represented too important a voice to be ignored.[73] The government may also have hesitated because the Orthodox request for secession rights represented a potential privilege for Jews not available to their Christian fellow citizens.

Despite the delay, compulsory membership in a religious community with which one did not identify could not be enforced once the Jew had been granted full, political emancipation. The law of secession from the Jewish communities was passed by the government in May 1876 and approved by the emperor in July. Passage of the law represented for many of the Orthodox a victory for minority rights.[74] For Hirsch, it provided Orthodox Jewry with the opportunity to assert their independence and even to demonstrate their strength in a free and open society.

A SPLIT OVER SEPARATION

In 1873 Samson Raphael Hirsch predicted that passage of a law of separation would not result in a significant number of withdrawals from the established Jewish communities. He was proven correct. In Karlsruhe, few joined the original twenty-five Orthodox Jews who received government sanction in 1869 to resign from their local and central community organizations.[75] The results in Prussia were no different. In Graudenz, twelve members resigned their community membership; in Heilbronn, one; in Perleberg, two; in Stargardt, one; in Naugard, four, one of whom rejoined shortly thereafter; in Gruenberg, one.[76] Curiously, in Stendal, Brandenburg, a community with forty-one members in 1871, all but two seceded and then reconstituted themselves into a new community.[77] Even in communities where autonomous Orthodox congregations already existed, secession did not necessarily follow. In Wiesbaden, forty-one members did withdraw,[78] but in Koenigsberg, no significant secession, if any at all, took place until 1899. According to the *Israelit*, the members of the independent Orthodox congregation in Koenigsberg were demonstrating, by remaining within the community, that the establishment of a separate synagogue had been a matter of principle and not of financial convenience.[79] Even in Berlin, there was virtually no response to the law. One report indicated the secession of five members.[80]

However, the law did have other consequences. In Cassel, the threat of secession seems to have stayed, at least temporarily, the attempt at reform.[81] In two communities, Graudenz and Crefeld, debates broke out over whether or not the existing community institutions and the current rabbis were Orthodox.[82] A Prussian study of the "practical effects" of the legislation concluded in 1883 that few had utilized the provisions of the law and that a majority of these had not seceded for religious reasons, but in order to be exempted from community taxes. The report also warned that in some cases wealthy members had attempted to influence community policies by threatening their resignations.[83]

The vast majority of Orthodox Jews in Germany were fully committed to the solidarity of the Jewish community. Their dilemma in the 1840s had been to find a way to function religiously once the local community had engaged a rabbi in whom the Orthodox did not place their religious trust, for this led to doubts about the acceptability of the institutions and rituals under his supervision. But the network of autonomous Orthodox congregations, inspired by the IRG of Frankfurt and sanctioned by sympathetic governments in the 1850s and 1860s, had solved these problems in a number of larger communities. Meanwhile, the communities of Breslau and Hamburg had already reached an accord fully recognizing the rights of both parties. The separatist law was now proving valuable to the Orthodox in other communities to encourage concessions from the ruling Reformers, but once these concessions were granted, few of the Orthodox made separatism into an independent principle. Samson Raphael Hirsch did, and the consequence was a bitter dispute over whether an Orthodox Jew was obligated by religious law to resign his membership in a Jewish community dominated by Reformers. The controversy divided the Orthodox Jews of Frankfurt and caused strife among the Orthodox rabbinate of Germany as well.

On September 17, 1876, Hirsch celebrated his twenty-fifth anniversary as rabbi of the IRG of Frankfurt. The festivities began the evening before when the community's school pupils marched in a torchlight procession in front of Hirsch's house to the accompaniment of military music (sic!). The following day, Hirsch was honored in his apartment by leaders of the congregation and visiting rabbis.[84] Later, in the synagogue, Hirsch used the occasion to propose that IRG members take advantage of the two-month-old law to secede from the Frankfurt Jewish community.[85] By September 26, Hirsch himself had resigned his membership, and several members of the IRG board decided to follow suit. A newspaper report of October 6 reported that eleven members had seceded, including four board members.[86] During the holiday season, Hirsch urged the entire membership of the IRG to do the same.[87] A dissenting party opposed to separation was formed immediately. Saemy Japhet described the differences of opinion:

By far the great majority of the members of the Society never intended to separate from their old community, and now their rabbi himself had done it without making the slightest effort to obtain the recognition of their just demands, without any struggle for their rights.[88]

Japhet's description echoes the view taken by most Orthodox leaders both before and after passage of the law that separation should be used as a vehicle for the purpose of yielding concessions from the community.

On October 15, 1876, a general meeting of the IRG membership was called, as requested by the opponents of separation, in the hope that negotiations could be conducted with the community.[89] The party opposed to secession was led by two of the founders of the IRG, Rabbi Moses Mainz and his son Michael. The younger Mainz argued at the general meeting that an Orthodox withdrawal would leave the numerous communal institutions totally in the hands of the Reformers. At this juncture, the strength of the secessionist party was fixed between 70 and 80 of the IRG's 360 members, but most secessionists favored the proposal of Emanuel Schwarzschild to maintain an association with certain of the community institutions. Hirsch, however, was opposed to even these ties.[90]

Schwarzschild submitted his proposals in a letter to the community board. Schwarzschild, together with Theodore Homburger and on behalf of the board of the IRG, wrote of their intention to resign their memberships in the community, but offered to continue to support "humanitarian institutions," specifically the hospital and cemetery, in return for the continued right to use those facilities.[91] The board's response on October 25 defended the community's past policies toward the Orthodox. The community provided for an independent Orthodox service and had recently decided to build larger facilities for the service as well as a ritual bath. Both the hospital and the cemetery were being maintained in an Orthodox manner. However, if these conditions were proving insufficient for the Orthodox to remain members because of the financial support provided for a Reform synagogue and school, the board was now prepared to deduct the proportion used for these expenses from the taxes of the IRG members.

The two sides were negotiating with different principles and objectives. The secessionist party of the IRG was not interested in monetary savings, and one report even indicates that they were prepared to contribute voluntarily the full equivalent of their former tax load as members. The Orthodox were attempt-

ing to demonstrate that community secessions were not finan-
cially motivated but a matter of principle against membership
in a Reform community. The board, however, responded with
a discounted tax for IRG members, placing its value on continued
membership and communal unity. In a letter of November 6
Schwarzschild and Homburger tried to explain the conceptual
difference between the sides. While opposed to any religious
association, they affirmed their desire to maintain a common
bond. "We do, however, believe that an ideal bond should continue to bind us with our co-religionists." In practice, they were
referring to the question of accessibility to the hospital and cemetery. The Orthodox petitioners explained that they surely did
not lack the resources to provide for their own cemetery, but
that they did not want to see the separation extended through
death and that exclusion from the community cemetery would
greatly deepen the separation between the living.

In November 1876 Hirsch published a treatise, *Der Austritt aus
der Gemeinde*, elaborating on the reasons behind his demand that
members of the IRG resign from membership in the Frankfurt
Jewish community.[92] Hirsch argued that passage of the Law of
Secession had transformed the Jewish community into a voluntary institution and that under these circumstances, an Orthodox Jew could not remain associated with a Reform Jewish
community. To the proposal to divorce religious matters from
the community's jurisdiction, Hirsch responded that any community must be either political or religious in nature, and that
in consequence of the emancipation of the Jews, no political
Jewish community could exist. In all matters, Jews now dealt
directly with the relevant civil authorities. "Whoever wishes the
reestablishment of Jewish political communities, seeks to return
the Jews to the old darkness."

The possibility that multiple resignations might lead to the
collapse of the community only strengthened Hirsch's convictions. If such a consequence were truly realistic, then his continued membership provided a significant support for a
community with whose principles he could not agree. Hirsch,
of course, did not miss the opportunity to ridicule the Reformers
for their dependence upon compulsory membership.[93]

Hirsch's continued urging through his writings and sermons

convinced few more of the necessity to secede from the community. By the year's end, between 70 and 80 of the IRG's approximately 350 members had resigned from the community.[94]

Meanwhile, the movement led by Rabbi Moses Mainz and his son Michael to negotiate an agreement with the community that would exempt Orthodox Jews from contributing toward the Reform synagogue and school was beginning to make progress. By the end of 1876, the board announced some further, but minor, concessions. Orthodox members could be exempted from expenses for the synagogue and school. In return, those choosing this option were denied voting rights in the community. However, the Orthodox were granted a single representative on the boards of the hospital and cemetery and were guaranteed by the board that these institutions would continue to be maintained in a manner religiously acceptable to that party.[95]

In mid-January, seventy IRG members agreed to the community proposal.[96] Hirsch considered this move as a major defeat, and it was against the party involved, led by the Mainzes, that Hirsch now focused his attacks. In fact, this party was far closer to Hirsch's position than the majority of the IRG's membership, for they had agreed to remain within the community only under certain conditions. Of approximately 360 IRG members, about 75 had seceded, 70 accepted the compromise, but about 200 chose to remain as they had always been—full paying members of both communities.[97]

A Frankfurt correspondent for the *Allgemeine Zeitung des Judenthums* analyzed the motivations behind the majority of IRG members who were prepared to continue paying double taxation when a significant reduction was easily available through the new compromise.[98] One group could not sign because they sent their children to the community school, while a second group attended one of the community-sponsored Orthodox services. The writer explained that some members were afraid to sign the agreement because of Hirsch. If this indeed was the case, then it clearly demonstrates the paradox that had developed, for by not accepting the compromise, they were actually providing direct support for Reform religious institutions. A final group was simply not opposed to retaining their community membership. Burial rights in the cemetery were also an important deterrent

against outright secession from the community. A member of
the IRG could retain those rights either by continuing his double
membership or by subscribing to the compromise, but not by
seceding from the community.

The question of the right to burial in the community cemetery
played a significant role in the controversy over secession in
Frankfurt and in a number of other communities. Having opposed passage of the Law of Secession, several community boards
felt free to punish the secessionists by revoking their burial rights
in their respective community cemeteries. In some communities,
boards even barred nonmembers from visiting the graves of their
relations. The Prussian authorities intervened and ordered that
wherever cemeteries were associated with a specific religion or
denomination, so that a Jew could not be buried elsewhere, the
community was obligated to accept the deceased for burial.[99] In
Frankfurt, there were no reports of such cruel provocation by
the community, but the response to Schwarzschild's proposals
indicates that the Frankfurt community would not permanently
agree to burial rights for nonmembers. In January 1877 the IRG
decided to purchase its own cemetery plot, adjacent to that of
the community.[100]

The IRG was, broadly speaking, now divided into three parties: less than one-fourth had agreed to the concessions offered
by the community, and more than one-half remained full members of both the IRG and of the community. Of those who seceded
from the community, only seven descended from native Frankfurt families; the remainder had migrated to Frankfurt from
smaller towns and villages in Germany. The founding membership of the IRG had consisted of approximately one hundred
families, many of whom were scions of Frankfurt's oldest families. Virtually none of the contemporary members stemming
from these families was willing to break the historic connection
with the community institutions. Obviously, the community
cemetery played a central role, as it contained the graves of close
relatives as well as of illustrious community notables. The cemetery then in use had been opened in 1828, and secession for a
native Frankfurter would have meant that he could not be buried
with parents or perhaps even with his spouse.[101]

Some writers have attempted further sociological analysis of the parties by contrasting the secessionists and their opponents as rural migrants and urbanites. This categorization is based on an incorrect statistical assumption. It is true that some 90 percent of those who seceded were non-Frankfurters, but probably no more than 25 to 30 percent of those IRG members that were not natives actually joined the ranks of the secessionists. If IRG membership included at least 250 families of newcomers and at most 80 of these seceded, then even among the non-Frankfurters, only 30 percent seceded.[102]

Any other sociological significance to the predominance of newcomers among the secessionists can be still further diluted. Almost half of those who seceded from the community can be unified into a category including Hirsch, his five sons, teachers and other employees of the IRG, and individuals whose businesses were integrally connected to the IRG, such as bakers, butchers, and grocers serving the congregation and subject to Hirsch's supervision.[103] Once this group is removed from consideration, there is no basis for drawing inferences on the character of the rural Jew and his apparent willingness to join the secessionists.

Hirsch's struggle to convince his congregants continued, while the failure of IRG members to withdraw from the community was proving an embarrassment. Already early in the dispute, the Wiesbaden Orthodox congregation congratulated itself for its swift action implementing the right of secession, while others hesitated. Special reference was made to the "father of Israelitische Religionsgesellschaften," where steps were being taken only "slowly and with difficulty." In early December, Lehmann published a special plea to the IRG membership to follow the dictates of its rabbi, thus rendering him the honor and gratitude to which he was entitled.[104] Later on in the controversy, Ludwig Philippson and his correspondents from Frankfurt, who had opposed the separatist law, took advantage of the opportunity to satirize Hirsch's position as a leading proponent of the law who now could not convince his own flock to follow.[105] According to several accounts, Hirsch was becoming increasingly isolated and bitter. His sermons focused on both the issue of secession and the necessity to obey his own rabbinical authority.[106]

Sometime in late February or early March, the board of the community extended significant new concessions to the Orthodox, not only in order to discourage secession, but also to end the necessity for Orthodox newcomers to Frankfurt to affiliate with the IRG at all. The board now offered to establish and maintain separate Orthodox institutions within the community. Also the hospital and cemetery would be religiously supervised by an Orthodox rabbi. In short, the new concessions integrated Orthodoxy back into the community framework.[107]

Hirsch's attacks continued to bear down on the party that had negotiated all along with the community and that had now attained such meaningful results. Negotiations with the community had now caused a serious threat both to Hirsch and to the IRG as a whole. The insistence of the party led by the Mainzes to negotiate with the community despite Hirsch's opposition constituted a fundamental affront to Hirsch. Rabbi Moses Mainz was a respected Talmudic scholar, and his challenge to Hirsch represented more than noncompliance with Hirsch's demands for secession. The requests from Hirsch's opponents that he prove his conclusions from rabbinical sources indicated a challenge to Hirsch's proficiency in texts or, more fundamentally, a challenge to Hirsch's rabbinical authority.[108]

The latest agreement with the community also threatened the future of the IRG as a whole. The community had undertaken to duplicate the religious facilities already offered, and the IRG now found itself with a competitor for Orthodox members. Hirsch dealt with the dangers to the future of Frankfurt Orthodoxy in his subsequent polemics. In sum, the active opposition of that party that, like Hirsch, refused to accept the status quo but differed with Hirsch on the desirability of a resolution within the community, constituted a far greater threat to both Hirsch and the congregation than the passive majority that quietly provided the Reformers with full, financial support.

The dynamics of the controversy gave Hirsch little opportunity for a compromise with his opponents, nor was Hirsch interested in granting concessions on this issue. Indeed, compromise would have been difficult. Orthodoxy had leaned heavily on Hirsch as its spokesman in the legislative battle for the new law, and it is not difficult to understand Hirsch's early refusal to negotiate with the community. Even Hildesheimer, who did little publicly to support Hirsch in the subsequent controversy, also did nothing to compromise his own earlier arguments on behalf of the bill.[109]

It is sometimes difficult for spokesmen to perceive the possibility of compromise, but in this case, the force of Hirsch's arguments had derived from a clear perception of his own role. Separatism represented for Hirsch the opportunity for the Orthodox to withdraw from the total community and to bind together the true adherents of traditional Judaism, but the accepted picture of the controversy, portraying Hirsch as a zealot on the offensive, ignores the role played by those on the other side, who fanned the flames of the dispute no less.[110] In fact, Hirsch was very much on the *defensive* in the controversy.

Hirsch's opponents were striking hard at him. The reluctance of the community toward secession had left him vulnerable, and the opposition went for broke. It is not enough to describe Hirsch as a fanatic insisting on what looks ostensibly as fulfillment of an abstract principle. Hirsch *was* a fanatic when it came to secession, but he was also a man under siege. Unlike the majority of the IRG membership, his opponents did not merely ignore his calls to secede from the community. Rather, they set out to undercut his position, and indeed they threw Hirsch on the defensive. The result of their continued negotiations was an opportunity for Frankfurt Orthodoxy to break its dependence on the IRG and, therefore, on Hirsch's leadership. It was in this objective that they soon found the influential support of the Wuerzburger Rav.

Hirsch's supporters had attempted to enhance their position in the strife by inviting the opinion of one of Germany's leading Talmudic scholars, Seligmann Baer Bamberger of Wuerzburg. Their action in bringing an outsider into an internal conflict can be understood only when we realize that they were responding to a challenge that was directed against Hirsch's capability as a judge of Jewish law. His followers sought to ascertain the views of an unimpeachable Talmudic scholar with the expectation that Hirsch's interpretation of religious law and, therefore, his ability to exercise rabbinic authority would be confirmed.

Bamberger first became involved in the Frankfurt dispute when he received a letter from several members of the IRG requesting his views on the acceptability of retaining membership in the local community. The request came in late January. By that time, the board had already issued its Supplementary Regulations, with financial concessions to the Orthodox, but had not yet reached the agreement to provide Orthodox facilities at the community's expense. On February 1 Bamberger responded to the query in complete agreement with Hirsch's position.

I have carefully examined the so-called Supplementary Regulations and found that nothing has changed the obligation of an Orthodox Jew to resign from a Reform community, just as has been expressed by your worthy Rabbi Hirsch.[111]

Members of Hirsch's party sought further support from Bamberger, and two of Hirsch's supporters called upon him in Wuerzburg, urging him to come to Frankfurt to persuade Moses Mainz of the halachic necessity of secession. Bamberger resisted that request, arguing that he would not accomplish in person what he had failed to accomplish in writing, but additional prodding from several sources, including his own son-in-law, who lived in Frankfurt, convinced Bamberger to travel to Frankfurt after all.[112]

The subsequent meeting between Bamberger and Mainz resulted in a reversal of Bamberger's views on the Frankfurt situation. The broad concessions now granted by the community had thoroughly altered the circumstances, and Bamberger issued a statement in the *Frankfurter Boersen- und Handelszeitung* of March 20, which stated that "if all the necessary guarantees were given for carrying out these concessions, it could no longer be deemed necessary to secede from the Reform community."[113] Bamberger's declaration virtually ended all hopes for Hirsch to convince any further IRG members to secede. The compromise reached by some members with the community had been vindicated by Germany's foremost Talmudic authority, and the majority of IRG members would certainly not see any conflict in retaining their dual memberships. Yet, this divisive chapter in the history of German Orthodoxy was far from over. Hirsch and Bamberger exchanged attacks, as did their respective followers.[114] The two sides talked about separation, but that was no longer the issue at stake. The slur of Hirsch's authority already implicit in the opposition of Moses Mainz was now out in the open.

Hirsch responded to Bamberger's declaration with quick publication of a twenty-six-page open letter. He argued that the decision that Orthodox Jews could remain members of the Frankfurt community amounted to full recognition of Reform as a valid expression of Judaism with the sole provision that the Reform leadership also provide for the needs of the Orthodox. Thus, in addition to recognizing Reform's legitimacy, Orthodoxy was placing itself in a position dependent upon the Reformers. Hirsch challenged Bamberger to explain the reversal in his position. In 1872 Bamberger had joined 389 other rabbis who responded to a request by Rabbi Solomon Spitzer of Vienna by declaring a prohibition of membership in a Reform community. Just seven weeks earlier, on February 1, 1877, Bamberger had affirmed Hirsch's position.[115]

Since the time of the conflict the appropriateness of Bamberger's interference has been considered the primary issue involved; yet, Hirsch gave scant attention in his essay to the problem of Bamberger's intervention in a local dispute outside his province. Since Bamberger had been invited to Frankfurt, in fact, urged to come, by Hirsch's own followers, Hirsch apparently did not consider it appropriate to attack Bamberger for his involvement. However, Bamberger's subsequent contradiction of Hirsch's ruling violated, according to Hirsch, the rabbinic dictum: "One cannot permit what his colleague has forbidden." Nevertheless, Hirsch's total objection to Bamberger's interference amounted to only twelve lines of his twenty-six-page polemic.[116]

Hirsch warned that the newest concessions by the board constituted a serious threat to the future of the IRG. He feared that Bamberger might not sympathize with the significance of the IRG for Orthodoxy in Frankfurt and the importance of its contribution to Orthodoxy throughout Germany. The IRG had prospered because of the principle of *Torah im derech Erez*, upon which it was founded. A principle "inscribed as the leading motto upon its flag, with which it entered, fighting, the arena of time; a principle with which you, Herr Rabbiner, are not in total agreement."[117] The suggestion that Bamberger did not agree with this basic principle was one of several passing references by Hirsch to the difference in outlook and approach between the two rabbis,[118] but despite the few allusions to broader issues, Hirsch's "open letter" remained a reasoned and organized statement of the specific questions of separatism and the harm that could potentially be inflicted upon the IRG.

Bamberger's "open answer" departed from Hirsch both in style and in content. It has often been said of Bamberger's response that he lacked the flair and strength of language to battle with Hirsch. Indeed, while Hirsch wrote with sweeping rational arguments, Bamberger steeped himself and the reader in legalistic ones. But the most remarkable characteristic of Bamberger's response is that, in fact, he did not answer Hirsch at all. Bamberger's essay had almost nothing to do with separatism. Rather, he transformed the debate into a question of rabbinic authority, and proceeded to cast doubts on Hirsch's rabbinical competence.

Bamberger divided his response into four points, the first of which was Hirsch's contention that an Orthodox Jew must, according to religious law, secede from a Reform community; but in this opening section, Bamberger dealt not with Hirsch's decree, but only with the manner of Hirsch's behavior in demanding compliance with his decision. Bamberger confronted Hirsch with the fact that hundreds of learned and pious Jews led by an accomplished Talmudic scholar, Rabbi Moses Mainz, joined by Orthodox Jews and rabbis outside Frankfurt had all decided not to resign from their local committees. With men of such caliber in disagreement with his position, Hirsch should have acted in accordance with rabbinical tradition and suggested bringing the matter before three acceptable authorities. Arbitration and not authoritarianism was the way for rabbis to carry on such a dispute.[119]

Bamberger next turned at length to the question of his contradicting the rabbi of a community by permitting to the IRG that which its rabbi had forbidden. In contrast with Hirsch's twelve lines of challenge on this point, Bamberger responded for five pages. Discussing the dictum that one cannot permit that which a colleague has forbidden, Bamberger explained that that rule did not apply to the case of a great scholar, who should not be restrained from reversing the decision of a lesser one. Almost to prove the point that Hirsch was the lesser scholar whose rulings could be overruled by Bamberger, Bamberger added that Hirsch had not quoted the complete rule, which, in fact, applied only to a case where the initial ruling had been accepted by the community. This had certainly not been the case in Frankfurt. Since according to Bamberger, Hirsch was not a greater scholar than Mainz, Bamberger's own involvement did not involve impinging upon the decision of another scholar, but amounted to deciding between two scholars with opposing views.[120]

Bamberger had little trouble explaining his about-face between February 1, when he had been in total agreement with Hirsch, and March 20, when he publicly rejected the halachic necessity to secede. In the Supplementary Regulations issued near the beginning of 1877, Orthodoxy had been left, as it had been before, to fend for itself outside the framework of Jewish communal life. But, subsequently, the board had offered new concessions to the Orthodox, pledging to provide the necessary institutions for the Orthodox at the community's expense. Bamberger reported that he then insisted upon certain guarantees from the community. He stipulated that these new institutions must be under Orthodox control without interference from the community. The board accepted the conditions and Bamberger saw fit to reverse his position.[121] Bamberger did not deny that Reformers must be viewed as *minim*, as sectarians, but he maintained that the complete separation urged by Hirsch was not the only form of protest available to the Orthodox. Bamberger called upon those who did not secede to declare openly their rejection of the Reform approach to Judaism and their hope that the Reformers could sooner or later return to the Orthodox way. In the meantime, the "bonds of friendship" within the Jewish community would be retained.[122]

Bamberger did not expound any further on the significance of Jewish unity, and so the question still remained as to why an Orthodox Jew should not, after all, secede from a Reform community once he had the right to do so. Bamberger explained that the establishment of religious institutions within the community provided for the needs of those Orthodox who chose not to join the IRG. The community was the obvious agency to fill those needs, and according to Bamberger, members who chose to support both were to be commended and not condemned.[123] Hirsch's suggestion that the accomplishments of the IRG were being slighted by Bamberger now proved correct, for few Jewish communities would conceive of completely duplicating religious facilities for the benefit of those who freely chose not to avail themselves of facilities already available.

Significantly, Bamberger concluded his essay by commenting on his own understanding of the principle of *Torah im derech Erez*, which urged the union of general and Torah education. Bamberger insisted that he indeed did value the contributions made by the IRG and that he accepted the principle on which it was governed. But Bamberger did not want any misunderstanding of the implications of that principle. He supplied several pointed examples: "I too desire that a rabbi in our times will attain a secular education, but I do not want this to come at the expense of his studies in Torah; on the contrary, they must remain intact, guarded from any abbreviation or condensation." The same was true of religious schools, which should instruct in the worldly sciences, but not at the expense of religious education.[124] In fact, in that same year, 1877, a dispute broke out among Orthodox leaders in Aschaffenburg and Unterfranken on what constituted the most pressing project to be undertaken by them at the time. One leader suggested opening a school which combined Torah and secular education. Bamberger objected and in its place called for the improvement of ritual baths.[125]

With his discussion of *Torah im derech Erez*, Bamberger concluded his answer to Hirsch, and the conclusion was appropriate. Bamberger's response had centered not on separatism, but on the legitimate basis and usage of rabbinic authority. Bamberger was not only Germany's greatest Talmudist of the age, he was also the last of a kind. Bamberger had attained the basics of a secular education, but only those elements he deemed necessary to serve his community. Most leading rabbis of his day in Germany were well acquainted with the culture of the society around them. Among the Orthodox rabbis, Jacob Ettlinger and Isaac Bernays had been among the first, but the prerequisite of a secular education was now regularly expected by Orthodox communities as well as Reform. Bamberger represented the last remnant of the older school of rabbi, almost exclusively steeped in Talmudic sources.

Bamberger had no love for the Reformers; he espoused no ideology of Jewish solidarity or community. In fact, I have found in Bamberger's letter book, located in the Central Archives for the History of the Jewish People, further indication that Bamberger's decision contradicted his most recent position. When consulted after passage of the secession law by a number of Orthodox Jews of Wiesbaden concerning membership in a community controlled by Reformers, Bamberger responded on December 17, 1876, that an Orthodox Jew "ought not to be a member of such a community." On January 8, 1877, he clarified his views further: "An Orthodox Jew may not be a member of such a community." Indeed, the insistence by Schwab and other later writers that Bamberger was no opponent of Orthodox secession only underscores the unlikelihood that that was the issue at hand.[126]

Rather, Bamberger's controversy with Hirsch reveals a deep hostility against the inroads of modernity into the ranks of traditional Orthodoxy. The controversy between Hirsch and Bamberger was a strife between new Orthodoxy and old.[127] Bamberger attacked Hirsch not in defense of community, but as a last defense of an old order against an upheaval of religious values. Tradition and community had combined forces against modernity and separation. Both sides represented Orthodoxy. Having presented Orthodox Judaism in a modern mode, Hirsch chose to separate himself from the party of Reformers by communal isolation; while Bamberger, who continued to understand Orthodoxy in predominantly traditionalist terms, could still afford to remain identified with the general community.

The law of 1876 was not the cause of the strengthening of Orthodoxy in Germany in the latter part of the nineteenth century. Rather, it was an expression of that strength. In the 1830s, the Reform leadership discovered that little could be attained for Jews or Judaism by separating themselves from the Jewish community. In the 1870s they admitted that little was left of their

Jewish identities without that community. In the 1830s they sought the demise of Orthodox Judaism. By the 1870s they eagerly sought an alliance of forces. Emancipation had created a crisis for the Reform leadership and the history of Reform Judaism over the next decades should be studied in the perspective of that crisis.

In the 1830s Orthodoxy, threatened by the changing political and cultural world around it, was hesitant to introduce religious innovations. In the 1840s it was threatened by the inroads made by the Reformers. By the 1850s it had proven to itself and to others that it would not be blown away by political or religious winds; but more positively, it had accepted the political mandate of the times. German Orthodoxy had determined that it was prepared to accept emancipation. But Orthodoxy had still not caught up with Hirsch.

All Orthodox leaders including Bamberger welcomed the law of separation, but only Hirsch approached it from a perspective of strength. For the others it was a guarantee of minority rights; for Hirsch, it represented the right to be fully independent— Orthodoxy could and would have the strength to stand on its own. If by the 1870s, for the Reformers, emancipation was transformed from an objective to a crisis; if for the Orthodox, it was a fact of life, for Hirsch, emancipation was an opportunity. In that he was unique, as early as 1836 and as late as 1877.

Epilogue

Although Hirsch was annointed by historical traditions as the founding father of Neo-Orthodoxy and emerged as its primary spokesman through his early writings, the development of Neo-Orthodoxy must be seen within the broader context of European Judaism. In fact, the term Neo-Orthodoxy actually derived from the religious developments within the Jewish community of Berlin. In the early 1850s Michael Sachs, preacher in the community synagogue and a member of the rabbinate, sought to introduce a number of innovations into the synagogue service for Sabbaths and festivals. Sachs, who already preached regularly as part of the service, also called for participation of a choir and the shortening of the service by elimination of some *piyutim* and passages of Talmudic learning. These changes were opposed by his two rabbinical colleagues, Joseph Oettinger and Elias Rosenstein, and the term Neo-Orthodox was used to designate Sachs's supporters in the disagreement.[1] Within the context of the Berlin strife, it is clear that Neo-Orthodoxy signified a break with old Orthodoxy. That simplistic observation, certainly implied by the term itself, can, however, be easily overlooked if Neo-Orthodoxy is merely identified as a response to save Orthodoxy from Reform encroachments.

What distinguished new Orthodoxy from the old? On the surface level, the differences between the two centered on questions of form, as Neo-Orthodoxy adopted the same sensitivity to decorum and aesthetics that was being manifested in Reform congregations. But more fundamental questions lay beneath these questions of form, and both Bamberger and Hirsch had understood that the conflict between them was reflected more in their different attitudes toward Jewish education than in superficialities of form—hence, the seemingly irrelevant emphasis on education in their polemics on secession. Educational values derive from a world view and it was there that the two sides differed: on the relation between Orthodoxy and the world outside.

Old Orthodoxy tended toward an almost sectarian withdrawal from the pressures of the world around into a rigid adherence to old customs and viewpoints. It is a significant characteristic of Germany Jewry that it could not offer a single, pure representative of old Orthodoxy. Even Bamberger had acquired some basic elements of a secular education and introduced innovations into the Wuerzburg synagogue. Thus when writers choose to contrast Hirsch with a representative of the old school, they turn to the Hungarian Hatam Sofer as their model.[2] But despite Bamberger's limited accommodations to the changing times, he accused Hirsch of supplanting traditional values and of effecting serious changes in educational content. For Bamberger, whatever adjustments would be made must still be rooted in the firm basis of traditional values.[3]

Neo-Orthodoxy accepted the premise that the Jew must be granted, or at least *will* be granted, a fuller role within the general society, and it maintained that accommodation to the new opportunities open to the Jew was a necessity. The state, interfering more than ever in the internal religious affairs of the community, had made clear its expectations of change in the separatist outlook of the Jew. The Neo-Orthodox program was adopted wherever the religious establishment responded to the pressures being exerted. Failure to do so would have brought displeasure from the authorities and have resulted in an internal schism led by those Jews most anxious to accommodate the new terms. Thus, Neo-Orthodoxy did not result from the religious strife between Orthodoxy and Reform. In fact, in several major communities, the adaptations introduced weakened any potential strength for the growth of a Reform movement. Put precisely, Neo-Orthodoxy resulted from the confrontation between tradition and modernity. It derived from a split with the older school, and both the term and the phenomenon should be identified with the development of Orthodoxy not only in Germany, but in England and France as well—or wherever Orthodoxy made the changes it deemed necessary for the full legal participation of the Jew in society.[4]

The various components of the Neo-Orthodox program—the vernacular sermon, increased decorum, patriotic prayers, rabbis with secular education—all characterized the religious services under the auspices of the United Synagogue and Chief Rabbi in England and under the *Consistoire* and *Grand Rabbin* in France. The religious program of these institutions derived from the outlook that emancipation demanded accommodation, although traditional values and practices were to be honored. One writer, reflecting a viewpoint more traditional than that of the United Synagogue, nevertheless described its religious position in this way:

Despite the various changes both in custom and ritual that have been introduced from time to time, the constituent congregations of the United Synagogue are essentially orthodox. . . . The degree of orthodoxy varies in the different synagogues. A few have introduced mixed choirs, some have been built without a central *Bemah* (Prayer and Reader's Stand), . . . and there have been several minor changes in the ritual. On the other hand, the services follow fairly closely the Orthodox pattern. They are well conducted, and usually by good Chazanim with choral accompaniment.[5]

S. Debre, Chief Rabbi of Paris in the late nineteenth century, offered a similar comment on religious services in France:

According to the majority, it was wise to eliminate from the services superfluous prayers, repetitions and those of the Piyutim which, in consequence of their incorrect style or their purport, no longer corresponded with the condition of the mind and heart of modern Jews: yet withal to touch with extreme caution the established order of things. This is the system which has prevailed and which still prevails today in France.[6]

Despite their similarities, the religious institutions in England and France differed from the developments in Germany in two essential points. First, they emerged not in pursuit of emancipation, but in its aftermath. This meant that the Jewish communities in England and France could approach the reevaluation of their religious position with a greater degree of self-confidence than could the German Jew through most of the nineteenth century. In fact, the *Consistoire* in France and the Orthodox-inclined Board of Deputies in England enjoyed governmental recognition as the official representatives of their Jewish communities. Thus, they did not see the need for the more extensive innovations proposed in Germany in pursuit of emancipation.

The second difference between the Jewish communities is that in England and France the Jewish establishment responded to emancipation in time to avoid a serious religious schism. This meant that until the arrival of East European immigrants around the turn of the century, the religious institutions of England and France represented neither Neo-Orthodoxy nor old Orthodoxy, but simply Jews and Judaism. Thus, although England and France produced men like Moses Montefiore and Adolphe Cremieux who were the nineteenth-century spokesmen for world Jewry, the intellectual stimulus and religious conflicts of Germany produced the leadership for the religious parties of Judaism. It was for this reason that although Neo-Orthodoxy was widespread throughout Western Europe and a product of the general confrontation between tradition and modernity, it has usually been identified as a German phenomenon, with the IRG of Frankfurt as its model and S. R. Hirsch as its spokesman.

Abbreviations ⸺

AJS Review	Association for Jewish Studies Review
ALBI	Archives of the Leo Baeck Institute, New York.
AZJ	Allgemeine Zeitung des Judenthums
CAHJP	Central Archive for the History of the Jewish People
DINJ	Der Israelit des neunzehnten Jahrhunderts
JJLG	Jahrbuch der juedisch-literarischen Gesellschaft
LBIYB	Leo Baeck Institute Yearbook
SUBF	Stadts- und Universitaetsbibliothek, Frankfurt
TZ	Treue Zionswaechter
WZJT	Wissenschaftliche Zeitschrift fuer juedische Theologie

Notes

INTRODUCTION

1. The Deists' position is described by S. Ettinger, "Jews and Judaism as seen by the English Deists of the 18th Century" (Hebrew), *Zion*, XXIX (1964), 182–207. For the later period, see Todd Endelman, *The Jews of Georgian England* (Philadelphia, 1979).

2. On Napoleon and the Jews, see Simon Schwarzfuchs, *Napoleon, the Jews and the Sanhedrin* (London, 1979) and Frances Malino, *The Sephardi Jews of Bordeaux* (University, Ala., 1978).

3. It was partly for this reason that the German rabbinate played a considerable role in the pursuit of emancipation, unlike its counterparts elsewhere. There is no full history of the emancipation controversy in Germany. The liberal position is described by Ismar Schorsch, *Jewish Reactions to German Anti-Semitism* (New York, 1972), pp. 1–13. Jacob Katz has described some aspects of the controversy with an emphasis on the conservative position in *From Prejudice to Destruction* (Cambridge, Mass., 1980), pp. 147–220.

4. See the important 1809 memo by Humboldt, published by Max J. Kohler in *Publications of the American Jewish Historical Society*, XXVI (1918), pp. 103–115. See also the discussion in Schorsch, *Jewish Reactions*, pp. 2–4.

5. On Dohm, see Ilsegret Dambacher, *Christian Wilhelm von Dohm* (Frankfurt, 1974). Michaelis is quoted in the second edition of Dohm's *Ueber die buergliche Verbesserung der Juden* (Berlin, 1783), part II, pp. 37–38.

6. Katz, *From Prejudice to Destruction*, p. 197.

7. *Ibid.*, pp. 197–198.

8. *Ibid.*, pp. 211–212.

9. Egon Caesar Corti, *The Reign of the House of Rothschild* (New York, 1928), p. 292.

10. Louis Finkelstein, *The Pharisees*, 3rd. ed. rev. (Philadelphia, 1962), especially I, l-lii.

11. *Urschrift und Uebersetzungen der Bibel* (1857) and in *Sadducaeer und Pharisaeer* (1863).

12. See Gerson Cohen's introductory essay to Jacob Mann, *Text and Studies in Jewish History and Literature* (reprinted: New York, 1972), especially pp. xvii-xxxii, and the relevant section in Meyer Waxman, *A History of Jewish Literature* (reprinted: New York, 1960), III, 596–601.

13. On the effects of the Geniza on Karaitic studies, see Cohen, Introduction to *Text and Studies* by Mann, especially, xxxii-xxxvii. But as Cohen emphasized, while "the revelations yielded by the opening of the Geniza . . . unquestionably revolutionized the subject, [they] were not made in a vacuum."

14. See the critical discussion of this thesis in the *Encyclopedia Judaica*, 16 vols. (Jerusalem, 1971) X, 762–763.

15. Scholem discussed the significance of Sabbatianism for later developments in *Major Trends in Jewish Mysticism* (New York, 1941), pp. 300–304, 330–334.

16. Jacob Katz, "The Possible Connection of Sabbataeanism, *Haskalah*, and Reform Judaism" (Hebrew), in *Studies in Jewish Religious and Intellectual History Presented to Alexander Altmann*, ed. Siegfried Stein and Raphael Loewe (University, Ala.), pp. 83–100.

17. For another example of this form of explanation, see Jakob Petuchowski, *The Theology of Habam David Nieto*, rev. ed. (New York, 1970), pp. XVI–XVII, where Petuchowski suggested a connection between an eighteenth-century quasi-Karaism and nineteenth-century Reform in England that had been transmitted by "family tradition."

18. "Alienated Intellectuals in the Camp of Religious Reform: The Frankfurt Reformfreunde," *AJS Review*, VI (1981), especially 79–86. See also the suggestion of Christian influence on the Reform synods during the eventful years of 1869 and 1871 in Meyer, "The Jewish Synods in Germany in the Second Half of the Nineteenth Century" (Hebrew). *Studies in the History of the Jewish People and the Land of Israel*, III (1974), 240–242.

19. Lou Silberman, *American Impact: Judaism in the United States in the Early Nineteenth Century* (Syracuse, N.Y., 1964). The lecture was published without pagination.

20. In discussing Christian influence, the emphasis is usually placed on radical elements within both the Christian and Jewish sectors who espoused an ideology of eliminating the distinctions between the various religious traditions. Thus, Meyer emphasized Christian influence

on the Jewish intelligentsia, correctly asserting that it was here that the influences were most strongly felt. There was a different kind of Christian influence that was more widely felt in the context of nineteenth-century Judaism. That was a far less intellectualized attempt at emulation of Christian services, especially enhancing the aesthetic nature of the service in the synagogue. This form of influence was felt extensively in Western countries and had great effects on a broad spectrum of Jewish groups. Even communities who reaffirmed their loyalty to tradition and to rabbinical leadership adopted a format that increased decorum and imitated Christian traits such as clerical robes. Such adaptations could be seen extensively even in the essentially traditional services conducted in England and France and in Frankfurt.

21. Leon Jick, *The Americanization of the Synagogue, 1820–1870* (Hanover, N.H., 1976).

22. Steven M. Lowenstein, "The 1840's and the Creation of the German-Jewish Religious Reform Movement," in *Revolution and Evolution, 1848 in German-Jewish History,* ed. Werner E. Mosse et al., (Tuebingen, 1981), pp. 255–297.

23. Support of the Orthodox party fits easily into the scholarship on state and religion in Germany, but the support given to the Reformers in the 1830s and early 1840s deserves more attention. The documents presented in this study imply a desire by state officials to weaken the frameworks of Jewish life, but such a policy too should be seen within the general context of a program encouraging enlightenment and rationalism in religion. See Franz Schnabel, *Deutsche Geschichte im Neunzehnten Jahrhundert,* 4 vols., 2nd edition (Freiburg, 1951), IV. Of special interest is pp. 97-105.

24. Already by the time of the 1854 rabbinical conference in Wiesbaden, a resolution was passed urging the writing of a history of Reform endeavors in the nineteenth century. Robert Liberles, "The Rabbinical Conferences of the 1850's and the Quest for Liturgical Unity," *Modern Judaism,* III (1983), 310. In fact, Jost was already at work on his *Judenthum und seine Sekten.* The nineteenth century is discussed in volume III, which appeared in 1859. For an even earlier example of the Reform view of its historical context within German Jewry, see Jost's *Neuere Geschichte der Israeliten* which deals with the period 1815–1845 (3 volumes, Berlin, 1846–1847). Later in the century, Immanuel Heinrich Ritter issued a multi-volume history *Geschichte der juedischen Reformation,* 4 vols. (Berlin, 1858–1902). The classic history of Reform in English is still David Philipson's 1907 history, *The Reform Movement in Judaism,* 2nd ed. (New York, 1967).

25. Friedrich Engels, *The German Revolution,* ed. Leonard Krieger (Chicago, 1967), p. 124.

26. On the Haskalah's criticisms of Jewish life, see Raphael Mahler, *A History of Modern Jewry 1780–1815* (London, 1971), pp. 152–176.

27. S. Ettinger, "The Modern Period," *A History of the Jewish People,* ed. H. H. Ben-Sasson (London, 1976), p. 783. See also Jacob Katz, *Out of the Ghetto,* (Cambridge, Mass., 1973), pp. 143–151. On Moses Mendelssohn, see the monumental study by Alexander Altmann, *Moses Mendelssohn* (Philadelphia, 1973).

28. M. S. Samet, "Mendelssohn, Weisel, and the Rabbis of their Time" (Hebrew), in *Studies in the History of the Jewish People and the Land of Israel,* I (1976), 233–257. Mahler, *Modern Jewry,* pp. 163–167.

29. For an overview of these new educational trends, see Mordechai Eliav, *Jewish Education in Germany in the Period of Enlightenment and Emancipation* (Hebrew, Jerusalem, 1960). On the religious implications of the schools, see chap. one below.

30. B. Mevorach, *Napoleon U'Tekufato* (Hebrew, Jerusalem, 1968), pp. 135–140.

31. On France, see Phyllis Albert, *The Modernization of French Jewry* (Hanover, N.H., 1977), pp. 128–129, and on Westphalia, see Arno Herzig, *Judentum umd Emanzipation in Westfalen* (Muenster, 1973), pp. 12–13. The school in Frankfurt is discussed in chapter one below.

32. Michael Meyer, *The Origins of the Modern Jew* (Detroit, 1967), pp. 132–134. For an example of muted opposition, see Mevorach, *Napoleon U'Tekufato,* pp. 138–140 and especially pp. 151–154. For examples of more active opposition in Westphalia, see Herzig, *Judentum in Westfalen,* pp. 13–14, and B. H. Auerbach, *Geschichte der israelitischen Gemeinde Halberstadt* (Halberstadt, 1866), pp. 145–150.

33. On the earlier but aborted attempt to establish independent Reform services in Berlin, see Michael Meyer, "The Religious Reform Controversy in the Berlin Jewish Community, 1814–1823," in LBI *Yearbook,* XXIV (1979), 139–155. The idea of religious change among Enlightenment figures is discussed by Moshe Pelli, *The Age of Haskalah* (Leiden, 1974), especially pp. 33–47.

34. On the polemics around the prayerbook issued in Hamburg, see Jakob Petuchowski, *Prayerbook Reform in Europe* (New York, 1968), pp. 84–98, and Pelli, *Age of Haskalah,* pp. 91–108.

35. Two fine surveys of modern Orthodoxy are Charles Liebman, "Orthodox Judaism in the Nineteenth and Twentieth Centuries," in *Encyclopedia of Religion* (forthcoming), and M. S. Samet, "Orthodox Jewry in Modern Times," *Mahalakhim,* nos. 1 and 3 (Hebrew, March 1969 and March 1970).

36. In the field of Jewish education, for example, there is abundant evidence of the earlier accomplishments of others in introducing secular subjects and progressive methods into Orthodox education. Mordechai

Eliav, *Jewish Education in Germany in the Period of Enlightenment and Emancipation* (Jerusalem, 1960), especially chapter 4, where he described the earlier accomplishments in Halberstadt and Hamburg. On Bernays, see Isaac Heinemann, "The Relationship between S. R. Hirsch and his Teacher, Isaac Bernays" (Hebrew), *Zion*, XVI (1951), 44–90, and Eduard Dukesz, "Zur Biographie des Chacham Isaak Bernays," *JJLG*, V (1907), 297–322. Judith Bleich has also argued that much of the program of modern Orthodoxy preceded Hirsch, focusing her analysis on Hirsch's teacher Jacob Ettlinger. Judith Bleich, *Jacob Ettlinger, His Life and Work: The Emergence of Modern Orthodoxy in Germany*. Unpublished Ph.D. Dissertation, New York University, 1974. Noah Rosenbloom has tried to minimize Bernays' influence on Hirsch and the extent of Hirsch's rabbinic learning under Ettlinger. Noah Rosenbloom, *Tradition in an Age of Reform* (Philadelphia, 1976), pp. 56–58. See my criticism in "Champion of Orthodoxy," *AJS Review*, VI (1981), 58.

37. Unpublished material on Bernays's negotiation with the board in Hamburg can be found in the Bach Collection, ALBI, file 8. The quotation is from letter 2.

38. Hirsch himself contributed to the view that he was solely responsible for saving Orthodoxy in Germany by slanting his own historical testimonies to indicate the isolation of Orthodox loyalists during the first half of the century. See the discussion on Hirsch's historical presentation in chap. two and four.

The contributions of Hirsch's contemporary Esriel Hildesheimer to the growth of modern Orthodoxy are analyzed in a forthcoming intellectual biography by David Ellenson.

39. Liberles, "Champion of Orthodoxy," 57–60.

CHAPTER ONE–THE TRIUMPH OF REFORM

1. The classical history of the Jews of Frankfurt which covers, however, only through 1824, is Isidor Kracauer, *Geschichte der Juden in Frankfurt A.M. (1150–1824)*, 2 vols. (Frankfurt, 1925–1927). On the Napoleonic period, see pp. 295–431. On the early history of the Philanthropin, see Herman Baerwald, *Geschichte der Realschule der israelitischen Gemeinde "Philanthropin" zu Frankfurt am Main 1804–1904* (Frankfurt, 1904) and Hugo Schaumberger and Arthur Galliner, "Aus der Geschichte des Philanthropins," in *Das Philanthropin zu Frankfurt am Main*, ed. Dietrich Andernacht (Frankfurt, 1964). For an overview of these new educational trends, see Mordechai Eliav, *Jewish Education in Germany in the Period of Enlightenment and Emancipation* (Hebrew, Jerusalem, 1960).

2. Isaak Markus Jost, *Geschichte des Judenthums und seiner Sekten* III

(Leipzig, 1859), 325. David Philipson, *The Reform Movement in Judaism*, 2nd ed. (New York, 1967), p. 13.

3. Baerwald, *Realschule*, pp. 22–23. On the society in Frankfurt, see, for example, *AZJ*, III (1839), 37, and IV (1840), 696. Ludwig Philippson was also involved in such a society; see *AZJ*, I (1837), 165, 261–262. On the efforts for vocational education in general, see Eliav, *Jewish Education*, pp. 280–287, and Adolf Kober, "Emancipation's Impact on the Education and Vocational Training of German Jewry," *Jewish Social Studies*, XVI (1954), 3–32, 151–176.

4. In reality, during some periods paying students were very much in the majority because of the school's financial difficulties. Baerwald, *Realschule*, p. 42.

5. Schaumberger and Galliner, "Philanthropins," p. 11.

6. V. D. Lipman, "The Age of Emancipation," in *Three Centuries of Anglo-Jewish History*, ed. V. D. Lipman (Cambridge, England, 1961), pp. 86, 90. Salmond S. Levin, "The Origins of the Jews' Free School," *Transactions of the Jewish Historical Society of England*, XIX (1955–1959), 112–114.

7. The development of the *Andachtstunde* is discussed in Baerwald, *Realschule*, pp. 50–52, and in Caeser Seligman, *Geschichte der juedischen Reformbewegung von Mendelssohn bis zur Gegenwart* (Frankfurt, 1922), pp. 72–73. Its contribution to communal life is described by Baerwald, *Realschule*; Philipson, *Reform Movement*, p. 13; and by Jost, *Judentum*, III, 375.

8. *DINJ*, II (1841), 163.

9. *Orient*, III (1842), 154. Baerwald, *Realschule*, p. 52.

10. Jacob Katz, *Jews and Freemasons in Europe* (Cambridge, Mass., 1970), pp. 55–56.

11. *Ibid.*, p. 69. Katz has reconstructed in this study a fascinating chapter of emancipation history and has presented a cogent argument that social emancipation could not be taken for granted in the first half of the nineteenth century.

12. *Ibid.*, pp. 92–93.

13. *Ibid.*

14. *Ibid.*, pp. 82–83, 89.

15. *Orient*, III (1842), 154–155. *AZJ*, X (1846), 326–327. Jost, *Judentum*, III, 375–376.

16. As late as 1820 in Frankfurt, only some Jewish bankers were being accepted socially by non-Jews. The revealing contrasts with the case of English Jewry are exemplified by the status of Jewish Freemasons in the two countries. In England, Jews had already been admitted to Masonic membership more than a full century prior to Rothschild's entry into Parliament and the culmination of emancipation efforts in

that country, while in Germany, the Masonic struggle ended only in 1848. Contrast the plight of the German Jewish Freemason as described by Katz with John H. Shaftesley, "Jews in English Regular Freemasonry, 1717–1860," *Transactions of the Jewish Historical Society of England*, XXV (1977), pp. 150–169. On Frankfurt, see Richard Schwemer, *Geschichte der Freien Stadt Frankfurt a.M.* II, (Frankfurt, 1910), 138.

17. *AZJ*, VIII (1844), 405. Ironically, the Orthodox Rothschilds had been admitted to the Casino in 1838. *Orient*, I (1840), 7. Later references to the *Orient* confused Floisheim's rejection with the Rothschilds. Contrast *Orient*, V (1844), 178 and 207.

18. On Riesser, see M. Rinott, "Gabriel Riesser—Fighter for Jewish Emancipation," in *LBIYB*, VII (London, 1962), 11–38. The fullest study of Philippson is still Meier Kayserling, *Ludwig Philippson* (Leipzig, 1898). See also Johanna Philippson, "Ludwig Philippson und die Allgemeine Zeitung des Judentums," in *Das Judentum in der Deutschen Umwelt*, ed. Hans Liebeschuetz and Arnold Paucker (Tuebingen, 1977), pp. 243–291.

19. The Jew law of 1824 restricted the community to fifteen marriages per year, no more than two of which could involve a non-Frankfurter. In 1831 widows and widowers were exempted from the restriction, and in 1834 all weddings between two Frankfurters were allowed. However, the limitation with regard to an outsider remained in effect until 1846. Jost, *Neuere Geschichte der Israeliten* (Berlin, 1846–1847), I, 93–94, and III, 284. The Frankfurt question before the Congress of Vienna is discussed in I. Kracauer, *Juden in Frankfurt*, II, chap. XVIII, and in Max J. Kohler's classic essay "Jewish Rights at the Congress of Vienna and Aix-La-Chapelle," *Publications of the American Jewish Historical Society*, XXVI (1918), 33–125. The legal condition of Frankfurt Jewry is compared with that in other states in Kracauer, *Geschichte der Juden*, II, 519–521, and in Johanna Heinrich Bender, *Zustand der Israeliten zu Frankfurt A.M.* (Frankfurt, 1833), pp. 132–139.

20. Schwemer, *Frankfurt*, vol. III, part I, chap. II.

21. *Ibid.*, pp. 26, 28.

22. On Souchay, see *Ibid.*, pp. 39–43. For references on the legal status of the Jews and efforts to improve it, see *AZJ*, I (1837), 97, 322; II (1838), 9, 17, 22.

23. Emancipation legislation was aimed at ending the distinctions within a state's population. The Edicts of Tolerance issued by Joseph II of Austria in 1781 and 1782 began by expressing the wish that all "subjects without distinction of nation and religion, as soon as they are accepted or tolerated in our states, will take part together in the common weal." In discussing the situation in revolutionary France, Jacob Katz observed that the Declaration of the Rights of Man did not

automatically apply to the Jews, "but at least the Jewish issue was now thrown into sharp focus and it was clearly felt that their old position could not be allowed to continue in the new circumstances. . . . With the disappearance of this whole structure of privileged groups the Jews became more of an anomaly than they had ever been." Jacob Katz, *Out of the Ghetto* (Cambridge, Mass., 1973), pp. 162–168. On the attitudes toward Jewish emancipation in the modern state, see Salo W. Baron, "Newer Approaches to Jewish Emancipation," *Diogenes*, XXIX (1960), 56–81. An exception to the rule that political emancipation was granted to the Jews en masse was the distinction in France between the Sephardim of Bordeaux and the Ashkenazim of Alsace, who were emancipated by separate legislation in 1790 and 1791. But the second act of emancipation shows that the distinction did not last.

24. The regressive policies of Frederick William IV of Prussia in the 1840s bore the same message for the Jews. In 1841 he declared his conclusion to the government that the efforts to improve the social situation of the Jews through individual assimilation can never be fruitful or successful. Though the king concluded that separation between Jews and Christians was inevitable, the Jews were determined to oppose his planned legislation and to demonstrate the fitness of the total group for full citizenship. Hoerst Fischer, *Staat und Heer in Preussen im fruehen 19. Jahrhundert* (Tuebingen, 1968), pp. 155–157, and Ismar Schorsch, "Ideology and History in the Age of Emancipation," in his edition of Heinrich Graetz, *The Structure of Jewish History and Other Essays* (New York, 1975), pp. 19–22. Reform spokesmen in the second generation were opposed to the idea of emancipation for only a segment of the population. Note the remarks by Leopold Stein in *Literaturblatt des Orients* (1843), 726–727, and by Ludwig Philippson in *AZJ*, XXIII (1859), 634–635.

25. *Regulativ, die Verwaltung der Israelitischen Gemeinde . . . betreffend* (Frankfurt, 1839), p. 3 (hereafter, *Regulativ*). Records of the deliberations, petitions, and memoranda pertaining to the Frankfurt Senate were all destroyed during World War II. Only the Senate Protocols, containing a succinct summary of the decisions reached, and those materials that were issued in printed format are still accessible. The printed materials are available in the History of Frankfurt Division of the Stadts- und Universitaetsbibliothek, Frankfurt.

26. *Actenstuecke die hiesige israelitische Religions-Gemeinde betreffend* (Frankfurt, 1839), pp. 8–10. (Hereafter *Actenstuecke*).

27. *AZJ*, III (1839), p. 256. *Actenstuecke*, p. 15.

28. *Actenstuecke*, p. 33. My emphasis.

29. *Ibid.*, "*dass er der Vorstand einer Religions-Gemeinde ist.*"

30. On Trier, see Paul Arnsberg, *Neunhundert Jahre "Muttergemeinde*

in Israel" Frankfurt am Main, Chronik der Rabbiner (Frankfurt, 1974), pp. 73–74. Other members of the rabbinate are listed in *AZJ* II (1838), 174, but at least three rabbinical personalities are omitted from this list: Beer Adler, Aaron Fuld, and Jacob Posen. These men were considered members of the Frankfurt rabbinate in other references and I do not understand their absence here.

31. *Actenstuecke*, pp. 39–40.

32. *Ibid.*, p. 32.

33. Trier's view ignored at least two mitigating factors for permitting the reconstruction project. First, there is disagreement over whether a women's section ("Ezrat Nashim") is to be considered a separate synagogue. See *Talmudic Encyclopedia* (Hebrew) III, p. 191 and n. 17. Secondly, although the demolition of a synagogue prior to construction of a new building is forbidden, there is a leniency with regard to demolition of a wall in order to enlarge the existing building. *Ibid.*, p. 200 and notes 346–347. This should certainly have been the case in Frankfurt, where the new wall, in fact, already existed as the outside wall of the women's synagogue.

34. On the agreement and its breakdown in 1844, see below in this chapter.

35. *AZJ* II (1838), 173–174.

36. *Ibid.*, p. 174.

37. *Ibid.*, p. 4. See also p. 89. On the relations between renovation and innovation, see *DINJ* II (1841), 91–92.

38. *Actenstuecke*, p. 31.

39. On the *Tzitzith Verein*, see Kurt Wilhelm, "An Early Nineteenth Century Frankfurt Benevolent Society," in *Between East and West: Essays Dedicated to the Memory of Beal Horwitz*, ed. Alexander Altmann (London, 1958), pp. 137–148 and the references in Solomon Geiger, *Dibhre Kehillot* (Hebrew, Frankfurt, 1862), pp. 37, 76. The society also conducted daily study sessions after morning and evening services.

40. Wilhelm, "Benevolent Society," p. 142, and Geiger, *Dibhre Kehillot* p. 76. According to Geiger, p. 37, the society still functioned in 1862.

41. Wilhelm, "Benevolent Society," p. 140.

42. *AZJ*, II (1838), 542.

43. *Ibid.*

44. *Ibid.*, p. 4. My emphasis.

45. *Ibid.*, p. 89.

46. *AZJ*, V (1841), 714n.

47. We next hear of Isaaksohn as a nominee for the position of deputy rabbi in 1843, but the board did not view his candidacy kindly. *Ibid.*, pp. 714–715; *Orient* V (1844), 123; David Einhorn also referred to

Isaaksohn's candidacy in his congratulatory letter to Stein. Letter of January 2, 1844, in the Stein Collection, ALBI.

48. Emanuel Schwarzschild, *Die Gruendung der Israelitischen Religions-gesellschaft* (Frankfurt, 1896), p. 15.

49. Philipson, *Reform Movement*, p. 76. On the unwillingness of the two camps to cooperate in the realm of reform, see the analysis in *DINJ*, II (1841), 162–163.

50. *Actenstuecke*, p. 3.

51. *Regulativ*, III, 4, A; and II, 4, A and B.

52. *Ibid.*, II, 1, and III, 1.

53. *Regulativ*, IV. The text reads: "*Jedenfalls muss der anzustellende Rabbinatscandidat von dem hiesigen Rabbinat, oder, in dessen Ermangelung, von dem Oberrabinern zweier bedeutender Staedte Deutschlands, in den juedisch—theologischen Kenntnissen geprueft und zum Lehramt tuechtig befunden worten seyn.*"

54. *Actenstuecke*, p. 30.

55. *Ibid.*

56. *AZJ*, III (1939), 180–182, especially 181.

57. *Ibid.*, pp. 113, 181.

58. *Protokolle des Grossen Raths* (1839), February 12, 1839, entry 145. The Senate's records are located in the Municipal Archives, Frankfurt. This document was published in *AZJ* III (1839), 181–182. An extract appears in Philipson, *Reform Movement*, p. 113.

59. Jost, *Judentum*, III, 350–351. On the growth of Reform in southern Germany, see Jost, *Israeliten*, III, 119–120. The most controversial instance of state interference on behalf of Reform took place in Weimar. See *Ibid.*, 226–227, and Jakob J. Petuchowski, *Prayerbook Reform in Europe* (New York, 1968), pp. 124–127.

60. Jost, *Judentum*, III, 367.

61. Schwemer, *Frankfurt*, II, 399–405 and 647–679.

62. *AZJ* III (1839), 207–208, 219–220. Jost, *Israelitische Annalen* I, (1839), 134, *Protokolle des Grossen Raths* (1839), February 12, 1839, entries 146, 147.

63. On Ihm's earlier involvement in religious issues, see Schwemer, *Frankfurt*, II, 191–197.

64. *Protokolle des Grossen Raths* (1839), February 12, 1839, entry 144.

65. *AZJ* III (1839), 256, 281. In fact, the number of Jews in Frankfurt was approximately 50 percent higher, but only local citizens were considered community members. See, for example, *AZJ*, XI (1848), 691.

66. A newspaper description divided Frankfurt Jewry into three categories: the financiers, whom the author identified with the Orthodox party, as we shall do in chap. 3; the intellectuals; and the *Geschaeftsleute*. *DINJ*, II (1841), 86–87.

67. *Orient*, VII (1846), 49.

68. A statistical study of the later roles played by the graduates of the Philanthropin and its sister schools would make a significant contribution to our understanding of the social dynamics of German Jewry in the first half of the nineteenth century. In the century 1804–1904, 5,200 boys and 3,100 girls graduated from the Philanthropin; already by 1812, 153 boys and 96 girls had graduated from the school. Baerwald, *Realschule*, p. 41.

69. *DINJ*, II (1841), 162–163.

70. The fullest account of the *Reformverin's* activities can be found in David Philipson, *Reform Movement*, chapter VI. See also the bibliographic references, p. 475, n 110. A recent examination can be found in Michael Meyer "Alienated Intellectuals in the Camp of Religious Reform: The Frankfurt Reformfreunde," *AJS Review*, VI (1981), 61–86.

71. Michael Creizenach had died on August 5, 1842, and the group had met by November of that year. The essay "Die Judenheit und das Judenthum—Bedenken eines Laien" appeared in *WZJT* III (1837) 161–171. For Jost's comment, see *Israeliten*, III, 212, n. 3, where he refers to the author as a *"denkender Reformfreund."*

72. *WZJT*, III, 165–166. The translation is based on Philipson, *Reform Movement*, p. 115, with changes.

73. *WZJT* III, 169–170.

74. *Ibid.*, pp. 170–171.

75. Jost, *Israeliten*, III, 212, but see *Orient* IV (1843), p. 398.

76. *AZJ*, VII (1843), 590, 766. *Orient* IV (1843), 148.

77. *Orient*, V (1844), 15.

78. *AZJ*, VII (1843), 405.

79. *Ibid.*, p. 438.

80. For Riesser's letter, see *Ibid.*, pp. 481–486.

81. *Ibid.*, p. 516.

82. The leaked correspondence was published in *Ibid.*, pp. 517–519.

83. The Reformers were not always so free to admit that their opposition to the Talmud stemmed from their desire to be liberated from rabbinic authority. But there was also opposition to the Talmud itself and in this same letter, Stern referred to the Talmud as a jelly that even the sharpest minds cannot cut through.

84. *Ibid.*, p. 519.

85. Philippson made a similar point, though from his more moderate perspective, in "Who are the real enemies of Reform?" in *AZJ*, X, (1846) 141–143.

86. Jost, *Israeliten*, p. 214; Philipson, *Reform Movement*, pp. 122–123.

87. *AZJ*, VII, 534. See also p. 548.

88. *Ibid.*, p. 438.

89. See below.

90. *AZJ*, VIII (1844), 26.

91. *Ibid.*, VII (1843), 638.

92. *Orient*, IV (1843), 398.

93. *Ibid.*, V (1844), 15. *Regulativ*, II, 1. On the *Reformverein*'s continued influence within the community, see note 123 below.

94. *Ibid.*, V, 14, and the response on p. 15; *AZJ*, VIII, (1844), 307. See also Jost, *Neuere Geschichte*, I, 101–102. Stein had actually written a lengthy critique of the *Reformverein* in which he, nevertheless, expressed respect for their objectives. See *Literaturblatt des Orients* (1843), pp. 721–727, 741–744, 762–766.

95. Dr. Josef Bergson summarized the previous literature in his *Die Beschneidung vom historischen, kritischen und medecinischen Standpunkt* (Berlin, 1844). See especially pp. 38–39. The events in Frankfurt precipitated an outpouring of polemical literature. The *Reformverein*'s position was defended in a pamphlet attributed to Philanthropin teacher Josef Johlson: Bar Amithai, *Ueber die Beschneidung* (Frankfurt, 1843) and in Samuel Holdheim, *Ueber die Beschneidung in religioesen, dogmatischen Beziehung* (Schwerin, 1844). Numerous attacks on the radicals' position were published in the Jewish press. For example, see note 112 below.

96. *AZJ* VII (1843), 166. Trier, *Rabbinische Gutachten ueber die Beschneidung* (Frankfurt, 1844), p. ix. For a summary of the edict, see *AZJ*, VII (1843), 144.

97. "*Israelitische Burger und Einwohner, insofern sie ihre Kinder beschneiden lassen wollen*"

98. Bender, *Zustand*, pp. 81, 86.

99. *AZJ* VII, (1843), 184–185.

100. *Ibid.*, pp. 198–200.

101. *Ibid.*, p. 201; Trier, *Gutachten*, pp. ix-x.

102. The request was submitted on August 4, September 15, and October 31, 1843, and again on February 9, 1844.

103. *AZJ*, VIII (1844), 182. The original text struck out the clause that the offense was caused "through non-observance of Jewish law." *Protokolle des Grossen Raths* (1844), February 13, 1844, entry 158.

104. *AZJ*, VIII (1844), 182. The reference to October 28 in the *AZJ* should read December 28. *Protokolle* (1843), entry 1324.

105. See note 96 above.

106. *Orient*, IV (1843), 148. *Allgemeine Deutsche Biographie* XXXIII, 316–317. On Schwarzschild's political position, see the references in Schwemer, *Frankfurt*, vol. III, part 1, and chap. 3 below.

107. Bergson, *Beschneidung*.

108. *Ibid.*, pp. 38–39. *Protokolle* (1844), March 5, 1844, entry 230. *AZJ* VIII (1844), 181–182.

109. Bar Amithai, *Beschneidung*, pp. 6–7.

110. Bergson, *Beschneidung*, pp. 60–63. Michaelis presented his interpretation in *Gruendliche Erklaerung des mosaichen Rechts*. On Michaelis, see the entry in *Encyclopedia Judaica* (1971), XI, 1490–1491.

111. Bergson, *Beschneidung*, p. 83.

112. See, for example, *AZJ*, VIII (1844), nos. 8–10.

113. Quoted by Ismar Schorsch in his introductory essay to Heinrich Graetz, *The Structure of Jewish History* (New York, 1975), pp. 18–19.

114. Schwemer, *Frankfurt*, vol. III, part I, pp. 78–79. *Encyclopedia of Religion and Ethics* (New York, 1908–1926), IV, 674.

115. Bergson, *Beschneidung*, p. 1.

116. Jost wrote of a number of deaths resulting from circumcision, while the *Orient* referred to a single recent death as prompting the city's concern. Jost, *Israeliten*, III, 218; *Orient* IV (1843), 56.

117. Schwemer, *Frankfurt*, vol. III, part I, pp. 383–384.

118. Philipson, *Reform Movement*, pp. 13–26. Especially valuable for an overview of communal regulations established by Reform dominated boards is Jakob Petuchowski's chapter on synagogue ordinances. *Prayerbook Reform in Europe* (New York, 1968), pp. 105–127. In an important revision of the events in Berlin, Michael Meyer has demonstrated that the king himself initiated inquiries into the Reform services and that the Orthodox turned to him only at a later stage. The point here, however, is not that the Orthodox did not involve government authorities in the conflict, but that both sides did. Michael A. Meyer, "The Religious Reform Controversy in the Berlin Jewish Community," *LBIYB* XXIV (1979), 139–155.

119. Adler was eulogized in *Israelit*, VII (1866), 104. On Fuld, see Marcus Horovitz's introduction in Hebrew to *Beit Aharon* (Frankfurt, 1890).

120. On *more judaico*, which remained partially in effect in Frankfurt until 1847 (!), see the entry and bibliography in *Jewish Encyclopedia* (1906), IX, 367–368. On the oath in Frankfurt, see Jacob Marcus, *Jew in the Medieval World* (Cincinnati, Ohio 1938), pp. 49–50 and Leopold Stein, *Der Eid More Judaico* (Frankfurt, 1847).

121. *Orient*, V (1844), 404.

122. *Orient*, VI (1845), 369; *AZJ*, IX (1845), 709. They did succeed in conducting High Holiday services in 1846. *AZJ*, X (1846), 644.

123. Schwemer, *Frankfurt*, vol. III, Part 1, pp. 78–79. Veit Valentin, *Frankfurt am Main und die Revolution von 1848/49* (Stuttgart, 1908), pp. 125–127. In following later activities of the *Reformverein* members, there is also evidence that their personal influence remained strong and that they had considerable influence on the community Board and its subsequently tense relations with Leopold Stein as community rabbi. Robert

Liberles, "Leopold Stein and the Paradox of Reform Clericalism," *LBIYB*, XXVII (1982).

124. Trier's accusations against the *Reformverein* are in *Gutachten*, pp. xii-xiv, and in *Protokolle* (1843), September 19, 1843, entry 990, where he refers to "the anarchistic efforts of the so-called *Reformverein.*"

125. The election was announced in *AZJ* VII (1843), 752.

126. The full agreement is reproduced in *AZJ* VIII (1844), 307–309.

127. Compare *Regulativ*, II, 4, B, c.

128. *Regulativ*, IV.

129. In subsequent years, Leopold Stein was himself quite disturbed over the long delay in construction. He assumed that the board was insufficiently committed to the building of a new synagogue. But, if so, why was the board prepared to accept the Rothschild agreement after struggling so long for expanded authority? I suggest that at least until the mid-forties the board was fully committed to a new synagogue, but without Orthodox support it lacked the necessary resources. In fact, despite the controversy between them, an apparently needed pledge of 20,000 gulden was still given by the Rothschilds toward the new building in 1853.

It is possible that after the mid-forties and the diversion of interests toward the political sphere, the board did demonstrate less interest in the project until construction of a new Orthodox synagogue forced the issue. On the Rothschild support in 1853, see *AZJ*, XVII (1853), 605. For Stein's views, see *Dienst-Verhaeltniss*, pp. 11–12.

130. *AZJ*, VII (1843), 765–766, and *Orient* V (1844), 123. See *Orient* VI (1845), 210–211, for reports that Stein was considered by some to be quite strict in his legal rulings.

131. *AZJ*, VIII (1844), 307; *Ibid.*, p. 223; and *Orient* V (1844), 123.

CHAPTER TWO–ORTHODOX COMEBACK

1. Samson Raphael Hirsch, *Gesammelte Schriften* III (Frankfurt, 1906), especially pp. 510–526. This section was omitted from the available English translation of the essay. Markus Horowitz, Hirsch's later Orthodox rival in Frankfurt, implicitly argued against the Hirschian view of total Orthodox collapse in his introduction to the collection of Aharon Fuld's writings, *Beit Aharon* (Frankfurt, 1890), pp. IV-VI. Note especially his references to earlier inclusions of secular studies within the traditional framework and on the literary efforts to fight the Reformers. He missed his opportunity, however, to present an alternative account when he terminated his study of *Frankfurter Rabbinen* with Pinchas Horowitz. His exclusion of Solomon Trier's rabbinate from this study remains a puzzle to me. *Frankfurter Rabbinen*, 2nd ed. (Jerusalem, 1969).

2. Hirsch, *Schriften*, III pp. 512–516. On the new burial ordinances introduced by the community and the ensuing controversy, see *AZJ*, V (1841), 715; VI (1842), 64–65.

3. Hirsch, *Schriften*, III p. 512.

4. Weill recounted his experiences in his informative and moving memoir *Ma Jeunesse* (Paris, 1870).

5. A recent study on Weill dates his arrival in Frankfurt to 1826 and some confirmation can be found from references in the memoir to Weill's first visit home on pp. 287 and 300. However, Weill also clearly stated that he turned seventeen shortly after his arrival in Frankfurt, which would then have been at the beginning of 1828. See pp. 215 and 229. Joë Friedemann, *Alexandre Weill, Écrivain Contestataire et Historien Engagé* (Strasbourg, 1980), pp. 29–30.

6. Weill, *Ma Jeunesse*, p. 199.

7. *Ibid.*, pp. 210–211.

8. *Ibid.*, pp. 206–207.

9. On the decline of the yeshivah in Frankfurt, see the personal lament of Rabbi Zvi Hirsch Horowitz in Mordechai Eliav, *Jewish Education in Germany in the Period of Enlightenment and Emancipation* (Hebrew, Jerusalem, 1960), pp. 149–150 and also 154–155. But whether or not Trier taught in the framework of the yeshivah, Weill's testimony informs us that rabbinical candidates did continue to come to Frankfurt for their training and ordination. I am grateful to Dr. Dietrich Andernacht, director of the Stadtsarchiv, Frankfurt, for calling this work to my attention. For additional testimony to the existence of advanced Talmudic studies in Frankfurt in the 1830s, see C. Seligmann, *Erinnerungen* (Frankfurt, 1975), p. 36.

10. Hirsch, *Schriften*, III, 513–514.

11. The incident was recounted by both sides with partiality. Compare Hirsch's account where he quoted an important 1838 memo from the board with that of I. M. Jost, *Neuere Geschichte der Israeliten von 1815 bis 1845*, (Berlin, 1846), I, 100–101.

12. *Protokolle des Grossen Raths*, Stadtsarchiv Frankfurt, (1843), May 2, entry 535, and *Protokolle des Engeren Raths* (1843), May 4, entry 853. The entries in the Senate protocols relate that the school was ordered closed in the first week of May 1843. The *Orient*, IV (1843), 299, reported in September 1843 a similar petition for a school teaching rabbinics.

13. According to this count, the Orthodox received 27 percent of the votes cast. The 1838 statistic is from chap. I, section ii; 1845, from chap. III, section i; and the 1850 figure from chap. III, section ii. The 1839 estimate of synagogue attendance is in *AZJ*, III (1839), 688. Reformers, too, referred to an Orthodox collapse by the late 1830s. For example, Jost, *Neuere Geschichte*, I, 100–101.

14. The inquiry is on *TZ*, II, 314 and the response on pp. 349–350 and 361–362.

15. On the Geiger-led conference, see "Die Rabbinerzusammenkunft," *WZJT*, III (1837), 313–332, 476–479. Quotation is from p. 321. See also Ludwig Geiger, *Abraham Geiger. Leben und Lebenswerk* (Berlin, 1910), pp. 45–46.

16. *AZJ*, VIII (1844), 27.

17. Geiger too had acknowledged in 1837 that a unanimous decision by the rabbis would have its influence. David Philipson, *The Reform Movement in Judaism*, 2nd ed. (New York, 1967), pp. 140–141.

18. *Protocolle der ersten Rabbiner-Versammlung* (Braunschweig, 1844), pp. 13–16. Both comments are quoted in Philipson, *Reform Movement*, p. 145. The term "synod," borrowed from Christian usage, connoted a body of higher authority constituted of both clergy and laymen. Note that it was the absence of laymen that curtailed the conference's authoritative standing!

Despite Ludwig Philippson's personal and pivotal involvement in convoking and planning the first of the conferences, he was able to return to the subject forty years later in a masterly series of articles recounting the history of rabbinical conferences and synods in nineteenth-century Germany. The objectivity implanted by the passing of time combined with a lucid and succinct style to make these essays the finest study we have to date of the early conferences. *AZJ*, XLVIII (1884), 213ff, 229ff, 245ff, 277ff, 293ff.

19. *Ibid.*, pp. 214–215 and especially 229.

20. On Ettlinger, see the unpublished doctoral dissertation by Judith Bleich: *Jacob Ettlinger, His Life and Work: The Emergence of Modern Orthodoxy in Germany* (New York University, 1974). A short biographical sketch by Jonah Emmanuel appeared in *Harav Yaakov Ettlinger* (Hebrew, Jerusalem, 1972), pp. 7–17.

21. An original copy of the declaration, *Shelomei Emunei Israel-Treue Glaeubige in Israel*, was available to me at the Jewish National Library, Jerusalem. For other protests and responses, see Philipson, *Reform Movement*, p. 461, n. 64, 69, and Jacob Katz, "Sources of Orthodox Trends," *The Role of Religion in Modern Jewish History*, ed. Jacob Katz (Cambridge, Mass. 1975), pp. 29–31 and documents.

22. The expression comes from Jeremiah 51:5. Literally translated "Israel is not a widower," it is usually interpreted as "Israel still has reserves of strength." My usage is based on the German text of the declaration, *"Noch ist Israel nicht verwais't."*

23. The German *Zionswaechter* continued publication until 1854; the Hebrew paper ceased publication in early 1857. On these papers, see Judith Bleich, "The Emergence of an Orthodox Press in Nineteenth-Century Germany," *Jewish Social Studies*, XLII (1980), 323–344.

24. *TZ*, I (1845), 97–98; III (1847), 303, 342.

25. *Ibid.*, III (1847), 101.

26. On Philippson, I. M. Jost, *Neuere Geschichte* III, (Berlin, 1847), 149–156; M. Kayserling, *Ludwig Philippson* (Leipzig, 1898), and Johanna Philippson, "Ludwig Philippson und die Allgemeine Zeitung des Judentums," *Das Judentum in der Deutschen Umwelt, 1800–1850*, ed. Hans Libeschuetz and Arnold Paucker (Tuebingen, 1977), pp. 243–291. Philippson even printed criticisms of the projects closest to him: on the theological faculty, see *AZJ*, II (1838), 153ff and 237–240, and on the Rabbinical Conferences, VIII (1844), 513–514.

27. *TZ*, II (1846), 241–246, 262.

28. For example, the failure to respond to the proposal for separation in *TZ*, III (1847), 353–354, and the total aimlessness on 225–227.

29. *Ibid.*, I (1845), 208; II (1846), 39–40. On Bamberger, see below in chap. seven.

30. *TZ.*, II (1846), 45.

31. *Ibid.*, pp. 62–63.

32. *Ibid.*, pp. 423–424. Enoch was referring to groups formed in the past year, but I do not believe that he discounted those established previously, since he tended to exaggerate the paper's role in initiating the momentum. For reports on the founding of the various groups, see *Ibid.*, II (1846), 62–63, 88, 190, 423–424; III (1847), 207, 208.

33. *Ibid.*, II (1846), 440, and III (1847), 207.

34. *Ibid.*, II (1846), 423–424, 440.

35. *Ibid.*, III (1847), 207.

36. *Ibid.*, I (1845), 211–212.

37. On the dispute in the Frankfurt conference, see *Protokolle und Aktenstuecke der zweiten Rabbinerversammlung abgehalten in Frankfurt am Main* (Frankfurt, 1845), pp. 18–72. An English summary is presented in Philipson, *Reform Movement*, pp. 164–173. Frankel's initiative to organize his own conference is reported on in *Orient*, VII (1846), 237, 245–246, 293; VIII (1847), 73; *AZJ*, X (1846), 523, 572.

38. *TZ*, III (1847), 81–83.

39. *Ibid.*, pp. 329–330, 337–339.

40. *Ibid.*, pp. 83–84.

41. *Ibid.*, II, 186–187.

42. *Ibid.*, pp. 423–424.

43. For early proposals in the Orthodox camp, see *ibid.*, II, 49–51, 60–61, and III, 225–227, 353–354. The development of the separatist idea is discussed below in chap. six.

44. *TZ*, III (1847), 194.

45. *Ibid.*, II (1846), 50. Similar views were expressed in Hungary by Moshe Schick. See *The Role of Religion*, pp. 30–31.

46. *Igrot Soferim*, edited by Shlomo Sofer (Hebrew, Tel-Aviv, 1970), part I, pp. 81–85.

47. *TZ*, III (1847), 225–227.

48. Samson Raphael Hirsch, *Nineteen Letters of Ben Uziel*, trans. Bernard Drachman (New York, 1899), p. 165. On the Hatam Sofer, see Jacob Katz's essay, "Contributions toward a Biography of R. Moses Sopher" (Hebrew), in *Studies in Mysticism and Religion presented to Gershom Scholem* (Jerusalem, 1967), especially pp. 142–145.

49. Jacob Toury, *Die politischen Orientierungen der Juden in Deutschland* (Tuebingen, 1966), pp. 20–21; *TZ*, II (1846), 159. Orthodox satisfaction with partial emancipation was also demonstrated among the religious Jews of London during this same period. Robert Liberles, "Origins of the Jewish Reform Movement in England," *AJS Review*, I (1976), p. 146.

50. *TZ*, III (1847), 73–75, 84–85, 91–92, 101–102.

51. *Ibid.*, pp. 84–85.

52. *Ibid.*, p. 92.

53. *Ibid.*, p. 101.

54. *Ibid.*, pp. 17–18.

55. Reported in indirect quotation in *TZ*, II (1846), 159.

56. Toury, *Orientierungen*, pp. 18–20; *TZ*, III (1847), 91–92.

57. *Shelomei Emunei Israel*.

58. Toury, *Orientierungen*, p. 20.

59. Michael Meyer has presented a summary of the conflict together with a number of important documents in "Rabbi Gedaliah Tiktin and the Orthodox Segment of the Breslau Community, 1845–1854," *Michael*, II (1973), 92–107.

60. *Ibid.*, p. 98.

61. *Ibid.*, pp. 94–95.

62. The prohibition originated with the synagogue ordinances issued in 1843 by Holdheim. Leopold Donath, *Geschichte der Juden in Mecklenburg* (Leipzig, 1874), pp. 234–235. For an English translation of the ordinances, see Jakob Petuchowski, *Prayerbook Reform in Europe* (New York, 1968), pp. 117–119.

63. There were contradictory reports in the *Treue Zionswaechter* as to whether permission for separate services in Schwerin was granted prior to or following Einhorn's election. Contrast *TZ*, II (1846), 339, with III (1847), 237–238. Other communities received permission only after the election. *Ibid.*, III (1847), 292–293, 302, 342.

64. Donath, *Juden in Mecklenburg*, pp. 244–245.

65. *Ibid.*, pp. 247–249.

66. Heinrich Silbergleit, *Die Bevoelkerungs und Berufsverhaeltnisse der Juden im Deutschen Reich* (Berlin, 1930), p. 14. On the development of the legislation and the relatively successful Jewish diplomatic efforts to

influence the new law, see Hoerst Fischer, *Judentum, Staat, und Heer in Preussen* (Tuebingen, 1968), chap. V, and Herbert Strauss, "Pre-Emancipation Prussian Policies towards the Jews, 1815–1847," *LBIYB*, XI (1966), pp. 107–136. Ismar Schorsch discussed the effects of the prolonged debate on inner Jewish life in "Ideology and History in the Age of Emancipation," introduction to Heinrich Graetz, *The Structure of Jewish History and Other Essays* (New York, 1975), pp. 19–31.

67. *AZJ*, XI (1847), 517–518. Ismar Freund, *Die Emanzipation der Juden in Preussen*, 2 vols. (Berlin, 1912), I, 250–251.

68. *TZ*, III (1847), 338.

69. Sections 35, 53ff. The text of the law is in Freund, *Emanzipation*, II, 501–520.

70. *Orient*, VIII (1847), 273–274.

71. *TZ*, III (1847), 303.

72. *Orient*, VIII (1847), 311.

73. *AZJ*, XLVIII (1884), 247–248.

74. Hermann Engelbert, *Statistik des Judenthums im Deutschen Reich* (Frankfurt, 1875), p. 68. These statistics are from circa 1871, and yet, despite the growing trend toward urbanization, they still indicate a population dispersed into numerous, small communities.

CHAPTER THREE–RESURGENCE IN FRANKFURT

1. Robert Liberles, "Leopold Stein and the Paradox of Reform Clericalism," *LBIYB*, XXVII (1982), 261–262.

2. The conditions laid down by Philippson for locating the conferences are in *AZJ*, VIII (1844), 69. The gratitude of the representatives at the first conference to the host community of Braunschweig was expressed in a letter reprinted in *ibid.*, p. 434. The documents in which the Frankfurt Board accepted responsibility for the second conference are in *ibid.*, IX (1845), 55. See also pp. 297–298.

3. *Ibid.*, IX, p. 516.

4. The address to Frankel and Trier's letter are in *Orient*, VI (1845), 351–352. Frankel's responses are in *ibid.*, pp. 342–343 and 349–350.

5. Schwarzschild incorrectly placed this incident without date at a much earlier point in his narrative. Schwarzschild, *Die Gruendung der Israelitischen Religionsgesellschaft zu Frankfurt am Main* (Frankfurt, 1896), pp. 9, 14–15, and *Archives Israelites*, X (1849), 309–310. See also Baron's discussion in "Jewish Communal Crisis in 1848," *Jewish Social Studies*, XIV (1952), 113.

6. Schwarzschild, *Gruendung*, pp. 11–12. An apocryphal explanation of Willy Rothschild's move to Frankfurt relates that the Orthodox Willy was proving an embarrassment to the Naples House due to his

donning of ritual fringes which he wore exposed, in accordance with tradition. The story is labeled legendary already by Jacob Rosenheim in his *Erinnerungen* (Frankfurt, 1970), p. 61. Indeed, one should note the move of all three sons of the Naples House to Frankfurt or Paris as a result of adverse local conditions. See Rosenheim, *ibid.*, pp. 60–65, for a description of Willy Rothschild's religious involvements.

7. Schwarzschild, *Gruendung*, pp. 14–15.

8. Richard Schwemer, *Geschichte der freien Stadt Frankfurt A.M., 1814–1866*, III, part I (Frankfurt, 1915), pp. 90, 189–195, 259–261, 279–280. According to Veit Valentin, Souchay resigned his Senate seat in order to have more flexibility in leading the opposition. Veit Valentin, *Frankfurt am Main und die Revolution von 1848/49* (Stuttgart, 1908), pp. 432–433.

9. Schwemer, *Frankfurt*, III, part 1, p. 194.

10. Valentin, *Frankfurt und 1848*, pp. 432–434.

11. *Ibid.*, pp. 433–436, 440.

12. *Protokolle des Grossen Raths* (1848), entries 551, 1029 and especially 1170 (from November 7, 1848), also (1849), May 1, 1849, entry 607. Schwarzschild, *Gruendung*, p. 14.

13. Leopold Stein, *Wahrheit, Recht, und Frieden* (Frankfurt, 1847), p. 10.

14. Leopold Stein, *Mein Dienst Verhaelthniss zum Israelitischen Gemeinde Vorstande zu Frankfurt a.M.* (Frankfurt, 1861), p. 17.

15. Jacob Toury, *Die politischen Orientierungen der Juden in Deutschland* (Tuebingen, 1966), pp. 59–60, 347. Schwemer, *Frankfurt*, III, part 1, pp. 250n, 262, 363.

16. On Heinrich Schwarzschild, see *Festschrift zur Jahrhundertfeier der Realschule der israelitischen Gemeinde, 1804–1904* (Frankfurt, 1904), pp. 63, 171.

17. See the discussion on the *Montagskraenzchen* in chap. one above and Schwemer, *Frankfurt*, III, part 1, pp. 78–79. For those active in the society, see the list in Schwemer, p. 290. Also *Orient*, IX (1848), 308–310, and Valentin, *Frankfurt und 1848*, pp. 270–271. On Stein's participation, see Schwarzschild, *Gruendung*, pp. 13–14.

18. Schwemer, *Frankfurt*, III, part 1, references in the index, but especially pp. 255, 274.

19. Valentin, *Frankfurt und 1848*, p. 441.

20. Schwarzschild, *Gruendung*, p. 18.

21. On the Senate's discussions, see Schwarzschild, *Gruendung*, pp. 17–19.

22. We shall hereafter use IRG as an abbreviation for the *Israelitische Religionsgesellschaft*.

23. These questions have been influenced by the work of George Rudé and others. George Rudé, *The Crowd in the French Revolution* (London, 1959), pp. 4–5.

24. *Gedaechtnisrolle, angefertigt anlaesslich der Grundsteinlegung zu einem Gotteshause am 30. September 1852.* Frankfurt a.m. Archives of the Leo Baeck Institute, New York.

25. Hirsch, *Gesammelte Schriften,* (Frankfurt, 1906), III, 526.

26. Saemy Japhet, "The Secession Movement of S. R. Hirsch," *Historia Judaica,* X (1948), 118.

27. On the petition, see below in this chapter.

28. Schwarzschild, *Gruendung,* pp. 26–27. Japhet claimed that eighty members were present at the meeting, but I have relied on Schwarzschild, who was actively involved at the time.

29. The list of eleven appears in Schwarzschild, *Gruendung,* p. 17, plus erratum after p. 48, and in Jubilee issue of *Israelit* (1908), pp. 34–35. For his supplementary list, see pp. 22–23, 25. Japhet's list is in "Secession," p. 118.

The name Gustav Hoflesch (C-4) is otherwise unknown to me and difficult to discern in the original.

30. Alexander Dietz, *Stammbuch der Frankfurter Juden* (Frankfurt, 1907). Also used was Wilhelm Dann, *Stammtafel & Register der Nachkommenschaft des Samuel Alexander Levi (Dann) aus Frankfurt A.M.* (Frankfurt, 1870).

31. Dietz, *Stammbuch,* pp. 52–53, 218–219, and Paul Arnsberg, *Bilder aus dem juedischen Leben im alten Frankfurt* (Frankfurt, 1970), pp. 52, 247.

32. Paul Arnsberg, *Jakob H. Schiff* (Frankfurt, 1969). Dietz, *Stammbuch,* pp. 23, 176–177, 280, 282, 316.

33. Those with immediate family were: Selig and Seligmann Schwarzschild; Lazarus and Salomon Posen; Ludwig, David, and Moses Rapp; Moses and Michael Mainz; Wolf, Salomon, and Loeb Bass; Meier and Benedict Goldschmidt. Anselm and Willy Rothschild, as well as Moses Michael and Nathan Marcus Oppenheim(er) were uncles and nephews, respectively. M. H. Bass and Meier Mainz were cousins of those already mentioned, and Juda and Menko Kulp were cousins.

34. Schwarzschild, *Gruendung,* p. 20.

35. *Protokolle des Grossen Raths* (1849), May 1, 1849, entry 607 states: "*Es ist von der Wiederbesetzung der erledigten Stelle eines Senats-Commissaers fuer die Angelegenheiten der israelitischen Gemeinde Umgang zu nehmen*" The entry proceeds to grant the board expanded powers. See also the entry of August 14, 1849, entry 1101—"*Von der Genehmigung eines Senatscommissaers nichtweiter abhaengig.*" Apparently, the position was eliminated out of the demands of the Jewish community for autonomy and equality. Relevant in this regard is the community's petition for a new governing regulation, *Protokolle* (1848), August 15, 1848, entry 809.

However, a less authoritative version of the position was apparently reestablished a few years later, for by 1853 the protocols do speak at various times of a supervisor for Jewish affairs. *Protokolle* (1853), entry 273; (1854), entry 832; (1861), entry 2296; (1863), entry 843; (1864), entry 1809; (1866), entry 364. This indicates that the position continued even after the granting of full emancipation in 1864.

36. *AZJ*, XIII (1849), 265–266.

37. *Gemeinde-Ordnung fuer die israelitische Religionsgemeinde in Frankfurt am Main* (1851), pp. iii-vi, SUBF.

38. *Ueber den Entwurf einer neuen Gemeinde-Ordnung fuer die israelitische Gemeinde*, SUBF.

39. Schwarzschild, *Gruendung*, pp. 22–23; *AZJ*, XV (1851), p. 113.

40. Schwarzschild, *Gruendung*, pp. 22–23, 25.

41. Board and Council memberships are listed in the annual *Staats-Kalendar der Freien Stadt Frankfurt* available in the SUBF. Michael Meyer has found in his analysis of the early membership of the Hamburg Temple Association that it also drew heavily from the middle class and especially from merchants. "The Establishment of the Hamburg Temple," *Studies in the History of Jewish Society Presented to Professor Jacob Katz* (Hebrew, Jerusalem, 1980), p. 120.

42. A number of contemporary newspaper references referred to the members of the Orthodox party generally and especially to the constituency of the IRG as "Geldmaenner." Such sources, often polemical in nature, merely complement the analysis offered here. *AZJ*, III (1839), 281; XV (1851), 498; XVI (1852), 547; and *Orient*, VI (1845), 131–132.

43. The following general discussion derives extensively from Jacob Toury's excellent analysis in his *Turmoil and Confusion in the Revolution of 1848* (Hebrew, Tel Aviv, 1968), pp. 120–148.

44. *Ibid.*, pp. 128–129.

45. *Ibid.*, pp. 131, 134–135.

46. *Ibid.*, pp. 134. For a listing and reproduction of the important caricatures, see Alfred Rubens, "The Rothschilds in Caricature," *Transactions of the Jewish Historical Society of England*, XXII (London, 1970), pp. 76–87.

47. Toury, *Turmoil*, pp. 139–140. My emphasis.

48. Alexander Weill, *Rothschild und die Europaeischen Staaten* (Stuttgart, 1844), pp. 11–12, 38–41.

49. Toury, *Turmoil*, pp. 145–148.

50. Salo Baron, "Revolution of 1848 and Jewish Emancipation," *Jewish Social Studies*, XI (1949), 205–206, and 224. In a note on p. 206, Baron lists a number of anti-Rothschild attacks appearing in the *Orient*. In addition, see *Orient*, VII (1846), p. 8.

51. *AZJ*, III (1839), 131–132 and 134–135.

52. Heinrich Heine, *Confessio Judaica*, ed. Hugo Bieber (Berlin, 1925), p. 9.

53. *Orient*, V (1844), 69, and *AZJ*, I (1837), 321. Other reports of hostility between the Rothschilds and the members of the *Reformverein* are in *Orient*, IV (1844), 268 and 398. Also *AZJ*, VIII (1844), p. 307.

54. Erich Achterberg, *Frankfurter Bankherren* (Frankfurt, 1956). On many of the Jewish bankers, see Hans-Dieten Kirchholtes, *Juedische Privat-banken in Frankfurt am Main* (Frankfurt, 1969).

55. *Wechsel und Merkantil-Ordnung der Freien Stadt Frankfurt* (Frankfurt, 1845) in *SUBF*, especially p. 32, and Edouard Souchay, *Anmerkungen zu den Wechsel-Gesetzen der Freien Stadt Frankfurt* (Frankfurt, 1845) also in *SUBF*, pp. 80–81.

56. *AZJ*, VIII (1844), 223.

57. Stein, *Mein Dienst Verhaeltniss*, pp. 8–10. Also, *Orient*, V (1844), 245; *AZJ*, VIII (1844), 465–466.

58. *AZJ.*, p. 607.

59. *Ibid.*, pp. 702–703.

60. *Ibid.*, p. 747.

61. *Orient*, V (1844), 404–405. Stein also placed great significance on the dispute over the new ordinance, declaring that "the seeds of separation and aversion had been sown." Stein, *Dienst Verhaeltniss*, p. 9.

62. See Fritz Stern's chapter on "Prussia" in *European Landed Elites in the Nineteenth Century*, ed. David Spring (Baltimore, Md., 1977), pp. 46–48, and *idem, Gold and Iron* (New York, 1977), p. 477.

63. Quoted in Stern, "Prussia," 54–55.

64. See chap. one.

65. Stern, "Prussia," p. 55.

66. Ernest K. Bramsted, *Aristocracy and the Middle Classes in Germany*, rev. (Chicago, 1964), pp. 182–199, especially 192.

67. *Jeschurun*, I (1854), pp. 97–98. The admiration stands despite the writer's denial: "*Wir sind gewiss die Letzten, die einer juedischen Aristokratie, zumal einer Geldaristokratie, das Wort reden wollen.*"

68. *AZJ*, XIV (1850), p. 582, article 20. For changes in these new regulations on matters of religion between April 1849 and September 1850, compare *AZJ*, XIII (1849), pp. 251–252, 265–266, and 385. In June 1849, there appeared a clause—"*Der Staat hat kein Recht, Geistliche oder Religionslehrer oder Beamte einer Religionsgesellschaft vorzuschlagen, zu waehlen, zu ernennen oder zu bestaetigen.*" This clause does not appear by 1850.

69. The petition was published under the title "Der erste Schritt zur Berufung Rabbiner Hirschs nach Frankfurt a.M.," in *Nachalath Z'wi*, VII (1937), pp. 271–274, and in *Hirsch—Jubilaeums-Nummer der Israelit* (1908), pp. 34–35. The Senate's discussions are in *Protokollen des Grossen Raths* (1850), Entries 140, 200, 267, 391, 440, 525, 601, 666. Schwarzschild's detailed account is on pp. 17–19.

70. For the later ruling, see *Grossen Rath* (1852), entry 49, section 2.

Since the government now required a civil marriage as prerequisite for the religious ceremony, it apparently at first denied the IRG rabbi this privilege as a concession to the community. *AZJ*, XIV (1850), 582–583, section 23.

A newspaper entry of September 1851 implies that Hirsch *was* to be given the right to conduct weddings, and by no later than 1861 Hirsch did enjoy that right. Testimony to this effect is given in an 1862 memorandum submitted by the IRG of Mainz petitioning for that same privilege. *CAHJP*, Samson Raphael Hirsch Collection, HM 4763, item 14, p. 32. See *AZJ*, XV (1850), 498.

71. From a reference in the text to the appointment some eighteen months before of the commission to formulate a new set of community ordinances, the document can be dated to approximately September 1850—a year before Hirsch's arrival in Frankfurt. *CAHJP*, Samson Raphael Hirsch Collection, HM 4763, item 43.

72. The full account of Sachs's interest in the position in Frankfurt is recorded in Schwarzschild, *Gruendung*, pp. 20–25.

73. Biographers of Sachs have paid no attention to this chapter in his career. Bernfeld refers to the invitation to come to Frankfurt as a complimentary indication of Sachs's stature, but the Frankfurt position was only made famous by its later occupant. Yet, Sachs's acceptance of that invitation reveals the extent of his frustrations in Berlin; his subsequent reneging reveals weak aspects within his personality. On Sachs, see S. Bernfeld's biography in Hebrew, *Michael Sachs—Events of his Life and his Literary Works* (Berlin, 1900), and Josef Eschelbacher, *Michael Sachs, Vortrag* (Berlin, 1908).

74. *Grossen Rath* (1850), entry 1182. The agreement was announced in *AZJ*, XIV (1850), p. 643, as well as in *Orient*, XI (1850), p. 177.

75. Sachs's plea stated that he found himself *"zwischen haeuslichen Unannehmlichkeit und oeffentlichen Pflichten stehend, sei seine Kraft gebrochen und er nicht im Stande, diesen Pflichten gerecht zu werden."* Schwarzschild, *Gruendung*, p. 24. Schwarzschild also contrasted Sachs's elaborate and prosaic letters to the board with the brief responses of Hirsch, who made no conditions and asked only that his family be taken care of. *Ibid.*, p. 27. If this last description is accurate, it would contrast greatly with Hirsch's previous negotiations for rabbinical positions as described by Heinrich Graetz. See Graetz, *Tagebuch*, pp. 76–79.

76. *Samson Raphael Hirsch—Jubilaeums-Nummer der Israelit* (Frankfurt, 1908), p. 36, letter III.

77. Hirsch's letter to Josaphat is in *ibid.*, p. 36, letter IV.

78. The attempt to convince Hirsch to remain is described best in his letter to the IRG board. The letter appeared in *Nachalath Z'wi*, VI (1936), pp. 252–256. For the IRG's response, see Schwarzschild, *Gruendung*, pp. 27–28.

CHAPTER FOUR–CHAMPION OF ORTHODOXY

1. "Samson Raphael Hirsch. Ein Lebensbild," in *Samson Raphael Hirsch—Jubilaeums-Nummer der Israelit* (Frankfurt, 1908), pp. 5–17. Frankfurter's father was named Zevi Hirsch and family members were variously named Frankfurter, Hirsch, and also Mendelssohn. Frankfurter himself used the name Hirsch in official documents. Josef Goldschmidt, *Geschichte der Talmud Tora Realschule in Hamburg* (Hamburg, 1905), p. 12n and n. 5 below. For the family history, see Eduard Duckesz, "Zur Geneologie Samson Raphael Hirsch," *JJLG*, XVII (1926), 103–131.

2. Duckesz, "Geneologie," pp. 115–123, and Duckesz, *Iwoh Lemoschaw* (Hebrew, Krakau, 1903), pp. 88–92. Goldschmidt, *Talmud Tora*, pp. 12–13.

3. Goldschmidt, *Talmud Tora*, pp. 12–36. Mordechai Eliav, *Jewish Education in Germany in the Period of the Enlightenment and Emancipation* (Hebrew, Jerusalem, 1960), pp. 134, 159–160.

4. Eliav, *Jewish Education*, p. 160.

5. Duckesz, "Geneologie," pp. 119–120. Frankfurter signed these reports as Mendel Hirsch.

6. CAHJP, AHW Collection, Item 542a, entries 283–284. Goldschmidt, *Talmud Tora*, pp. 46ff.

7. Goldschmidt, *Talmud Tora*, pp. 22, 32–41; Helga Krohn, *Die Juden in Hamburg 1800–1850* (Frankfurt, 1967), pp. 28–31. The importance of these family relations will be explained below.

8. David Philipson, *The Reform Movement in Judaism*, 2nd ed. (New York, 1967), pp. 29–34. On the polemical controversy, see Jakob J. Petuchowski, *Prayerbook Reform in Europe* (New York, 1968), pp. 86–98. On the controversy in Hamburg, see Michael A. Meyer. "The Establishment of the Hamburg Temple," *Studies in the History of Jewish Society Presented to Professor Jacob Katz* (Hebrew, Jerusalem, 1980), pp. 218–224.

9. *Hirsch Jubilaeums-Nummer*, p. 6. For an English summary, see I. Grunfeld's introduction to *Judaism Eternal*, 2 vols. (London, 1956), p. xxiii. The credibility of this source will be established through a parallel source to be introduced below.

10. Philipson, *Reform Movement*, pp. 11–18.

11. Monika Richarz, *Der Eintritt der Juden in die akademischen Berufe* (Tuebingen, 1974), pp. 106–107.

12. Ludwig Geiger, *Abraham Geiger. Leben und Lebenswerk* (Berlin, 1910), pp. 5–10. Years later, Abraham fondly recalled his studies with his brother. See the poem composed in honor of Solomon's sixtieth birthday in Abraham Geiger, *Nachgelassene Schriften*, 5 vols. (Berlin, 1875–

1878), V, 373–374. See also the comment in his childhood memoir, I, 301.

13. *Ibid.*, I, 302.

14. Raphael Breuer, *Unter seinem Banner* (Frankfurt, 1908), p. 213.

15. Grunfeld in *Judaism Eternal*, I, xxv. See the discussion on Hirsch's elementary education in Noah H. Rosenbloom, *Tradition in an Age of Reform* (Philadelphia, 1976), pp. 53–56, and Mordechai Breuer's review in *Tradition*, XVI (1977) no. 4, pp. 140–149, especially 140–141. On the problem, but not the solution, see Robert Liberles, "Champion of Orthodoxy: The Emergence of Samson Raphael Hirsch as Religious Leader," *AJS Review*, VI (1981), 58.

16. Richarz, *Eintritt*, pp. 92, 96, 106, 188. Geiger, *Schriften*, V, 27.

17. Richarz, *Eintritt*, pp. 188–190.

18. Geiger, *Schriften*, V, 19.

19. Richarz, *Eintritt*, p. 107n. See also pp. 111, 118, 190. Geiger, *Schriften*, V, 27.

20. *Ibid.*, p. 19.

21. Ludwig Geiger, *Leben und Lebenswerk*, pp. 13–18. Two letters are in *Schriften*, V, 48–50, and 77–79. The third letter, dated February 26, 1832, has been called to my attention by Dr. Murray Rossman. Isak Markon, "Ein unveroeftentlicher Brief von Abraham Geiger an Samson Raphael Hirsch," Bar Ilan University, Sanger Collection 0115. The original letter is also at Bar Ilan in the Hirsch Collection.

22. "Unveroeffentlicher Brief" and Geiger, *Schriften*, V, 54–55. Ullmann was later rabbi in Koblenz; Frensdorff became director of the teachers' seminar in Hannover; Hess apparently died young and is not otherwise identifiable. Geiger described all three in his diary, *Schriften*, V, 20–22. See also Ludwig Geiger, *Leben*, p. 14.

23. *Schriften*, p. 78.

24. Leo Trepp, *Die Oldenburger Judenschaft* (Oldenburg, 1973), p. 131.

25. Samson Raphael Hirsch, *The Nineteen Letters of Ben Uziel*, trans. Bernard Drachman (New York, 1899), pp. 212–213.

26. *Ibid.*, p. 173. For Hirsch's critical comments on the Orthodoxy of his age, see the eighteenth letter of Ben Uziel. In this regard, see the review of Rosenbloom's study on Hirsch by Aryeh Rubinstein, "Orthodox Critic," *The Jerusalem Post Magazine*, February 11, 1977, p. 14.

27. "Neues Stadium des Kampfes in dem Judenthume unserer Zeit," *WZJT*, II (1836), 209–225.

28. *Ibid.*, 225. The second work was S. L. Steinheim, *Die Offenbarung nach dem Lehrbegriffe der Synagogue, ein Schiboleth* (Frankfurt, 1835).

29. *WZJT*, II (1836), 351–359, 518–548, and III (1837), 74–91. Gottlieb Klein explained the discrepancy between the two reviews by suggesting that Geiger had only seen the early chapters of *The Nineteen Letters*

when he wrote the first review. However, that essay contains quotations from the seventeenth letter! See p. 224. For Klein, see *Leben und Lebenswerk*, p. 287.

30. *WZJT*, II (1836), p. 352.

31. *Ibid.*, p. 353.

32. *Ibid.*, p. 355.

33. *Ibid.*, pp. 354ff.

34. See, for example, the review by Jost in *Annalen*, I (1839), 73–78, and also the comment on 351; the series of exchanges in the literary supplement to the *AZJ*, III (1839); and H. B. Fassel, *Herev Be-Tzayon* (Leipzig, 1839).

35. For example, Hirsch, *Letters*, pp. 213–214, 216–217.

36. *WZJT*, III (1837), 88–91.

37. Isaac Heinemann, "Mehkarim al R. Shimshon Raphael Hirsch," *Sinai*, XXIV (1949), 249–271. Also Noah Rosenbloom, *Tradition*, pp. 80–81. Hirsch's polemical writings from this period include: *Erste Mitteilungen* (1838); *Postscripta* (1840); and *Zweite Mitteilungen* (1844).

38. *Hirsch Jubilaeums-Nummer*, p. 6. The finest studies of Hirsch's writings and thought can still be found in the various essays of Isaac Heinemann. On *Horeb*, see especially his chapter on Hirsch in *Taamei HaMitzvot BeSifrut Israel*, 2 vols. (Hebrew, Jerusalem, 1956), II, 91–161.

39. Hirsch, *Letters*, pp. 103–105.

40. Michael Creizenach, *Shulchan Aruch oder encyclopedische Darstellung des Mosaischen Gesetzes*, 4 vols. (Frankfurt, 1833–1840).

41. *Ibid.*, I, vii, x.

42. From the author's Foreword to *Horeb*, pp. clv–clvi. All references to Hirsch's writings have been made to the available English translations, although the translations themselves have at times been modified.

The seriousness with which Hirsch took Creizenach's work is indicated in Hirsch's first literary polemic against the Reformers, the *Erste Mittheilungen*, which is devoted to a refutation of the first volume of Creizenach's *Schulchan Aruch*.

43. *Horeb*, pp. clvii–clviii.

44. *Ibid.*, p. clviii.

45. Isaac Heinemann, *Taamei HaMitzvoth*, p. 91, and "Samson Raphael Hirsch: The Formative Years of the Leader of Modern Orthodoxy," *Historia Judaica*, XIII (1951), p. 46.

46. For Grunfeld's understanding of the title, see *Horeb*, pp. xxx–xxxi. Rosenbloom correctly posed the question of why the title *Horeb* and not Sinai. For his answer, see *Tradition*, pp. 125–126.

47. The letter appeared in English in *Horeb*, pp. cxli–cxlv. It had previously appeared in Hebrew with minor differences in *Sinai*, XIV (1944), 62–64.

48. *Horeb*, I, 154.

49. *Nineteen Letters*, p. 208.

50. The prospectus is in *Nachalath Z'wi*, II (1932), 257–260.

51. Hirsch indicated at the end of this passage that it came from Malachi 3:23. However, there are several changes in nuance from the biblical passage, one of which was the transformation of Elijah as one who will come at the end of days to Elijah as a reappearing savior.

52. Hirsch, *Judaism Eternal*, II, 129. The passage originally appeared in *Jeschurun*, I (1854), 322–323.

53. The essay appeared in *Jeschurun*, XIV (1868), 205–215. It is available in English in *Judaism Eternal*, II, 291–300. On the traditional identification of Phinehas with Elijah, see the references in Louis Ginzberg, *The Legends of the Jews*, 7 vols. (Philadelphia, 1946–1947), III, 389; IV, 195; and the notes in VI, 138; and especially 316–317.

54. *Judaism Eternal*, II, 292.

55. *Ibid.*, p. 296.

56. *Ibid.*, II, 129.

57. *Ibid.*, II, 300, and *Horeb*, p. cxliii.

58. *Judaism Eternal*, II, 291–292. The biblical account is in Numbers, chap. 25.

59. Ginzberg, *Legends*, III, 385, 388–389.

60. See note 1 above.

61. In fact, contrast Hirsch's rendition with the traditional Midrash in which Aaron's wife Elisheba counts among her joys "her grandson, Phinehas, priest of war." Ginzberg, *Legends*, III, 187, based on Zevahim 102a. My gratitude to Dr. Carmi Horowitz for calling this Midrash to my attention.

62. An additional literary clue to Hirsch's perceived estrangement from his father is provided when Hirsch *misquoted* the biblical passage describing Elijah's flight to Horeb, for Hirsch added the words actually spoken by Elijah earlier in the chapter: "I am no better than my fathers." Hirsch effectively moved this phrase from I Kings 19:4 to 19:14, so that these words were now spoken by Elijah at Horeb, which was not the case in the biblical account. "Karmel und Sinai," *Nachalath Z'wi*, II (1932), 258–259. In studying the dynamics of Hirsch's personality, an objective evaluation of the father-son relationship would prove not only speculative, but far less relevant than Hirsch's perception of that relationship as revealed in his literary testimony.

63. For the difficulties Hirsch faced in Nikolsburg, see Rosenbloom, *Tradition*, pp. 83–94. Josaphat's letter to Hirsch is in *Jubilee Israelit*, p. 36, letter III.

64. *Gedaechtnisrolle, angefertigt anlaesslich der Grundstein legung zu einem Gotteshause am 30, September 1852* (Frankfurt, 1852). Archives of the Leo Baeck Institute, New York.

CHAPTER FIVE–MODEL COMMUNITY

1. Emanuel Schwarzschild, *Die Gruendung der Israelitischen Religions-gesellschaft* (Frankfurt, 1896), pp. 28–29.

2. On conflicts over the question of synagogue location in other communities, see H. Hammer-Schenk, *Untersuchungen zum Synagogen-bau, 1800–1871*, (Bamberg, 1974), passim.

3. Guenther Vogt, *Frankfurter Buergerhaeuser des Neunzehnten Jahr-hunderts* (Frankfurt, 1970), pp. 17, 123–126, and Fried Leubbecke, *Das Antlitz der Stadt* (Frankfurt, 1952), pp. 130–131.

4. *Gedaechtnisrolle, angefertigt anlaesslich der Grundsteinlegung zu einem Gotteshause am 30, September 1852.* (Frankfurt, 1852), ALBI.

5. Schwarzschild, *Gruendung*, p. 31. Hammer-Schenk, *Synagogen-bau*, p. 159. It is unfortunate that the important and fascinating theme of synagogue architecture has been so badly treated in Hammer-Schenk's work. After observing that the small entrances on both sides of the synagogue building were similar to those found in Mannheim, Hammer-Schenk comments that the desire to give an impression of being closed off played a role in the design of the building, since it corresponded to the reactionary attitudes of the IRG. But the synagogue in Mannheim with similar entrances was a liberal synagogue! To have it both ways, the author concludes: "The similarity of the Orthodox synagogue in Frankfurt with the liberal one in Mannheim demonstrates that architectural forms were independent of the religious tendency of the community." See pp. 159–161.

6. Schwarzschild, *Gruendung*, p. 35. *Programm fuer die Einweihung der Synagoge* (20 September 1853), SUBF.

7. Hammer-Schenk, *Synagogenbau*, p. 482, n. 256; Schwarzschild, *Gruendung*, pp. 35, 43, 45; *Frankfurter Journal*, no. 233 (September 30, 1853), p. 2.

8. *Synagogen-Ordnung fuer die Synagoge Beth Tefilat Jeschurun* (Frankfurt, 1853) and *Synagogen-Ordnung fuer die Synagoge der IRG im Frankfurt a.M.*, (1874), SUBF. On synagogue ordinances in general, see Jakob Petuchowski, *Prayerbook Reform in Europe* (New York, 1968), chap. VI. A selection from the revised IRG code appears on pp. 123–124.

9. For Reform prohibitions on removing shoes in the synagogue, see the ordinances of Wuertemberg (9/g) and Birkenfeld (6/5). For Hold-heim's formulation, see Mecklenburg (11/f). These references are in Petuchowski's work. The IRG rulings on clothing are in the 1853 edition, sections 8 and 19.

10. *Synagogen-Ordnung* (1874), sections 14–18. Herman Schwab, *Memories of Frankfurt* (London, 1955), p. 16.

11. Herman Schwab, *Aus der Schuetzenstrasse* (Frankfurt, 1923), pp. 40–41.

12. *AZJ*, XVII (1953), 540, and Saemy Japhet, "The Secession Movement of S. R. Hirsch," *Historia Judaica*, X (1948), 106. That Hirsch may not have always thought his sermons through in advance fits what we know about his writing as well. In explaining how Hirsch could have been so prolific while maintaining an intensive rabbinical schedule, one writer commented that one need only glance at his manuscripts to answer this question. "One finds . . . no corrections, not one word stricken out; all came ready, out of the head and heart, as a fully formulated whole." Students of Hirsch's writings may not be surprised. *Hirsch—Jubilaeums-Nummer* (1908), p. 14.

13. On Japhet, see Isaac Heinemann's necrology, *Jeschurun*, N.F. V (1918), 241–244.

14. On Reform's approach to synagogue music, see *Encyclopedia Judaica* (1971), XII, 644.

15. Japhet, *Schire Jeschurun* (1864), III; (1881), see table of contents.

16. Schwab, *Memories of Frankfurt*, p. 25. *History of Orthodox Jewry in Germany* (London, 1950), p. 89.

17. Schwab, *Memories of Frankfurt*, pp. 21, 25–26, and in the German edition, *Schuetzenstrasse*, p. 54.

18. *Synagogen-Ordnung* (1853), section 22; (1874), section 33; Petuchowski, *Prayerbook Reform*, pp. 108–109.

19. The Frankfurt liturgical variations are incorporated in the "Roedelheim Siddur," *Sefat Emet*. Solomon Geiger described the Frankfurt customs in detail in *Dibhre Kehillot* (Hebrew, Frankfurt, 1862). On attitudes toward these local customs in Hirsch's time, compare Japhet and Heinemann, *Historia Judaica*, X (1948), 119, 127 and note 9, 130 n. 15. On Horovitz, see J. Unna's introduction to Horovitz, *Frankfurter Rabbinen*, 2nd ed. (Jerusalem, 1969), and David Ellenson, "Accommodation, Resistance, and the Halakhic Process: A Case Study of Two Responsa by Rabbi Marcus Horowitz," *Jewish Civilization: Essays and Studies*, ed. Ronald A. Brauner (Philadelphia, 1981), pp. 83–100.

20. Noah Rosenbloom, *Tradition in an Age of Reform* (Philadelphia, 1976), pp. 69; 420 n. 15. For a discussion of the *Kol Nidre* question in the nineteenth century and on Hirsch's eliminating the prayer once or twice in his younger days, see Petuchowski, *Prayerbook Reform*, pp. 334–347, especially 337–338.

21. *Die Israelitische Synagogengemeinde (Adass Jisroel) zu Berlin, 1869–1904* (Berlin, 1904), p. 22.

22. *Jeschurun*, N.F. V, 241, quoted in Schwab, *Orthodox Jewry*, p. 89.

23. Schwab, *Orthodox Jewry*, p. 88, based on *Hirsch—Jubilaeums-Nummer*, p. 21.

24. *Der Israelit* (1860), 96; *Historia Judaica*, X (1948), 119; Jacob Rosenheim, *Erinnerungen* (Frankfurt, 1970), p. 31, 37.

25. Rosenheim, *Erinnerungen*, p. 31.

26. *Ibid.*, and Schwab, *Schuetzenstrasse*, pp. 16, 40–41.

27. Information based on *Staats und Adress Handbuch der Freien Stadt Frankfurt*, published annually through 1866, and Alexander Dietz, *Stammbuch der Frankfurter Juden* (Frankfurt, 1907). The board elected at the first general meeting in 1851 is identical with that listed in the *Handbuch* for 1855 and included in our survey. The *Handbuch* is available in SUBF.

28. Meier Schueler, *Zur Geschichte der Israelitischen Religionsgesellschaft in Frankfurt a.M.* (1940), p. 23. Manuscript in CAHJP. I wish to thank Professor Jacob Katz for calling this manuscript to my attention.

29. "Liste der... Ausgetreten," *Frankfurt Intelligenz-Blatt* (February 18, 1877).

30. Schwarzschild, *Gruendung*, p. 11. He did not elaborate on the Orthodoxy of nonnative Frankfurters.

31. *Israelit*, VII (1866), 104; *Hirsch—Jubilaeums-Nummer*, p. 36, Letter III; Schwab, *Orthodox Jewry*, p. 42.

32. Rosenbloom has fabricated a scandalous falsehood out of this material, declaring that "Hirsch's act... was tantamount to an endorsement of an incongruous but common concept in his day—the Schinkenorthodoxie, ham-eating orthodoxy." But Rosenbloom clearly did not examine the available by-laws when he wrote that one could "violate Jewish law and simultaneously belong to or even hold office in the traditionalist bastion of the Israelitische Religionsgesellschaft." Rosenbloom, *Tradition*, p. 102.

33. *Statuten der Israelitischen Religionsgesellschaft* (1875), sections 4, 27, SUBF.

34. *Instruktion fuer die Baecker und Conditoren der IRG* (1886), section 1, and *Instruktion fuer die Restauranteure der IRG* (1887), section 1. Both are available in SUBF.

35. "Liste der Ausgetretenen"; *Statuten*, section 29, *Zweite Gedaechtnisrolle. Angefertigt anlaesslich der Grundsteinlegung zum Erweiterungsbau des Gotteshauses* (Frankfurt a.M., 1874), in Archives of the Leo Baeck Institute, New York.

36. Emanuel Schwarzschild, *Die Angriffe des Herrn Rabbiner Sueskind ...beleuchtet von S.* (Frankfurt, 1876), p. 11.

37. Selmar Spier, *Vor 1914, Erinnerungen an Frankfurt* (Frankfurt, 1961), p. 62.

38. For the earlier period, see Schwarzschild, *Die Gruendung*, p. 11; for the later, *An Hohen Senat, Vorstand* (1858), pp. 7–8, SUBF.

39. For Geiger's comments, see Heinemann's references in *Historia Judaica*, X (1948), 127.

40. Later accounts are all based on A. Sulzbach, "Zur Geschichte der Schulanstalten," *Festschrift zur Jubilaeums Feier der Unterrichts-anstalten der IRG zu Frankfurt a.M.* (Frankfurt, 1903), pp. 3–5.

41. CAHJP Samson Raphael Hirsch Collection, HM 4763.

42. The documents are in Sulzbach, *Schulanstalten*, pp. 33–35.

43. *Ibid.*, pp. 34–35. The development of Hirsch's educational philosophy and of the school curriculum has been traced and analyzed in Eleazer Stern, *"Torah im derech Erez": The educational ideal in its development*, unpublished Ph.D. thesis, Hebrew University of Jerusalem (1970), especially pp. 53–73.

44. Rosenheim, *Erinnerungen*, pp. 15–16.

45. Mordechai Eliav, *Jewish Education in Germany in the Period of Enlightenment and Emancipation* (Hebrew, Jerusalem, 1960), pp. 231–232.

46. Eliav, *Jewish Education*, especially pp. 159–161.

47. Schwab, *Schuetzenstrasse*, pp. 14–15; Spier, *Vor 1914*, pp. 67–72; Rosenheim, *Erinnerungen*, pp. 22–33. This interpretation conforms, I believe, to the conclusions reached by Mordechai Breuer, who examined the influence of the state authorities on the IRG's school curriculum. Breuer concluded that the success of the school in inculcating an Orthodox way of life into its graduates was more a function of internal and external social factors, rather than of the precise religious content of the school's curriculum. Following Rosenheim, I am suggesting that the extent of integration into the IRG community was such a primary social factor. "Ideal and Reality in Orthodox Education in 19th Century Germany" (Hebrew), *Annual of Bar-Ilan University Studies in Judaica and the Humanities*, XVI-XVII (1979), 317–335.

48. Schwarzschild, *Die Gruendung*, pp. 42–46.

49. Friedrich Bothe, *Aus Frankfurts Sage und Geschichte* (Frankfurt, 1911), pp. 64–65, 74–79.

50. *Statuten*, p. 5.

51. *Zweite Gedaechtnisrolle.*

52. Schwarzschild, *Gruendung*, p. 46.

53. *Statuten*, section 4, 27.

54. *Ibid.*, p. 4 and sections 1, 2, 32.

55. *AZJ*, XXXIX (1875), 153. Contrast sections 31–32 of the proposed version (1874) with section 32 of the adopted version (1875).

56. *Statuten* (1875), sections 24, 26. These clauses were not in the proposed version. On the controversy over Mendel Hirsch as successor, see Japhet, "Secession Movement," p. 107, and Rosenheim, *Erinnerungen*, pp. 25, 41–42.

57. S. Sueskind, *Die Statuten der IRG zu Frankfurt a.M. Beleuchtet* (Wiesbaden, 1876), p. 4. On Sueskind, see Adolf Kober, *Zur Geschichte der Juden Wiesbadens in der ersten Haelfte des 19 Jahrhunderts* (Wiesbaden, 1913), pp. 27–28.

58. Sueskind, *Statuten*, pp. 4–5, 8–10.
59. *Statuten*, section 2. Sueskind, *Statuten*, pp. 3–4, 7–8.
60. Sueskind, *Statuten*, p. 4.
61. Isaac Hirsch, *Heimleuchtung des Herrn Rabbiner Sueskind von einem "Paganus"* (Frankfurt, 1876), pp. 4–5.
62. *Ibid.*, pp. 12–18.
63. *Ibid.*, p. 22; Schwarzschild, *Angriffe*, p. 7.
64. "Ein Satzungsentwurf von Rabbiner Hirsch," *Nachalath Z'wi*, I (1931), 38.
65. Meier Schueler, *Geschichte*, p. 23.
66. Wilhelm Hanauer, *Zur Statistik der juedischen Bevoelkerung in Frankfurt a.M.* (Frankfurt, 1910), p. 1.
67. *Ibid.*, p. 4.
68. Josef Unna, *Statistik der Frankfurter Juden bis zum Jahre 1866* (Frankfurt, 1931), p. 24.

CHAPTER SIX—THE POLITICS OF SEPARATISM

1. Abraham Geiger, *Nachgelassene Schriften*, 5 vols. (Berlin, 1875–1878), V, pp. 54–55. A selection of Geiger's letters is available in English in Max Wiener, *Abraham Geiger and Liberal Judaism* (Philadelphia, 1962). This letter is in Wiener, pp. 99–100.
2. *Ibid.*, p. 108. Geiger went on to explain that this historical position was, in fact, totally consistent with his personal views. Michael Meyer discussed this aspect of Geiger's thinking in "Abraham Geiger's Historical Judaism," in *New Perspectives on Abraham Geiger*, ed. Jakob Petuchowski (New York, 1975), especially pp. 6–8.
3. Wiener, *Geiger*, p. 89.
4. *Ibid.*, p. 110.
5. Geiger, *Schriften*, V, 117, 188ff, 251. This point has been developed by Jakob Petuchowski in "Abraham Geiger the Reform Jewish Liturgist" in *New Perspectives*, pp. 42–54, and in "Abraham Geiger and Samuel Holdheim," *LBIYB*, XXII (1977), especially pp. 139–142.
6. David Philipson, *The Reform Movement in Judaism*, 2nd ed. (New York, 1967), p. 257.
7. Samuel Holdheim, *Geschichte der Entstehung und Entwickelung der juedischen Reformgemeinde in Berlin* (Berlin, 1857). The community's legal position is discussed in detail on pp. 212–242.
8. *Ibid.*, pp. 216–217.
9. *Ibid.*, pp. 228–233, where Holdheim also explained his main objections to the congregation's response.
10. *Ibid.*, pp. 228–229.
11. *Ibid.*, pp. 228, 234.

12. Philipson, *Reform Movement*, p. 257. Philipson's formulation is based on Moritz Levin, *Die Reform des Judenthums* (Berlin, 1895), pp. 98–99. But Levin also pointed out that double taxation represented the free choice of the Reform congregation. Both writers, in attributing the lack of growth of Reform congregations in Germany to double taxation, also ignore that the secession law of 1876 eventually alleviated the burden of double taxation. Pointedly, the Reformers voluntarily chose not to take advantage of such arrangements. See Holdheim, *Geschichte*, pp. 241–242, and *AZJ*, XIII (1854), 311. For a comprehensive review of the complicated problem of double taxation in Berlin, see Moritz Tuerk, "Das erste Gemeindestatut und die Genossenschaft fuer Reform im Judentum," in *Festschrift zum 70 Geburtstage von Moritz Schaefer* (Berlin, 1927), pp. 241–257.

13. Philipson, *Reform Movement*, p. 257.

14. Jakob Petuchowski, *Prayerbook Reform in Europe* (New York, 1968), chap. III, especially pp. 42–43.

15. Letter to Rabbi Ullmann in Colbenz, Geiger, *Nachgelassene Schriften*, V, 55.

16. Direct evidence for this approach can be found in the controversy between Reformers and Orthodox over passage of the Law of Secession, discussed in chap. seven. Notice should also be given to Leopold Stein's objections to the *Reformverein* that one segment of the community must not achieve emancipation at the expense of the whole. *Literaturblatt des Orients* (1843), 726–727.

17. See chap. two.

18. *AZJ*, XII (1848), 437–438.

19. Holdheim, *Reformgemeinde*, pp. 216–217.

20. See Philippson's article, "Die Organisirung der juedischen Religions-gemeinde," *AZJ*, XII (1848), 337–338.

21. *Protokolle des Grossen Raths* (1851), entry 711 (July 1).

22. Salo Baron has argued that the 1848 revolution had a positive impact on Jewish communal life: "Contrary to expectation, the revolution of 1848 reinforced rather than weakened the Jewish communal structure." But of the examples brought by Baron: the unification of Sephardic and Ashkenazi congregations in Paris never materialized; the German synod was held only in 1869 and the Joint Rabbinical Conference scheduled for 1848 was never convened; the Berlin initiative for a centralized organization of Prussian Jewry received little support; the Prague community resisted the calls to decentralize its power in Bohemia, and S. R. Hirsch's attempts to restructure the community in Moravia "led to no tangible results." True, the *École Rabbinique* of Metz was eventually reorganized, but such attempts preceded the revolution and the seminary was moved to Paris only in 1859. The one area in

which there apparently was significant reform was in opening the financial books of the community to a broader scope of supervision. On the whole, it appears that the communal reforms precipitated in 1848 were as short-lived as the revolutionary success. What can be argued is that the political emancipation of European Jewry did not weaken communal structure to the extent usually described. On the relation between emancipation and a continuing community structure, see Ismar Schorsch, *Jewish Reactions to Germany Anti-Semitism, 1870–1914* (New York, 1972), pp. 29–30, and Uriel Tal, *Christians and Jews in Germany* (Ithaca, N.Y., 1975), pp. 110–117. Baron's thesis is in "Aspects of the Jewish Communal Crisis in 1848," *Jewish Social Studies*, XIV (1952), especially pp. 133–144.

23. See, for example, Jost, *Neuere Geschichte der Israeliten*, 3 vols. (Berlin, 1846–1847), I, 101.

24. But see *Treuer Zionswaechter*, II (1846), 50, where one of the first Orthodox writers in the press to recognize the significant growth of Reform reached the opposite conclusion and supported the call for Orthodox separation.

25. On Hamburg, see M. M. Haarbleicher, *Aus der Geschichte der Deutsch-Israelitischen Gemeinde* (Hamburg, 1866), pp. 405–406, 456ff, 502ff, and Helga Krohn, *Die Juden in Hamburg 1848–1918* (Hamburg, 1974), pp. 40–49. On Berlin, see n. 12 above.

26. Michael A. Meyer, "Rabbi Gedaliah Tiktin and the Breslau Community (1845–1854)," *Michael*, II (Tel Aviv, 1973), 92–107.

27. Moritz Tuerk, "Gemeindestatut," Krohn, *Juden in Hamburg*, pp. 56–64. The case of Hamburg will be discussed in greater detail below in this chapter.

28. The legal reversals suffered during the period are discussed in Jacob Toury, *Soziale und politische Geschichte der Juden in Deutschland 1846–1871* (Duesseldorf, 1977), pp. 299–308.

29. See chap. three.

30. *Nachalath Z'wi*, VII (1937), 273.

31. *Protokolle des Grossen Raths* (1851), entry 711 (July 1).

32. The election of Hirsch is noted in *Protokolle des Grossen Raths* (1851), entry 654 (June 17). The initial request for the transfer of authority is in entry 1005 (September 30). A previous attempt to expand the authority of the IRG rabbi was made while Michael Sachs was still the rabbi-designate of the congregation. Then the IRG petitioned for Sachs's right to conduct weddings which would be recognized by the authorities. That petition was also refused. *Protokolle* (1850), 1298 (December 17).

33. *Protokolle des Grossen Raths* (1852), entry 49 (January 13).

34. Contrast, for example, the active intervention by the authorities

in Mecklenburg once they had reached a similar reevaluation of the religious conflict. Leopold Donath, *Geschichte der Juden in Mecklenburg* (Leipzig, 1874), pp. 247–249.

35. The following petitions were available in SUBF. *An Hohen Senat der freien Stadt Frankfurt, Gehorsamster Bericht des Vorstands der Israelitischen Gemeinde* (1854); *An Hohen Senat der freien Stadt Frankfurt, Gehorsamster Vorstellung und Bitte des Vorstandes der Israelitischen Gemeinde* (1855); *An Hohen Senat der freien Stadt Frankfurt, Gehorsamster Bericht und Bitten von Seiten des Vorstandes der israelitischen Gemeinde dahier* (1858); *An Hohen Senat der freien Stadt Frankfurt, Gehorsamster Vorstellung von Seiten des Vorstandes der Israelitischen Religions-Gesellschaft dahier* (1858). Future references will indicate the date of the petition and the side from which it came.

36. *An Senat, Vorstand* (1856), p. 6; (1858), p. 19. *An Senat, IRG* (1858), pp. 32–33.

37. *An Senat, IRG* (1858), p. 18.

38. *Ibid.*, pp. 12, 20.

39. *An Senat, Vorstand* (1854), p. 4.

40. *An Senat, Vorstand* (1858), p. 7.

41. *An Senat, IRG* (1858), pp. 39–40.

42. *Ibid.*, p. 34. Samson Raphael Hirsch, "Juedisches Gemeindewesen," *Gesammelte Schriften*, I (Frankfurt, 1908), especially 212–222. For an English translation, see the collection of Hirsch's essays *Judaism Eternal*, 2 vols. (London, 1967), II, 97–107.

43. Salo W. Baron, *The Jewish Community*, 3 vols. (Philadelphia, 1942), I, 348–356. Jacob Katz, *Tradition and Crisis* (New York, 1961), pp. 157–167.

44. *AZJ*, V (1841), 714–716; VI (1842), 64–65; *Orient*, III (1842), 155. On the historical process in France, see Phyllis Albert, *The Modernization of French Jewry* (Hanover, N.H., 1977). For an example of the influence of French rationalization in Germany, see the statutes of Westphalia under Napoleonic rule in Petuchowski, *Prayerbook Reform in Europe*, pp. 106–111.

45. Ludwig von Roenne and Heinrich Simon, *Die frueheren und gegenwaertigen Verhaeltnisse der Juden in den saemmtlichen Landestheilendes Preussischen Staates* (Breslau, 1843), pp. 128–137.

46. *An Senat, Vorstand* (1858), pp. 8–9.

47. *An Senat, IRG* (1858), p. 23.

48. *Protokolle des Grossen Raths* (1858), entry 213 (July 13).

49. Leopold Stein, *Mein Dienst-Verhaeltniss zum Israelitischen Gemeinde Vorstande zu Frankfurt a.M.* (Frankfurt, 1861). Robert Liberles, "Leopold Stein and the Paradox of Reform Clericalism," *LBIYB*, XXVII (1982), 261–279.

50. *Protokolle des Grossen Raths* (1861), entry 460 (July 30).

51. Wiener, *Geiger*, pp. 56–58.

52. *Gesetz und Statuten—Sammlung der Freien Stadt Frankfurt*, IX, 221–224, in SUBF.

53. Richard Schwemer, *Geschichte der Freien Stadt Frankfurt, 1814–1866*, III, part 2, (Frankfurt, 1918), 209. A previous law affecting the rights of both groups had been passed in 1853. That law had granted Jews complete voting rights, but had left restrictions on the right to be elected and on positions that Jews could hold. Schwemer, pp. 75–76. On the controversy that followed passage of the 1853 act and on Bismarck's involvement, see *ibid.*, pp. 77–78, and Otto Joehlinger *Bismarck und die Juden* (Berlin, 1921), pp. 16–17.

54. *Israelit*, VI (1865), 43–44.

55. *Ibid.*, pp. 63–64, 204.

56. See n. 52 above.

57. This view was based on clauses 14–15 of the 1812 law, Freund, *Die Emanzipation der Juden in Preussen*, 2 vols. (Berlin, 1912), II, 456. For opinions from the 1830s and 1840s, see Roenne and Simon, *Verhaeltnisse*, pp. 78–79. This matter remained unchanged in Prussia by the 1847 law. See clause 59 in Freund, II, 516.

58. Krohn, *Juden in Hamburg*, pp. 40–64. Haarbleicher, *Deutsch-Israelitische Gemeinde*, p. 457.

59. *Ibid.*, pp. 458–459.

60. *Ibid.*, pp. 462ff, Krohn, *Juden in Hamburg*, pp. 56ff.

61. Krohn, pp. 49–50.

62. See n. 45 above.

63. Samson Raphael Hirsch, *Der Austritt aus der Gemeinde* (Frankfurt, 1876), pp. 13–14.

64. Haarbleicher, *Deutsch-Israelitische Gemeinde*, pp. 502ff; Krohn, *Juden in Hamburg*, pp. 60ff.

65. *Protokolle des Grossen Raths* (1866), entry 364 (January 23).

CHAPTER SEVEN–UNIFICATION AND SEPARATION

1. *Israelit*, XIII (1872), 1070–1071.

2. Richard Schwemer, *Geschichte der Freien Stadt Frankfurt* vol. III, part 2 (Frankfurt, 1918). For the period under discussion, see pp. 186–527.

3. *Ibid.*, pp. 203–208.

4. *Ibid.*, p. 230.

5. *Ibid.*, p. 206.

6. *Ibid.*, p. 258.

7. *Ibid.*, p. 259.

8. *Ibid.*, pp. 260–262.

9. *Ibid.*, pp. 308–309. For the Jewish element in the flight from Frankfurt, see Jacob Toury, *Die politischen Orientierungen der Juden in Deutschland* (Tuebingen, 1966), pp. 132–133, and Hans-Dieten Kirchholtes, *Juedische Privatbanken in Frankfurt am Main* (Frankfurt, 1969), p. 55. On the arrangements for Swiss citizenship, see Selmar Spier, *Vor 1914, Erinnerungen an Frankfurt* (Frankfurt, 1961), p. 25. But see *AZJ*, XXX (1866), p. 474.

10. Schwemer, *Geschichte*, III, part 2, pp. 352–356.

11. *Ibid.*, pp. 382–418. Fritz Stern, *Gold and Iron* (New York, 1977), pp. 90–92.

12. Otto Joehlinger, *Bismarck und die Juden* (Berlin, 1921), p. 18. Stern, *Gold and Iron*, p. 100.

13. Schwemer, *Geschichte*, III, part 2, pp. 449–451.

14. *AZJ*, XXXI (1867), 601. See also *ibid.*, XXXV (1871), 738–739, 901.

15. *Israelit*, XI (1870), 121, 564.

16. *Ibid.*, VIII (1867), 206–207 and also 219–221.

17. Abraham Geiger, *Nachgelassene Schriften*, 5 vols. (Berlin, 1875–1878), V, 300. See the discussion in Ludwig Geiger, *Abraham Geiger. Leben und Lebenswerk* (Berlin, 1910), pp. 193–195.

18. Abraham Geiger, *Schriften*, V, 300–301.

19. Klaus Gerteis, *Leopold Sonnemann*, Studien zur Frankfurter Geschichte, Heft 3 (Frankfurt, 1970), pp. 56–68.

20. Abraham Geiger, *Schriften*, V, 311–312. Ludwig Geiger, *Leben*, pp. 200–203.

21. The volumes of Hirsch's commentary appeared as follows: Genesis, 1867; Exodus, 1869; Leviticus, 1873; Numbers, 1876; Deuteronomy, 1878. For an English edition of the commentary, see Hirsch, *The Pentateuch Translated and Explained*, trans. Isaac Levy, 2nd ed. (New York, 1971).

22. For the *Midrash*, see *Exodus Rabbah*, I, 8. In English, see *Midrash Rabbah* (Soncino edition, London, 1939) III, 9. The interpretation based on the new king coming from a new dynasty is in, among others, U. Cassuto, *A Commentary on the Book of Exodus* (Jerusalem, 1967); S. L. Gordon, *Hamishah Humshei Torah* I (Hebrew, Tel Aviv, 1938); A. S. Hartum, *Sifre Hamikrah* II (Tel Aviv, 1963); and J. H. Hertz, *The Pentateuch and Haftorahs* II (London, 1935).

Gordon and Hertz both refer to a native dynasty overthrowing an invading usurper. Hirsch's contemporaries were Jacob Zevi Mecklenburg, *Haketav Vehakabbalah* (Jerusalem, 1961) and Meir Loeb Malbim, *HaTorah VehaMitzvah* (Jerusalem, 1956).

23. Hirsch, *Pentateuch*, II, chapter I, verse 8. The author transliterated from Hebrew script.

24. *Ibid.*, verse 9.

25. Emil Lehmann, *Hoere Israel!* (Dresden, 1869). The organization's secretary at that time wrote an account of the founding of the *Gemeindebund* and of its early years of activity: Bernhard Jacobsohn, *Der Deutsch-Israelitsche Gemeindebund nach Ablauf des ersten Decenniums seit seiner Begruendung* (Leipzig, 1879). For a comprehensive study of the *Gemeindebund*, see Ismar Schorsch, *Jewish Reactions to German Anti-Semitism, 1870–1914* (New York, 1972), pp. 23–52. As example of the freely drawn association between community reform and religious innovation in Lehmann, see, for example, the closing section of his essay, where he discussed the community's obligations toward the dietary laws and the ritual bath.

26. Jacobson, *Gemeindebund*, p. 7. Schorsch, *Jewish Reactions*, p. 25.

27. On the effects of the war on the growth of interest in the new defense organization, see the analysis of Schorsch, *Jewish Reactions*, pp. 25–29.

28. *Israelit*, XI (1870), 387–389, 408–409.

29. *Israelit*, XII (1871), 331–332, 344–346. *Juedische Presse*, II (1871) 333–335.

30. See the discussion by Hildesheimer in this article on the question of centralization, in which he holds that the two extreme positions are equally dangerous: Both the complete centralization of France and the chaotic decentralization of Hungary have harmed Jewish interests. On Hildesheimer's experiences in Hungary, see Mordechai Eliav, "Rabbi Hildesheimer and his Influence on Hungarian Jewry" (Hebrew), *Zion*, XXVII (1962), 59–86.

31. *Juedische Presse*, II (1871), 440, 463–465.

32. E. Munk, "Die Juedische Gemeinde und der Gemeindebund," *ibid.*, pp. 512, 528–529.

33. Contrast *Israelit*, XIII (1872), 433 and 458.

34. Schorsch, *Jewish Reactions*, p. 33. Jacobsohn, *Gemeindebund*, p. 7.

35. Jacobsohn, *Gemeindebund*, pp. 7–8.

36. See Enoch's discussion of the *Gemeindebund*'s interference in religious matters in *Juedische Presse*, II (1871), 440.

37. *Juedische Presse*, II (1871), 440.

38. Jacobsohn, *Gemeindebund*, pp. 13–14.

39. In the 1880s, cooperation did begin between the *Gemeindebund* and that sector of Orthodoxy led by Ezriel Hildesheimer. Schorsch, *Jewish Reactions*, pp. 34–35.

40. *Israelit*, XIII (1872), 433–434. Schorsch, *Jewish Reactions*, pp. 33–34, 222, n 48.

41. *Israelit*, XIII (1872), 458.

42. *Israelit*, XI (1871), 683–684, 693.

43. Ludwig Philippson, "Politische und sociale Zustaende," *AZJ*, XXXIV (1870), 409–411, 431–434, 449–452.

44. *Ibid.*, p. 26.

45. *Ibid.*, pp. 26–27, quoted in Schorsch, *Jewish Reactions*, p. 220 n. 26. For Philippson's muted response to the synods, see M. A. Meyer, "The Jewish Synods in Germany in the Second Half of the Nineteenth Century" (Hebrew), *Studies in the History of the Jewish People and the Land of Israel*, III (1974), 239–274, especially pp. 259–261.

46. For the events in Baden and a synopsis of the ensuing polemics, see Adolf Lewin, *Geschichte der badischen Juden, 1738–1909* (Karlsruhe, 1909), pp. 385–394. A number of the documents relevant to the government's decision were published in the contemporary press. *Israelit*, XI (1870), 57–60, and *AZJ*, XXXIV (1870), 78–80, 86–88, 166–170.

47. Lewin, *Badische Juden*, pp. 388–389.

48. Excerpts from the pamphlet were published in *Israelit*, XI (1870), 369–373. Quotation from p. 372.

49. Lewin, *Badische Juden*, pp. 392–393.

50. Schorsch, *Jewish Reactions*, pp. 25–29.

51. On the tendency toward strife, see the series "Was ist und will der fanatismus der neueren juedischen Orthodoxen?" *AZJ*, XXXIV (1870), 509–512, 529–532, 549–552, and his discussion on the current status of the strife on pp. 201–204.

52. On the hope and need for unity, see the series "Zum deutsch-israelitische Gemeindebund," *ibid.*, pp. 25–27, 41–43, 78–80. The last article deals with the separatist question.

53. *Ibid.*, pp. 79–80. On the inevitability of a separatist law, see also pp. 125–126.

54. *Juedische Presse*, I (1870), 149–150.

55. *AZJ*, XXXV (1871), 649. For a review of existing legislation, see H. Makower, *Ueber die Gemeinde—Verhaeltnisse der Juden in Preussen* (Berlin, 1873).

56. *Israelit*, XIII (1872), 781–782.

57. Z. Wolff, "Staat und Kirche und das Judengesetz des Jahres 1847," *Juedische Presse*, II (1871), 461–463, 472–473, 477–478, 495–496, 502–503.

58. Philippson explained his proposals in *AZJ*, XXXV (1871), 649–654. The circular is reprinted there on pp. 671–672.

59. *Juedische Presse*, II (1871), 469–472.

60. The text of clause 53 is in Freund, *Die Emanzipation der Juden in Preussen*, 2 vols. (Berlin, 1912), II, 515. Statements that the clause was never utilized are in *Israelit*, XIII (1872), 782; XIV (1873), 573–575; XVI

(1875), 575–576. Hirsch, *Denkschrift ueber die Judenfrage in dem Gesetz Betreffend den Austritt aus der Kirche* (Berlin, 1873), p. 7. Makower, *Gemeinde-Verhaeltnisse*, p. 32. On the 1853 decision, see *Israelit*, XVI (1875), 575–576, and XVIII (1877), 780.

61. Georg Franz, *Kulturkampf, Staat, und Katholische Kirche in Mitteleuropa* (Muenchen, 1956), pp. 233–235.

62. While the law allowed for secession from a church, the memorandum explicitly stated that secession from a parish was not included: *"wie das Gesetz sich nur auf den Austritt aus der Kirche, nicht auf den Austritt aus der Parochie bezieht."* The passage is quoted in Makower, *Gemeinde-Verhaeltnisse*, p. 3, and in *AZJ*, XXXVII (1873), 401. Contrast Uriel Tal, *Christians and Jews in Germany* (Ithaca, N.Y., 1975), p. 112. In fact, much of the subsequent debate between community and Orthodox leadership centered on whether a law enabling separation from the Jewish communities provided Jews equality with Christians or with extra privileges, but both sides agreed that Christians did *not* enjoy the right of secession from their local communities without resigning from their particular church. Compare Makower, *Gemeinde-Verhaeltnisse*, p. 3, with Hirsch, "Das Prinzip der Gewissensfreiheit" in Hirsch, *Gesammelte Schriften*, 4 vols. 2nd ed. (Frankfurt, 1922), IV, 269–270; also Manuel Joel, *Lasker's Resolution* (Breslau, 1875), p. 7, with Emanuel Schwarzschild, *Herr Rabbiner Dr. Joel und die Lasker'sche Resolution* (Frankfurt, 1875), pp. 5–7. In sum, secession from a parish was a consequence of secession from the church; it was not permitted independently of secession from the church.

63. *Israelit*, XIV (1873), 246–247.

64. *Ibid.*

65. *Ibid.*, pp. 261–264.

66. *Denkschrift ueber die Judenfrage in dem Gesetz betreffend den Austritt aus der Kirche* (Berlin, 1873). The pamphlet's authorship was not immediately known. Philippson at first assumed that the author was connected to the Berlin Adass Yisroel, but later identified its origins as Frankfurt. *AZJ*, XXXVII (1873), 206–207, 387. See also p. 222 for its central role in the Orthodox campaign. The essay is printed in Hirsch's *Gesammelte Schriften*, IV, 250–265.

67. *Denkschrift*, p. 6.

68. *Ibid.*, p. 11.

69. Hermann Makower, *Gemeinde-Verhaeltnisse*, pp. 30–36, 107–115. Philippson's proposals are in *AZJ*, XXXVII (1873), 531–532, 797–801. The Jewish community of Berlin formally submitted proposals quite close to those of Makower, who was the community's president. *Ibid.*, pp. 768–769, 800–801.

70. *Ibid.*, pp. 731–732, where Philippson compared his proposals to those of Makower.

71. Hirsch, "Das Prinzip der Gewissensfreiheit," *Schriften*, IV, 287–288.

72. *Israelit*, XIV (1873), 675.

73. On the delay, see *Ibid.*, XV (1874), 106–107, 258–259, 445–446, and XVI (1875), 155, 202–203, 231–232.

74. The Prussian law is printed in Ismar Freund, *Die Rechtstellung der Synagogengemeinden in Preussen und die Reichsverfassung* (Berlin, 1926), pp. 39–42. The parallel Hessian law is discussed in Leopold Katz, *Die Rechtliche Stellung der Israelite nach dem Staatskirchenrecht des Grossherzogtums Hessen* (Giessen, 1906), pp. 61–70.

75. Hirsch, *Denkschrift*, p. 10. Lewin, *Badische Juden*, pp. 392–393.

76. *Israelit*, XVII (1876), 1188, and XVIII (1877), 751. *AZJ*, XL (1876), 738–739, 817, 836; XLI (1877), 57, 150–151.

77. *Israelit*, XVII (1876), 1049, *Encyclopedia Judaica* (1971), XV, 379.

78. *Israelit*, XVII (1876), 960, 1041.

79. *Bericht ueber die Verhaeltnisse der Synagogen Gemeinde zu Koenigsberg i. Pr. in den Jahren 1893 bis 1899* (Koenigsberg, 1900), pp. 12–15. *Israelit*, XVIII (1877), 505.

80. *AZJ*, XLI (1877), 57–58. The Adass Jisroel of Berlin did not respond to passage of the 1876 law. No significant trend toward secession was demonstrated until the congregation was legally recognized as a synagogue community in 1885. See the long discussion on the inadequacies of the 1876 law and the difficulties involved in the process of secession in *Die Israelitische Synagogengemeinde (Adass Jisroel) zu Berlin, 1869–1904* (Berlin, 1904), pp. 20–26. Also Max Sinasohn, *Adass Jisroel Berlin* (Jerusalem, 1966), pp. 25–26.

81. *Israelit*, XVII (1876), 1078–1079.

82. *Ibid.*, XVIII (1877), 72 and 122.

83. Salo W. Baron, "Freedom and Constraint in the Jewish Community. A Historic Episode," in *Essays and Studies in Memory of Linda R. Miller* ed. by Israel Davidson (New York, 1938), pp. 15–17.

84. *Israelit*, XVII (1876), 905–907.

85. Saemy Japhet, "The Secession from the Frankfurt Jewish Community under Samson Raphael Hirsch," *Historia Judaica*, X (1948), 109–110.

86. *Israelit*, XVII (1876), 913. *AZJ*, XL (1876), 723. The board consisted of five members.

87. Japhet, "Secession," p. 110. According to Japhet's account, written at the age of ninety and some fifty-nine years after the event, Hirsch made the announcement on the festive holiday of Simchat Torah and shocked the congregation with the news. However, Simchat Torah fell on October 11 in 1876, and the news of Hirsch's resignation from the community had been published in the September 27 edition of the

Israelit, so that either Hirsch only used the occasion to urge the rest of the congregation to secede or the event did not occur on Simchat Torah at all.

88. *Ibid.*

89. *Ibid.*, pp. 110–111. Regardless of the caution necessary, Japhet's account cannot be ignored both because it is the most complete record we have of these events and because it frequently reveals cogent historical analysis that can be corroborated by other evidence. See, for example, his discussion of the "myth of the eleven founders" presented in chap. three of this study. Schwarzschild glossed over the entire separatist affair in his own memoir.

90. Japhet, "Secession," pp. 110–111. *AZJ*, XL (1876), 709, 723.

91. The correspondence was printed in *Israelit*, XVII (1876), 1096–1098. *AZJ*, XL (1876), 723–724, 754–756.

92. Samson Raphael Hirsch, *Der Austritt aus der Gemeinde* (Frankfurt, 1876).

93. *Ibid.*, pp. 12–13.

94. *AZJ*, XLII (1877), 39.

95. Japhet, "Secession," pp. 112–113. The community's proposal, "Supplemental Regulations of the Jewish Community" were printed in *AZJ*, XLI (1877), 6–7, and *Israelit*, XVIII (1877), 1–2. An original copy is located in the SUBF.

96. *AZJ*, XLI (1877), 86.

97. *Ibid.*, pp. 135–136. While that account speaks of 400 members, I have followed Japhet's figure of 355, which is closer to Hirsch's figure of 325 given in 1874. Japhet, "Secession," p. 119. Hirsch, *Schriften*, IV, 287.

98. *AZJ*, XLI (1877), 135–136.

99. On the question of visiting rights, see *Israelit*, XVIII (1877), 44, 219, 481–482, 692, 1099.

100. *Israelit*, XVIII (1877), 23. CAJHP, Samson Raphael Hirsch Collection, HM 4763, Item 34.

101. A list of those who seceded was published in the *Frankfurter Intelligenz-Blatt* (February 18, 1877). Japhet, "Secession," pp. 118–119. Julius Huelsen, *Der Alte Judenfriedhof in Frankfurt A.M.* (Frankfurt, 1932), p. 7.

102. Such a broad interpretation of the social dynamics of secession was offered by Yeshayahu Wolfsberg, "Popular Orthodoxy," *LBIYB*, I (1956), 251–253. See Japhet, "Secession," p. 118. Dr. W. Hanauer, *Zur Statistik der juedischen Bevoelkerung in Frankfurt a.M.*, p. 1; Dr. Josef Unna, *Statistik der Frankfurter Juden* (Frankfurt, 1931), pp. 11, 24.

103. The list referred to above indicates the place of origin and profession of those who seceded. It was obviously published by opponents of secession, but its authenticity was not challenged.

104. *Israelit*, XVII (1876), 1117–1119.

105. *AZJ*, XLI (1877), 285–286, 315.

106. Japhet, "Secession," pp. 104–107, 119, *AZJ*, XLI (1877), 235–236.

107. Seligmann Baer Bamberger, *Offene Antwort* (Wuerzburg, 1877), pp. 17–18. Japhet, "Secession," pp. 114–115. For an account of these further developments in the negotiations, see Isaac Heinemann, "Supplementary Remarks on the Secession from the Frankfurt Jewish community under Samson Raphael Hirsch," *Historia Judaica*, X (1948), 123–134.

108. Japhet, "Secession," p. 112.

109. See his letters to Hirsch during this period in *Rabbiner Esriel Hildesheimer Briefe*, ed. Mordechai Eliav (Jerusalem, 1965), pp. 116, 119–120.

110. See, for example, Rosenbloom, *Tradition in an Age of Reform*, pp. 111–113, or even Schwab, who did not seem to grasp the threat to the IRG.

111. Bamberger, *Offene Antwort*, p. 14.

112. *Ibid.*, pp. 18–19. Japhet, "Secession," pp. 113–115.

113. Bamberger, *Antwort*, p. 16.

114. For a list of the polemical literature from both sides, see *Literatur ueber die Juden in Frankfurt* (Frankfurt, 1914), pp. 13–14.

115. Samson Raphael Hirsch, *Offener Brief an Sr. Ehrwuerdigen Herrn Distrikts-Rabbiner S. B. Bamberger* (Frankfurt, 1877), pp. 11–15. Hirsch appended to his letter the text of the rabbinical statement pertaining to membership in the Vienna community.

116. *Ibid.*, pp. 19–20.

117. *Ibid.*, p. 22.

118. *Ibid.*, p. 6.

119. Bamberger, *Offene Antwort*, pp. 4–7.

120. *Ibid.*, pp. 7–11. On the legal significance of *Mara D'atra*, see David Weiss Halivni, "The Role of Mara D'atra in Jewish Law," *Proceedings of the Rabbinical Assembly (1976)*, XXXVIII (New York, 1977), pp. 124–129.

121. Bamberger, *Antwort*, pp. 12–20, 25.

122. *Ibid.*, pp. 22–23.

123. *Ibid.*, pp. 23–24.

124. *Ibid.*, pp. 25–27.

125. *Israelit*, XVIII (1877), 271–272, 363–364.

126. CAHJP, GA S 14.3 (5). Entry 2735 (December 17, 1876) and 2739 (January 8, 1877).

127. On Bamberger, see the Hebrew essay by Mordechai Eliav, "Rabbi Isaac Dov Halevi Bamberger—the Man and his Times," *Sinai*, XLIII (1979), 61–71; and S. Schmidt, " 'The Wuerzburger Rav' His Personality

and Life Work," *The Bamberger Family*, 2nd ed. (Hebrew, Jerusalem, 1979), pp. 8–14.
On the general acceptance of modernity in German Orthodoxy, see Ismar Schorsch, "Emancipation and the Crisis of Religious Authority," in *Revolution and Evolution. 1848 in German-Jewish History* (Tuebingen, 1981), pp. 205–247.

EPILOGUE

1. On the conflict in Berlin, see Ludwig Geiger, *Geschichte der Juden in Berlin* (Berlin, 1871), I, 204–205, and Josef Eschelbacher, *Michael Sachs* (Berlin, 1908), pp. 24–26. The first references I have found using the term neo-Orthodoxy are in the *AZJ*, XVIII, (1854), 69, 94, 129, 143. See also the polemics against neo-Orthodoxy in XIX, (1855), 39–40, 508–509.

2. Rabbi Samuel Salant of Jerusalem described his visit to Bamberger's synagogue in this way: "When I entered the synagogue, I saw Reb Seligmann Baer standing there in vestments like a Christian preacher. I also noticed that, contrary to time-honored tradition, the reading desk stood directly in front of the Ark instead of in the middle of the synagogue. All this seemed strange to me" Naphtali Carlebach, *Joseph Carlebach and his Generation* (New York, 1959), pp. 225–226. On the Hatam Sofer, see Jacob Katz's essay in Hebrew, "Contributions towards a Biography of R. Moses Sofer," in *Studies in Mysticism and Religion Presented to Gershom G. Scholem* (Jerusalem, 1967), pp. 115–148. For a comparison of Hirsch with the Hatam Sofer, see Isaac Heinemann, "Samson Raphael Hirsch: The Formative Years of the Leader of Modern Orthodoxy," *Historia Judaica*, XIII (1961), especially 45–47.

3. Seligmann Baer Bamberger, *Offene Antwort* (Wuerzburg, 1877), pp. 26–27.

4. Contrast with the entry "Neo-Orthodoxy," *Encyclopedia Judaica* (1971), XII, 956–958.

5. Bernard Homa, *Orthodoxy in Anglo-Jewry, 1880–1940* (London, 1969), pp. 47–48. The essay is partial to the viewpoint of the immigrants to England from eastern countries. Unfortunately, Aubrey Newman's *The United Synagogue, 1870–1970* (London, 1976) fails to provide a description of religious practices in England.
The religious outlook of Nathan Adler, the first to hold the title of Chief Rabbi in England, is described extensively in Leo Trepp, *Die Oldenburger Judenschaft* (Oldenburg, 1973), pp. 88–118.

6. S. Debre, "The Jews of France," *Jewish Quarterly Review*, III (1891), 388.

Bibliography

ARCHIVES

Central Archive for the History of the Jewish People, Jerusalem

Altona, Hamburg, Wandsbeck Collection
Gesamtarchiv, Bayern
Samson Raphael Hirsch Collection
Schueler, Meir, "Zur Geschichte der Israelitischen Religionsgesellschaft in Frankfurt, A.M."

Leo Baeck Institute, New York City

Bach Collection.
"Gedaechtnisrolle angefertigt anlaesslich der Grundsteinlegung zu einem Gotteshause am 30 September 1852." Frankfurt, 1852.
"Zweite Gedaechtnisrolle angefertigt anlaesslich der Grundsteinlegung zum Erweiterungsbau des Gotteshauses." Frankfurt, 1874.
"Plan der Freien Stadt Frankfurt von Carl Juegel." 1849.
Leopold Stein Collection.

Stadtsarchiv, Frankfurt

File of Juda Samuel Adler
File of Samson Raphael Hirsch
Protokollen des Engeren Raths, 1833–1866

Protokollen des Grossen Raths, 1833–1866
Protokollen des Magistrates, 1868–1877

PERIODICALS CONSULTED

Allgemeine Zeitung des Judenthums. Leipzig, 1837–1877.
Der Israelit. Mainz, 1860–1877.
Der Israelit des neunzehnten Jahrhunderts. Meiningen; Kassel; Hersfeld;
    Frankfurt; 1839–1848.
Israelitische Annalen. Frankfurt, 1839–1841.
Jeschurun. Frankfurt, 1854–1870.
Juedische Presse. Berlin, 1869–1877.
Der Orient. Leipzig, 1840–1851.
Der Treue Zions-Waechter. Altona, 1845–1854.
Wissenschaftliche Zeitschrift fuer Juedische Theologie. Frankfurt, Stuttgart,
    1835–1839.

PRIMARY SOURCES

Actenstuecke, die hiesige israelitische Religions Gemeinde betreffend. Frank-
    furt, 1839.
An die Angehoerigen der israelitischen Religionsgemeinde hiesiger Stadt.
    Frankfurt, 1849.
*An einen Hohen Senat der freien Stadt Frankfurt . . . Gehorsamster Bericht des
    Vorstands der israelitischen Gemeinde, das Verhaeltniss der Mitglieder
    der israelitischen Religionsgesellschaft zur israelitischen Gemeinde . . .
    betreffend.* Frankfurt, 1854.
*An Hohen Senat der Freien Stadt Frankfurt . . . Gehorsamster Vorstellung und
    Bitte des Vorstandes der israelitischen Gemeinde, das Verhaeltniss der
    Mitglieder der Religionsgesellschaft zur israelitischen Gemeinde betref-
    fend.* Frankfurt, 1855.
*An Hohen Senat der freien Stadt Frankfurt . . . Gehorsamster Bericht und Bitte
    von Seiten des Vorstandes der israelitischen Gemeinde dahier, das Ver-
    haeltniss der Mitglieder der Religionsgesellschaft zur israelitischen Ge-
    meinde betreffend.* Frankfurt, 1858.
*An Hohen Senat der freien Stadt Frankfurt . . . Gehorsamste Vorstellung und
    Bitte von Seiten des Vorstandes der israelitischen Religionsgesellschaft
    dahier, das verhaeltniss ihrer Mitglieder zu der hiesigen israelitischen
    Gemeinde . . . betreffend.* Frankfurt, 1858.
Bamberger, Seligmann Baer. *Offene Antwort auf den an ihn gerichteten
    Brief des Herrn S. R. Hirsch.* Wuerzburg, 1877.
Bar Amithai. *Ueber die Beschneidung in historischer und dogmatischer Hin-
    sicht.* Frankfurt, 1843.

Bender, Johann Heinrich. *Der fruehere und jetzige Zustand der Israeliten zu Frankfurt am Main*. Frankfurt, 1833.

Bergson, Joseph. *Die Beschneidung vom historischen, kritischen und medecinischen Standpunkt*. Berlin, 1844.

Betrachtungen einer Muecke, Entgegnung auf den offenen Brief des Herrn Rabbiners Samson Raphael Hirsch. Frankfurt, 1877.

Betrachtungen ueber das Rechtsverhaeltniss der israelitischen Religionsgesellschaft zur israelitischen Gemeinde. Frankfurt, 1865.

Charbonah, M. S. *Harav B'Zion. Briefe einen juedischen Gelehrten und Rabbinen ueber das Werk Horeb*... Leipzig, 1839.

Creizenach, Michael. *Schulchan Aruch oder encyclopedische Darstellung des Mosaischen Gesetzes*. 4 vols. Frankfurt, 1833–1840.

Einweihung des erweiteren Beth Tefilat Jeschurun. Frankfurt, 1874.

Der Entwurf der neuen israelitischen Gemeinde-Ordnung. Frankfurt, 1850.

Frankfurter israelitische Gemeindezustaende. Frankfurt, 1854.

Freund, Ismar. *Die Emanzipation der Juden in Preussen*. 2 vols. Berlin, 1912.

————. *Die Rechtstellung der Synagogengemeinden in Preussen und die Reichsverfassung*. Berlin, 1926.

Geiger, Abraham. *Nachgelassene Schriften*. 5 vols., Edited by Ludwig Geiger. Berlin, 1875–1878.

Geiger, Solomon. *Dibhre Kehillot* (Hebrew). Frankfurt, 1862.

Gemeinde Ordnung fuer die israelitische Religionsgemeinde in Frankfurt am Main. Frankfurt, 1851.

Graetz, Heinrich. *Tagebuch und Briefe*. Edited by Reuven Michael. Tuebingen, 1977.

Heinleuchtung des Herrn Rabbiner Sueskind. Von einem "Paganus." Frankfurt, 1876.

Hildesheimer, Rabbiner Esriel. *Briefe*. Edited by Mordechai Eliav. Jerusalem, 1965.

Hirsch, Samson Raphael. *An den loeblichen Vorstand der Israelitischen Religionsgesellschaft*. Frankfurt, 1877.

————. *Der Austritt aus der Gemeinde*. Frankfurt, 1876.

————. *Denkschrift ueber die Judenfrage in dem preussischen Gesetz betreffend den Austritt aus der Kirche*. Berlin, 1873.

————. *Erste Mittheilungen aus Naphtali's Briefwechsel*. Altona, 1838.

————. *Gesammelte Schriften*. 6 vols. Edited by Naphtali Hirsch. Frankfurt, 1902–1912.

————. *Horeb*. 2nd ed. 2 vols., Translated by I. Grunfeld. London, 1962.

————. *Judaism Eternal*. 2 vols., Edited and translated by I. Grunfeld. London, 1956.

————, "Karmel und Sinai." *Nachalath Z'wi*, II. (1932), 257–260.

————. *Nineteen Letters of Ben Uziel*. Translated by Bernard Drachman. New York, 1899.

————. *Offener Brief an Herrn Distrikts-Rabbiner S. B. Bamberger.* Frankfurt, 1877.

————. "Phinehas-Elijahu." *Jeschurun*, XIV (1868), 205–215.

————. *Das Prinzip der Gewissensfreiheit.* Frankfurt, 1874.

————. *Die Religion im Bunde mit dem Fortschritt, von einem Schwarzen.* Frankfurt, 1854.

————. *Zweite Mittheilungen aus einem Briefwechsel ueber die neuste juedische Literatur.* Altona, 1844.

Holdheim, Sammuel. *Geschichte der Entstehung und Entwickelung der Juedischen Reformgemeinde in Berlin.* Berlin, 1857.

Igrot Soferim. Edited by Shlomo Sofer. (Hebrew) Tel-Aviv, 1970.

Instruktion fuer die Baecker und Conditoren der Israelitischen Religionsgesellschaft. Frankfurt, 1886.

Instruktion fuer die Restaurateure der Israelitischen Religionsgesellschaft. Frankfurt, 1887.

Jacobsohn, Bernhard. *Der Deutsch-Israelitische Gemeindebund nach Ablauf des ersten Decenniums seit seiner Begruendung von 1869 bis 1879.* Leipzig, 1879.

Japhet, I. M. *Schire Jeschurun.* Frankfurt, 1856; 2nd ed., 1881.

Japhet, Saemy. "The Secession from the Frankfurt Jewish Community under Samson Raphael Hirsch." *Historia Judaica*, X (1948), 99–122.

Joel, Manuel. *Lasker's Resolution.* Breslau, 1875.

Lehmann, Emil. *Hoere Israel!* Dresden, 1869.

Makower, Hermann. *Ueber die Gemeindeverhaeltnisse der Juden in Preussen.* Berlin, 1873.

"Der neue Entwurf fuer die Gemeindeordnung der hiesigen israelitischen Religionsgemeinde." *Frankfurter Intelligenzblatt.* March 9, 1850.

Philalethes. *Ausgleich, nicht Austritt.* Frankfurt, 1876.

Programm fuer die Einweihung der Synagoge, Beth Tefilat Jeschurun. Frankfurt, 1853.

Protocolle der ersten Rabbiner-Versammlung, abgehalten zu Braunschweig. Braunschweig, 1844.

Protokolle und Aktenstuecke der zweiten Rabbinerversammlung abgehalten in Frankfurt am Main. Frankfurt, 1845.

Regulativ, die Verwaltung der israelitischen Gemeinde . . . betreffend. Frankfurt, 1839.

Die religioesen Wirren in der israelitischen Gemeinde zu Frankfurt a.M. Frankfurt, 1854.

Roenne, Ludwig von, and Simon, Heinrich. *Die frueheren und gegenwaertigen Verhaeltnisse der Juden in dem saemmtlichen Landestheilen des Preussischen Staates.* Breslau, 1843.

Rosenheim, Jacob. *Erinnerungen*. Frankfurt, 1970.

"Ein Satzungsentwarf von Rabbiner Hirsch" *Nachalath Z'wi*, I (1931), 33–40, 113–117

Schwarzschild, Emanuel. *Die Angriffe des Herrn Rabbiner Sueskind zu Wiesbaden gegen die Statuten der Israel. Religionsgesellschaft*. Frankfurt, 1876.

————. *Die Gruendung der Israelitischen Religionsgesellschaft*. Frankfurt, 1896.

————. *Herr Rabbiner Dr. Joel und die Lasker'sche Resolution*. Frankfurt, 1875.

Shelomei Emunei Israel. Treue Glaeubige in Israel. 1845.

Souchay, Edouard. *Anmerkungen zu den Wechsel-Gesetzen der Freien Stadt Frankfurt*. Frankfurt, 1845.

Spier, Selmar. *Vor 1914, Erinnerungen an Frankfurt*. Frankfurt, 1961.

Statuten der israelitischen Religionsgesellschaft. Als Manuscript gedruckt. Frankfurt, 1874.

Statuten der israelitischen Religionsgesellschaft. Frankfurt, 1875.

Stein, Leopold. *Mein Dienst Verhaeltniss zum Israelitischen Gemeinde Vorstande zu Frankfurt a.M.* Frankfurt, 1861.

————. *Wahrheit, Recht, und Frieden*. Frankfurt, 1847.

Sueskind, Samuel. *Die Statuten der israelit. Religionsgesellschaft*. Wiesbaden, 1876.

Synagogen-Ordnung fuer die Synagoge Beth Tefilat Jeschurun. Frankfurt, 1853.

Synagogen-Ordnung fuer die Synagoge der Israelitischen Religionsgesellschaft. Frankfurt, 1874.

Trier, Solomon. *Rabbinische Gutachten ueber die Beschneidung*. Frankfurt, 1844.

Ueber den Entwurf einer neuen Gemeinde-Ordnung fuer die israelitische Gemeinde. Frankfurt, 1850.

Der Vostand der israelitischen Gemeinde in Frankfurt a.M. an Herrn Emanuel Schwarzschild und Genossen. Frankfurt, 1876.

Wechsel und Merkantil-Ordnung der Freien Stadt Frankfurt. Frankfurt, 1845.

Weill, Alexandre. *Ma Jeuness*. Paris, 1870.

————. *Rothschild und die Europaeischen Staaten*. Stuttgart, 1844.

Zusatz—Bestimmungen zu dem Regulativ der israelitischen Gemeinde. Frankfurt, 1877.

SECONDARY SOURCES

Achterberg, Erich. *Frankfurter Bankherren*. Frankfurt, 1956.

Albert, Phyllis. *The Modernization of French Jewry*. Hanover, N.H., 1977.

Arnsberg, Paul. *Bilder aus dem juedischen Leben im alten Frankfurt*. Frankfurt, 1970.

———. *Jakob H. Schiff*. Frankfurt, 1969.

———. *Neunhundert Jahre "Muttergemeinde in Israel"* Frankfurt am Main, *Chronik der Rabbiner*. Frankfurt, 1974.

Baerwald, Herman. *Geschichte der Realschule der israelitischen Gemeinde "Philanthropin" zu Frankfurt am Main, 1804–1904*. Frankfurt, 1904.

Baron, Salo. "Aspects of the Jewish Communal Crisis in 1848." *Jewish Social Studies*, XIV (1952), 99–144.

———. "Church and State Debates in the Jewish Community of 1848." *Mordechai M. Kaplan Jubilee Volume*. Edited by Moshe Davis. New York, 1953, pp. 49–72.

———. "Freedom and Constraint in the Jewish Community." *Essays and Studies in Memory of Linda R. Miller*. Edited by Israel Davidson. New York, 1938, pp. 9–23.

———. "The Impact of the Revolution of 1848 on Jewish Emancipation." *Jewish Social Studies*, XI, (1949), 195–248.

———. *The Jewish Community*. 3 vols. Philadelphia, 1942.

———. "Newer Approaches to Jewish Emancipation." *Diogenes*, XXIX (1960), 56–81.

Bleich, Judith. "The Emergence of an Orthodox Press in Nineteenth-Century Germany." *Jewish Social Studies*, XLII (1980), 323–344.

———. *Jacob Ettlinger, His Life and Work: The Emergence of Modern Orthodoxy in Germany*. Ph.D. dissertation, New York University, 1974.

Bothe, Friedrich. *Aus Frankfurts Sage und Geschichte*. Frankfurt, 1911.

Breuer, Mordechai. "Prakim Mitoch Biographia" (Hebrew). *Harav Shimshon Raphael Hirsch: Mishnato veShitato*. Edited by Jonah Immanuel. Jerusalem, 1962.

Breuer, Raphael. *Unter Seinem Banner*. Frankfurt, 1908.

Carlebach, Naphtali. *Joseph Carlebach and his Generation*. New York, 1959.

Dann, Wilhelm. *Stammtafel & Register der Nachkommen des Samuel Alexander Levi (Dann) aus Frankfurt A.M*. Frankfurt, 1870.

Dietz, Alexander. *Stammbuch der Frankfurter Juden*. Frankfurt, 1907.

Donath, Leopold. *Geschichte der Juden in Mecklenburg*. Leipzig, 1874.

Duckesz, Eduard. *Iwoh Lemoschaw* (Hebrew). Krakau, 1903.

———. "Zur Geneologie Samson Raphael Hirsch." *Jahrbuch der juedischeliterarischen Gesellschaft*, XVII (1926), 103–131.

Eliav, Mordechai. *Jewish Education in Germany in the Period of Enlightenment and Emancipation* (Hebrew). Jerusalem, 1960.

———. "Rabbi Hildesheimer and his Influence on Hungarian Jewry" (Hebrew). *Zion*, XXVII (1962), 59–86.

———. "Rabbi Isaac Dov Halevi Bamberger—the Man and his Times" (Hebrew). *Sinai*, XLIII (1979), 61–71.

Engelbert, Hermann. *Statistik des Judenthums im Deutschen Reich.* Frankfurt, 1875.

Eschelbacher, Josef. *Michel Sachs.* Berlin, 1908.

Festschrift zur Jahrhundertfeier der Realschule der israelitischen Gemeinde, 1804–1904. Frankfurt, 1904.

Fischer, Hoerst. *Judentum, Staat, und Heer in Preussen im fruehen 19 Jahrhundert.* Tuebingen, 1968.

Franz, Georg. *Kulturkampf, Staat, und Katholische Kirche in Mitteleuropa.* Muenchen, 1956.

Friedmann, Joë-Yehoshua. *Alexandre Weill, Écrivain Contestaire et Historien Engagé.* Strasbourg, 1980.

Geiger, Ludwig. *Abraham Geiger. Leben und Lebenswerk.* Berlin, 1910.

———. *Geschichte der Juden in Berlin.* 2 vols. Berlin, 1871.

Gerteis, Klaus. *Leopold Sonnemann.* Frankfurt, 1970.

Goldschmidt, Josef. *Geschichte der Talmud Tora Realschule in Hamburg.* Hamburg, 1905.

Haarbleicher, Moses Martin. *Aus der Geschichte der Deutsch-Israelitischen Gemeinde.* Hamburg, 1866.

Halivni, David Weiss. "The Role of the Mara D'atra in Jewish Law." *Proceedings of the Rabbinical Assembly (1976),* XXXVII, 124–129.

Hammer-Schenk, Harold. *Untersuchungen zum Synagogenbau 1800–1871.* Bamberg, 1974.

Hanauer, Wilhelm. *Zur Statistik der juedischen Bevoelkerung in Frankfurt A.M.* Frankfurt, 1910.

Harav Yaakov Ettlinger (Hebrew). Jerusalem, 1972.

Harav Shimshon Raphael Hirsch: Mishnato veShitato. Edited by Jonah Immanuel. Jerusalem, 1962.

Heinemann, Isaac. "I. M. Japhet." *Jeschurun* N.F. (1918), 240–244.

———. "Mekharim al R. Shimshon Raphael Hirsch." *Sinai,* XXIV (1949), 249–271.

———. "The Relationship between S. R. Hirsch and his Teacher, Isaac Bernays." (Hebrew). *Zion,* XVI (1951), 44–90.

———. "Samson Raphael Hirsch: The Formative Years of the Leader of Modern Orthodoxy." *Historia Judaica,* XIII (1951), 29–54.

———. "Supplementary Remarks on the Secession from the Frankfurt Jewish Community under Samson Raphael Hirsch." *Historia Judaica,* X (1948), 123–134.

———. *Taamei HaMitzvot BeSifrut Israel* (Hebrew). Jerusalem, 1956.

Horovitz, Markus. *Frankfurter Rabbinen,* 2nd ed. Jerusalem, 1969.

———. "Toledot Aharon," Introduction to Aharon Fuld, *Beth Aharon.* Frankfurt, 1890.

Die Israelitische Synagogengemeinde (Adass Jisroel) zu Berlin, 1869–1904. Berlin, 1904.

Joehlinger, Otto. *Bismarck und die Juden*. Berlin, 1921.

Jost, Isaak Markus. *Geschichte des Judenthums und seine Sekten*. 3 vols. Leipzig, 1857–1859.

———. *Neuere Geschichte der Israeliten*. 3 vols. Berlin, 1846–1847.

"Judenheit und das Judenthum—Bedenken eines Laien." *WZJT*, III (1837), 161–171.

Katz, Jacob. *Jews and Freemasons in Europe*. Cambridge, Mass., 1970.

———. "Contributions towards a Biography of R. Moses Sofer" (Hebrew). *Studies in Mysticism and Religion Presented to Gershom Scholem*. Jerusalem, 1967.

———. *From Prejudice to Destruction*. (Cambridge, Mass., 1980).

———. *Out of the Ghetto*. Cambridge, Mass., 1973.

———, ed. *The Role of Religion in Modern Jewish History*. Cambridge, Mass., 1975.

———. *Tradition and Crisis*. New York, 1961.

Katz, Leopold. *Die rechtliche Stellung der Israeliten nach dem Staatskirchenrecht des Gross Herzogtums Hessen*. Giessen, 1906.

Kayserling, Meier. *Ludwig Philippson*. Leipzig, 1898.

Kirchholtes, Hans-Dieten. *Juedische Privatbanken in Frankfurt am Main*. Frankfurt, 1969.

Kober, Adolf. "Emancipation's Impact on the Education and Vocational Training of German Jewry." *Jewish Social Studies*, XVI (1954), 3–32, 151–176.

———. "Jews in the Revolution of 1848 in Germany." *Jewish Social Studies*, X (1948), 135–164.

Kohler, Max J. "Jewish Rights at the Congress of Vienna and Aix-La-Chapelle." *Publications of the American Jewish Historical Society*, XXVI (1918), 33–125.

Kracauer, Isidor. *Geschichte der Juden in Frankfurt A.M.* 2 vols. Frankfurt, 1925–1927.

Krohn, Helga. *Die Juden in Hamburg, 1800–1850*. Frankfurt, 1967.

———. *Die Juden in Hamburg, 1848–1918*. Hamburg, 1974.

Levin, Moritz. *Die Reform des Judenthums*. Berlin, 1895.

Lewin, Adolf. *Geschichte der Badischen Juden, 1838–1909*. Karlsruhe, 1909.

Liberles, Robert. "Champion of Orthodoxy: The Emergence of Samson Raphael Hirsch as Religious Leader." *AJS Review*, VI (1981), 43–60.

———. "Leopold Stein and the Paradox of Reform Clericalism." *LBIYB*, XXVII, (1982).

———. "Origins of the Jewish Reform Movement in England," *AJS Review*, I (1976), 121–150.

———. "The Rabbinical Conferences of the 1850's and the Quest for Liturgical Unity." *Modern Judaism*, III (1983), 309–317.

Lowenstein, Steven M. "The 1840's and the Creation of the German-Jewish Religious Reform Movement." *Revolution and Evolution, 1848 in German-Jewish History*. Edited by Werner E. Mosse, Arnold Paucker, Reinhard Rürup. Tuebingen, 1981, pp. 255–297.

Meyer, Michael. "Abraham Geiger's Historical Judaism." In *New Perspectives on Abraham Geiger*. Edited by Jakob Petuchowski. New York, 1975.

————. "Alienated Intellectuals in the Camp of Religious Reform: The Frankfurt Reformfreunde," *AJS Review*, VI, 61–86.

————. "The Establishment of the Hamburg Temple." *Studies in the History of Jewish Society in the Middle Ages and in the Modern Period* (Hebrew) Jerusalem 1980, pp. 218–224.

————. "The Jewish Synods in Germany in the Second Half of the Nineteenth Century" (Hebrew). *Studies in the History of the Jewish People and the Land of Israel*, III (1974), 239–274.

————. "Rabbi Gedaliah Tiktin and the Orthodox Segment of the Breslau Community, 1845–1854." *Michael*, II (1973), 92–107.

————. "The Religious Reform Controversy in the Berlin Jewish Community, 1814–1823." *LBIYB*, XXIV (1979), 139–155.

Petuchowski, Jakob, ed. *New Perspectives on Abraham Geiger*. New York, 1975.

————. *Prayerbook Reform in Europe*. New York, 1968.

Philippson, Johanna. "Ludwig Philippson und die Allgemeine Zeitung des Judentums." *Das Judentum in der Deutschen Umwelt 1800–1850*. Edited by Hans Lieberschuetz and Arnold Paucker. Tuebingen, 1977, pp. 243–291.

Philipson, David. *The Reform Movement in Judaism*. 2nd ed. New York, 1967.

Richarz, Monika. *Der Eintritt der Juden in die Akademischen Berufe*. Tuebingen, 1974.

Rinott, Moshe. "Gabriel Riesser—Fighter for Jewish Emancipation." *LBIYB*, VII (1962), 11–38.

Rosenbloom, Noah. *Tradition in an Age of Reform*. Philadelphia, 1976.

"Samson Raphael Hirsch—Jubiliaeums-Nummer." *Der Israelit*. Frankfurt, 1908.

Schaumberger, Hugo, and Galliner, Arthur. "Aus der Geschichte des Philanthropins." *Das Philanthropin zu Frankfurt am Main*. Edited by Dietrich Andernacht. Frankfurt, 1964.

Schmidt, S. " 'The Wuerzburger Rav'—His Personality and Life Work." *The Bamberger Family*. 2nd ed. Jerusalem, 1979.

Schnabel, Franz. *Deutsche Geschichte im Neunzehnten Jahrhundert*. 4 vols. Freiburg im Breisgau, 1933–1937.

Schorsch, Ismar. "Emancipation and the Crisis of Religious Authority."

In *Revolution and Evolution. 1848 in German-Jewish History*. Edited by Werner E. Mosse, Arnold Paucker, and Reinhard Rürup. Tuebingen, 1981, pp. 205–247.

———. "Ideology and History in the Age of Emancipation." Introduction to Heinrich Graetz, *The Structure of Jewish History*. New York, 1975.

———. *Jewish Reactions to German Anti-Semitism*. New York, 1972.

Schwab, Herman. *Aus der Schuetzenstrasse*. Frankfurt, 1923.

———. *History of Orthodox Jewry in Germany*. London, 1950.

———. *Memories of Frankfurt*. London, 1955.

Schwemer, Richard. *Geschichte der Freien Stadt Frankfurt a.M.*, 3 vols. in 4. Frankfurt, 1910–1918.

Seligmann, Caesar. *Geschichte der juedischen Reformbewegung von Mendelssohn bis zur Gegenwart*. Frankfurt, 1922.

Silbergleit, Heinrich. *Die Bevoelkerungs und Berufsverhaeltnisse der Juden im Deutschen Reich*. Berlin, 1930.

Sinasohn, Max, ed. *Adass Jisroel Berlin; Entstehung, Entfaltung, Entwurzelung 1869–1939*. Jerusalem, 1966.

Stern, Eleazer. *"Torah-im-derech Erez": The Educational Ideal in its Development* (Hebrew). Ph.D. thesis, Hebrew University, 1970.

Stern, Fritz. *Gold and Iron; Bismarck, Bleichroeder, and the Building of the German Empire*. New York, 1977.

———. "Prussia." In *European Landed Elites in the Nineteenth Century*. Edited by David Spring. Baltimore, 1977.

Strauss, Herbert. "Pre-Emancipation Prussian Policies Towards the Jews, 1815–1847." *LBIYB*, XI (1966), 107–136.

Sulzbach, Abraham. "Zur Geschichte der Schulanstalten." *Festschrift zur Jubilaeums Feier der Unterrichtsanstalten der IRG zu Frankfurt A.M.* Frankfurt, 1903.

Tal, Uriel. *Christians and Jews in Germany*. Ithaca, N.Y., 1975.

Toury, Jacob. " 'Deutsche Juden' im Vormarz." *Bulletin of the Leo Baeck Institute*, 1965, pp. 65–87.

———. *Die politschen Orientierungen der Juden in Deutschland*. Tuebingen, 1966.

———. *Soziale und politische Geschichte der Juden in Deutschland, 1847–1871*. Duesseldorf, 1977.

———. *Turmoil and Confusion in the Revolution of 1848* (Hebrew). Tel-Aviv, 1968.

Trepp, Leo. *Die Oldenburger Judenschaft*. Oldenburg, 1973.

Tuerk, Moritz. "Das erste Gemeindestatut und die Genossenschaft fuer Reform im Judentum." *Festschrift zum 70 Geburtstage von Moritz Schaefer*. Berlin, 1927.

Unna, Josef. *Statistik der Frankfurter Juden zum Jahre 1866*. Frankfurt, 1931.

Valentein, Veit. *Frankfurt am Main und die Revolution von 1848/49.* Stuttgart, 1908.

Wiener, Max. *Abraham Geiger and Liberal Judaism.* Philadelphia, 1962.

———. *Juedische Religion im Zeitalter der Emanzipation.* Berlin, 1933.

Wilhelm, Kurt. "An Early Nineteenth Century Frankfurt Benevolent Society." *Between East and West: Essays dedicated to the Memory of Bela Horwitz.* Edited by Alexander Altmann. London, 1958, pp. 137–148.

Wolfsberg, Yeshayahu. "Popular Orthodoxy." *LBIYB*, I (1956), 237–254.

Index

About the Author

ROBERT LIBERLES, most recently Visiting Associate Professor in the Department of Religious Studies at Yale University (1983–1985) is Lecturer in the Department of History at Ben Gurion University. His articles have appeared in the *Association for Jewish Studies Review*, *Modern Judaism*, and the *Leo Baeck Institute Yearbook*.

Recent Titles in
Contributions to the Study of Religion
Series Editor: Henry W. Bowden